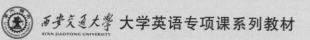
西安交通大学 大学英语专项课系列教材

中国文化翻译实践教程

Chinese Culture Translation Practice Coursebook

总主编 孙长虹
主　编 靳　蓉　许　明
参　编（按姓氏笔画）
　　　　王雪梅　尹转云　杨　芳　张丽娟
　　　　庞云青　赵晓英　焦晓凌

图书在版编目(CIP)数据

中国文化翻译实践教程 / 孙长虹总主编;靳蓉,许明主编. — 西安:西安交通大学出版社,2024.5

ISBN 978-7-5693-3570-5

Ⅰ.①中… Ⅱ.①孙…②靳…③许… Ⅲ.①中华文化—英语—翻译—教材 Ⅳ.①K203

中国国家版本馆CIP数据核字(2023)第252339号

书　　　名	中国文化翻译实践教程
	ZHONGGUO WENHUA FANYI SHIJIAN JIAOCHENG
总 主 编	孙长虹
主　　编	靳　蓉　许　明
责任编辑	庞钧颖
责任校对	张静静
封面设计	任加盟
出版发行	西安交通大学出版社
	(西安市兴庆南路1号　邮政编码 710048)
网　　址	http://www.xjtupress.com
电　　话	(029)82668357　82667874(市场营销中心)
	(029)82668315(总编办)
传　　真	(029)82668280
印　　刷	陕西金和印务有限公司
开　　本	880mm×1230mm　1/16　印张　14.25　字数　452千字
版次印次	2024年5月第1版　2024年5月第1次印刷
书　　号	ISBN 978-7-5693-3570-5
定　　价	59.80元

如发现印装质量问题,请与本社市场营销中心联系。

订购热线:(029)82667874　(029)82665371

投稿热线:(029)82668531

版权所有　侵权必究

前　言

中国是一个文化大国,承载着悠久璀璨的历史文明和博大精深的文化经典。这些文化瑰宝中蕴含的思想观念、人文精神和道德规范等,不仅深刻塑造了中国人的思想和精神内核,也为解决人类普遍问题提供了宝贵的借鉴与启示。随着我国经济的快速发展和综合国力的不断提升,世界了解中国的愿望日益高涨。

党的二十大报告强调要坚守中华文化立场,提炼展示中华文明的精神标识和文化精髓,加快构建中国话语和中国叙事体系,讲好中国故事、传播好中国声音,展现可信、可爱、可敬的中国形象。因此,如何向世界介绍中国及优秀中华传统文化、在国际上展现良好的中国形象,具有十分重要的现实意义。许多英语水平较高的中国青年学者在国际交流中,并不能很好地用英语介绍自己的母语文化,更遑论讲好中国故事、传播好中国声音。要消除这种"中国文化失语症"现象,增强中华文明的传播力和影响力,就需要在英语教学中融入文化教学,尤其是将中国文化导入外语教学,使母语文化与目的语文化在英语教学中并重。《中国文化翻译实践教程》正是为适应这种现实需要编写而成的。语言承载的是文化,语言学习中的听、说、读、写、译无不蕴含着文化特征。本教材通过教学内容的合理设计,以科学的态度、巧妙的形式讲好中国故事,弘扬好中国文化,引导学生坚定文化自信。

本教材突出知识性和实用性,题材广泛,内容多样,与时代紧密结合。教材特色主要体现在以下方面。

1. 以 CBI 教学理念为理论指导

CBI(Content-Based Instruction)是以内容为依托的外语教学理念。它是一种将语言指导和学科指导结合在一起的教学方法。本教材的编写以 CBI 教学理念为指导,力图将中国传统文化教育与英语学习有机结合起来,使语言和内容的教学相统一。在培养学习者汉译英翻译能力的同时,本教材力求拓宽学习者的文化视野,使学习者更好地了解中国文化知识,提升用英语表述中国文化的能力,为未来讲好中国故事、弘扬中国文化打下坚实的语言基础。

2. 输入与输出相结合,提升综合能力

本教材的编者精心选择了与各单元文化内容相契合的听力材料和阅读材料,并相应设计了口语讨论题及阅读题,克服了目前大部分翻译教材只着眼于语言的输出而缺乏输入的弊端。学习者经过语言输入再进行翻译的输出,效率大大提高,从而实现听、说、读、写、译能力的同步提升。

3. 教材中融入思政元素

本教材积极响应国家的教育方针,在着重培养学生汉译英能力的同时,提高学生的综合文化素养,帮助学生树立正确的世界观、人生观和价值观,将思想品德培养有机融入中国文化翻译实践课程教学。

4. 技巧与实战并重

本教材围绕中国优秀传统文化,辅以汉译英翻译技巧讲授和训练,以提高学习者汉译英翻译实战能力为目标。每一单元均设有翻译技巧模块,并配以大量的实例加以分析。同时,各单元还配有大量针对不同主题的段落翻译练习,力求在实战中提高学习者的翻译能力。

《中国文化翻译实践教程》可作为英语专业学生必修或选修课教材、非英语专业的后续拓展教材、面向各专业开设的通识教育课程教材及英语学习者了解中国文化的自学材料。本教材内容涉及翻译技巧、汉英语言与文化差异对比及中国文化相关主题翻译,主题包括中国的历史地理、语言文字、哲学思想、古今教育、科技成就、文学艺术、节日民俗、生活方式、风景名胜、民间传说、民间工艺和生态环境,共14个单元。每单元都附有大量练习,供学生课后研习。练习包括思考题、词汇层面的翻译、句子层面的翻译以及篇章层面的翻译,形式多样,旨在结合各章所学内容,加深学生对中国文化与翻译策略的理解,从而提升学生"讲好中国故事"的能力。

本教材的编者都是西安交通大学外国语学院长期参与翻译教学和实践工作的一线教师,具有丰富的翻译教学和实践经验。各编者在教材的编写过程中付出了巨大努力,但由于水平所限,编写时间仓促,教材中难免有疏漏与不足之处,诚望各位专家、学者和广大使用者提出宝贵意见,以期不断完善。在教材的编写过程中,我们也参阅并借鉴了大量国内外相关文献资料和同类教材,在此向所有相关作者表示感谢。

编 者
2024 年 4 月

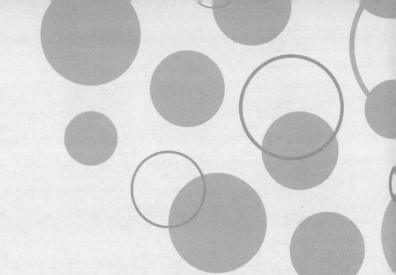

目 录

Unit 1　翻译概述 ··· 1
　翻译的概念和性质 ··· 1
　翻译的种类 ··· 2
　翻译的标准 ··· 2
　翻译的基本方法 ·· 5
　文化与翻译 ··· 9
　翻译的可译性与不可译性 ··· 10
　译者的素养 ··· 12
　拓展阅读 ··· 16

Unit 2　汉英语言及文化差异对比 ·· 19
　汉英语言体系差异 ··· 19
　汉英语言类型差异 ··· 20
　汉英词法差异 ·· 20
　汉英句法差异 ·· 24
　汉英思维差异 ·· 27
　汉英文化差异 ·· 28

Unit 3　历史地理 ·· 31
　Related Words and Expressions ··· 31
　Lead-in Activities ··· 33
　翻译技巧：增译法（Amplification）··· 36
　段落翻译 ··· 38
　拓展阅读 ··· 42
　翻译佳作赏析 ·· 44

  翻译练习 ·· 44

Unit 4　语言文字 ·· 46
  Related Words and Expressions ·· 46
  Lead-in Activities ·· 47
  翻译技巧:减词法/省略法(Omission) ·· 52
  段落翻译 ·· 55
  拓展阅读 ·· 58
  翻译佳作赏析 ·· 61
  翻译练习 ·· 62

Unit 5　哲学思想 ·· 64
  Related Words and Expressions ·· 64
  Lead-in Activities ·· 65
  翻译技巧:合译法(Combination) ·· 67
  段落翻译 ·· 69
  拓展阅读 ·· 73
  翻译佳作赏析 ·· 76
  翻译练习 ·· 78

Unit 6　古今教育 ·· 80
  Related Words and Expressions ·· 80
  Lead-in Activities ·· 82
  翻译技巧:连动句(Sentences with Serial Verbs) ·· 84
  段落翻译 ·· 89
  拓展阅读 ·· 91
  翻译佳作赏析 ·· 95
  翻译练习 ·· 96

Unit 7　科技成就 ·· 98
  Related Words and Expressions ·· 98
  Lead-in Activities ·· 101
  翻译技巧:被动句(Sentences with Passive Voice) ·· 104
  段落翻译 ·· 107
  拓展阅读 ·· 109
  翻译佳作赏析 ·· 110
  翻译练习 ·· 111

Unit 8　文学艺术 ·· 113
  Related Words and Expressions ·· 113

Lead-in Activities	115
翻译技巧：分译法（Division）	117
段落翻译	118
拓展阅读	123
翻译佳作赏析	128
翻译练习	128

Unit 9　节日民俗 ········ 131

Related Words and Expressions	131
Lead-in Activities	133
翻译技巧：调整语序（Adjusting Word Order）	135
段落翻译	137
拓展阅读	140
翻译佳作赏析	145
翻译练习	145

Unit 10　生活方式 ········ 147

Related Words and Expressions	147
Lead-in Activities	148
翻译技巧：无主句（Sentences without Subject）	150
段落翻译	151
拓展阅读	154
翻译练习	156

Unit 11　风景名胜 ········ 157

Related Words and Expressions	157
Lead-in Activities	159
翻译技巧：词性转换（Word Conversion）	161
段落翻译	164
拓展阅读	168
翻译佳作赏析	173
翻译练习	173

Unit 12　民间传说 ········ 175

Related Words and Expressions	175
Lead-in Activities	176
翻译技巧："是"字句（是-Sentences）	178
段落翻译	179
拓展阅读	184

翻译佳作赏析 ·· 185
翻译练习 ·· 186

Unit 13　民间工艺 ·· 189
Related Words and Expressions ·· 189
Lead-in Activities ··· 190
翻译技巧:"把"字句(把-Sentences) ·· 192
段落翻译 ·· 193
拓展阅读 ·· 199
翻译佳作赏析 ··· 200
翻译练习 ·· 201

Unit 14　生态环境 ·· 203
Related Words and Expressions ·· 203
Lead-in Activities ··· 204
翻译技巧:否定句(Negation Sentences) ·· 206
段落翻译 ·· 207
拓展阅读 ·· 209
翻译佳作赏析 ··· 214
翻译练习 ·· 215

Bibliography ·· 217

Unit 1

翻译概述

> **Unit Goals**
>
> In this unit, you are going to
> - be acquainted with some basic knowledge of translation, including the concept of translation, the types of translation, the criteria of translation and the methods of translation;
> - understand the relationship between culture and translation and get to know the importance of cultural awareness in the process of translating;
> - learn about the translatability and untranslatability in translation;
> - know the prerequisites for being a qualified translator.

　　翻译是一项古老的活动,在人类进步的历程中发挥着重要作用。在全球化语境下,要保持自己的文化特性和民族精神,在激烈的国际竞争中立于不败之地,我们就必须了解世界,同时让世界了解自己。翻译是国际交流至关重要的媒介,起着不可替代的桥梁和纽带作用。翻译也是一项复杂的、创造性的活动,涉及译者的语言水平、文化素养、思维方式、审美情趣、知识结构、认知水平、风俗习惯等诸多因素。本单元将概括介绍有关翻译的基本知识,为学习者打好理论基础。

翻译的概念和性质

　　我国著名翻译家张培基先生在《英汉翻译教程》一书中,从语言学的角度对翻译进行了如下定义:"翻译是运用一种语言把另一种语言所表达的思维内容准确而完整地重新表达出来的语言活动。"

　　美国翻译理论家尤金·奈达(Eugene A. Nida)则这样定义翻译:"Translating consists in reproducing in the receptor language the closest natural equivalent of the source language message, first in terms of meaning, and secondly in terms of style."。(翻译是在接受语中寻找和源语信息尽可能接近的、自然的对等话语,首先是就意义而言,其次是就其风格而言。)

　　很多人认为翻译很容易,只要懂得某一门外语(比如英语),有一本双语词典,就可以进行翻译活动。实际上,翻译绝不像人们所认为的那么简单。翻译是一种跨语言、跨文化、跨社会的交际活动,翻译的过程不仅是语言转换的过程,还是反映不同社会特征的文化转换过程。

　　翻译是一门科学,也是一种技能,更是一门艺术。翻译是一门科学,因为它涉及思维和语言,反映了认识主体与客体之间的关系,这种关系可以用受一定规律支配的语言加以描述,因此,翻译是有科学规律可循的。同时,翻译是严谨的、一丝不苟的,比如一些科技术语、成语、度量单位或部分社交用语已经有了特定的翻译模式,具有严格的标准。翻译是一种技能,因为原文的信息需要用目的语以恰当的方式再现。在再现的过程中,由于目的语和源语的差异及目的语和源语所在文化背景的不同，译者和作者对语言的认识和使用语言的习惯不可能一致，所以信息的损失不可避免。为使信息的损失尽可能减少，译者需要灵活运用减词、增词、并句、分句等技巧。只有具备强烈的翻译技能意识并在翻译理论的指导下不懈地坚持翻译实践，译者才能提高翻译水平，不断完善译文质量。翻译是一门艺术，因为它是译者对原文进行再创造的过程。从源语到目的语的转换并不是简单的机械操作，需要译者对信息进行选择、判断，在理解原文信息和作者创作意图的基础上，克服语言和文化差异，再现原文信息，否则只能反映表层的意思，无法触及深层的含义。在翻译过程中，译者会采用独特的处理方法体现自己的风格，这也反映了翻译的独创性。

翻译的种类

翻译可以从不同的角度分成不同的种类。

根据所涉及的语言，翻译可分为语内翻译（intralingual translation）和语际翻译（interlingual translation）。语内翻译指同一语言的各个语言变体之间的翻译，如将方言译成民族共同语，或将古代语译成现代语。语际翻译指不同语言之间的翻译活动，如将汉语文本译为外语文本，或将外语文本译为汉语文本。通常所说的翻译大都指语际翻译。

根据活动方式，翻译可分为口译和笔译两类。口译一般指口头翻译，其基本方式有两种：一是连续传译（consecutive interpretation），用于会议发言、商务谈判、学术研讨等场合，发言人讲完部分或全部内容之后，由口译人员进行翻译；二是同声传译（simultaneous interpretation），通常用于大型正式会议，要求译员利用专门设备，不间断地边听边译。笔译就是笔头翻译，多用于社会科学、文学艺术和科学技术等文献资料的翻译。

根据翻译材料的文体，翻译可分为应用文体、科技文体、论述文体、新闻文体和艺术文体的翻译。其中每一大类又包含许多小类，并各有特点。除了必须保证译文准确性，应用文体翻译还要求译文格式规范，严谨紧凑；科技文体翻译要求译文合乎规范并具有专业特色；论述文体要求译文逻辑清晰、语言庄重；新闻文体翻译要求译文格式正确、语义清晰、用词生动；艺术文体翻译要求译文生动流畅、富有文采。

根据处理方式，翻译可分为全译、节译、摘译、编译和译述。全译是指译者将原文原封不动地翻译出来，没有任何删节。节译是指对原文进行局部删节的翻译，但应保持原文内容相对完整。摘译是指译者根据实际需要，摘取原文的中心内容或个别章节、段落进行翻译。编译是指译者把一个甚至几个文本的相关内容进行编辑加工，根据要求进行概述性的传译。译述是最为灵活的处理方式，一般指译者仅表达出原文的主要内容或大意，不拘泥于原文的论述格式或语言表现。

翻译的标准

翻译标准是翻译活动必须遵循的准绳，是衡量译文质量的尺度，是译者不断努力以达到的目标。切实可行的翻译标准对发挥译者主观能动性、提高翻译质量具有重要的意义。

Ⅰ. 西方传统的翻译标准

西方最早的翻译标准可追溯到古罗马时代。古罗马翻译家和演说家西塞罗（Marcus Tullius Cicero）就提出"翻译不应拘泥于原文的词语，而应注重原文的思想"，"不可逐字死译，而要符合译文的语言规则和特性"，主张"翻译要保留语言总体风格和力量"。古罗马诗人贺拉斯（Quintus Horatius Flaccus)也认为"忠实原著的译者不会逐字直译"。

文艺复兴时期，关于西方翻译标准的探讨有了进一步发展。德国神学家马丁·路德(Martin Luther)提倡用大众化语言进行翻译，强调译文必须通畅易懂。法国学者艾迪安·多莱(Etienne Dolet)提出五条具体的翻译原则：①充分理解原文内容；②精通源语和目的语；③避免逐字对译；④采用通俗语言形式；⑤讲求译文整体和谐。

从18世纪开始，西方翻译理论研究更为广泛、深入，一些著名翻译理论家系统地提出了各自的翻译标准。英国翻译家乔治·坎贝尔(George Campbell)提出了翻译三原则：①必须准确再现原文的意义；②在符合译作语言特征的前提下，尽可能移植原作的精神和风格；③译作要具有原作的特征，显得自然流畅。此外，英国翻译理论家亚历山大·泰特勒(Alexander Tytler)在其所著的《论翻译的原则》中也提出了类似的三原则：① 译文应完整地再现原文的思想内容；② 译文的风格和笔调应与原文保持一致；③ 译文应和原文一样流畅自然。

19世纪英国知名的翻译家和文论家马修·阿诺德(Matthew Arnold)指出，要做到忠实于原文，必须使译文与原文风格特征契合统一，不能把传达原作风格排斥在忠实于原文的概念范围之外。阿诺德强调要揭示原作风格，译者就必须抓住原作者的创造个性，绝不能用自己的世界观去替代原作者的世界观。他还提出译文语言要自然，不可硬译，使译文产生古怪和不自然的效果。

Ⅱ. 中国传统的翻译标准

在中国翻译史上，最早的翻译标准可追溯到三国时期的佛经翻译家支谦提出的"因循本旨，不加文饰"，这可谓是"直译论"的先声。唐代佛经翻译家玄奘则提出"既须求真，又须喻俗"的翻译标准，要求译文既要忠实，又要通俗易懂，易为读者所接受。

清代翻译家严复在《天演论》的《译例言》中提出："译事三难：信、达、雅。"从此"信、达、雅"成为翻译界长期推崇的翻译标准。所谓"信、达、雅"，意即译文应忠实准确，通顺流畅，文字典雅。时至今日，"信"与"达"仍然是翻译界普遍遵循的翻译标准，但对"雅"争议颇多，因为一味追求译文的古雅而忽视原文的具体风格特征就违背了"信"的原则。一些翻译家对严复的三字标准进行了修正，其中翻译家思果提出翻译应做到"信、达、贴"。"贴"意即"贴切"，就是说译文要符合原文的语境和风格。原文雅，译文就雅；原文不雅，译文就不雅。

鲁迅和瞿秋白提倡"信"与"顺"的翻译原则，即"忠实"和"通顺"。傅雷提出的"神似"和钱钟书提出的"化境"是文学翻译的更高标准，要求译者除文字形式可有所不同外，要将原文的思想、感情、风格、神韵都原原本本地化到译文境界，不留下丝毫翻译痕迹，但真正的"化境"很难实现，可谓是翻译的最高理想。

Ⅲ. "忠实"与"通顺"

从以上翻译标准可以看出，古今中外的学者关于翻译标准的看法在本质上基本一致，无不强调译文的"忠实"和"通顺"。我国翻译教学界一直把"忠实"和"通顺"作为翻译的基本原则，这也是翻译学习者必须努力达到的标准。

"忠实"首先是指译文要忠实于原文的内容，要完整而准确地把原文的内容表达出来，不得改变或歪曲原文。"忠实"还指保持原作的风格——民族风格、语体风格、作者个人的语言风格。对这些风格，译者不得任意破坏和改变，不能以译者的风格代替原作的风格。原作若是通俗的口语体，译文就不能是文绉绉的书面体；原作若文雅，译文就不能粗俗；原作若富有某种文化色彩，译文也要尽可能将其保留。

"通顺"指的是译文语言必须流畅、易懂，遣词造句应当符合译语的语法规范和表达习惯，切不可逐词死译、硬译，避免出现文理不通、逻辑不清、晦涩难懂的现象，而是应在忠实于原文的前提下，摆脱原文结构形式的束缚，按照目的语的行文规范和表达习惯组织译文。但需注意，译文的通顺程度要和原文的通顺程度保持一致。例如在文艺作品中，作者有时故意采用一些表达不规范的语言以刻画人物或渲染气氛，译文就不能片面追求通顺而改变原作语言风格，应尽可能体现原作的语言特征，这正是"忠实"的具体体现。

实际上，"忠实"与"通顺"之间是一种相互依存的关系："忠实"而不"通顺"，读者看不懂，"忠实"便失去了意义；"通顺"而不"忠实"，脱离原作的内容与风格，"通顺"也就失去了作用，使译文成为编纂或杜撰。因此，应当将"忠实"和"通顺"看作是统一的整体。

下文将通过一些译例来讨论翻译的标准。

例 1 Rubber is not hard; it gives way to pressure.

原译 橡胶不硬，屈服于压力。

改译 橡胶不硬，受压会变形。

评析 give way 本义为"屈服""让步"，原译仅照搬原文的字面意思，没有摆脱原文语言形式，似乎忠实于原文，但译文读起来生硬、奇怪；改译则考虑了 rubber 的特性，根据上下文的语境，准确地翻译出了原文的意思。改译后，译文读起来更加流畅自然，符合汉语的表达习惯。

例 2 There will be television chat shows hosted by robots, and cars with pollution monitors that will disable them when they offend.

原译 将会有机器人控制的电视聊天节目，以及带有污染监视器的汽车在冒犯时，司机就不能工作了。

改译 将出现由机器人主持的电视谈话节目以及装有污染监控器的汽车，当这些汽车排污超标，监控器就会使其停止行驶。

评析 原译过分拘泥于原文的句子结构和字面意思，因而未能翻译出原文所要表达的含义，读起来逻辑不清、晦涩难懂。正确的翻译方法是在准确理解原文的基础上，跳出原文的框架，根据汉语习惯和上下文的逻辑关系，通过适当调整句子结构并寻找贴切的表达方式来准确再现原文的意思。根据汉语习惯，原句中两个主语各自的后置定语 hosted by robots 和 with pollution monitors 可以分别放到其中心词前来翻译。monitor 是"监视器"的意思，但是汉语中，"监视污染"搭配不当，可改为"检测或者监控污染"，所以这里 pollution monitors 可翻译为"污染监控器"或者"污染检测器"。此外，that will disable them when they offend 应根据汉语习惯先翻译其中的时间状语从句，when they offend 中的 they 指"汽车"，但这个从句直译成"当汽车冒犯时"毫无意义。根据上下文，此句实际上是说"汽车排污超标"。同样，disable 的意思是"使丧失能力"或"使伤残"，根据语境，该词在这里指"使汽车不能行驶"。

例 3 听到这话，他心里一跳，脸色也变了。

原译 Hearing this, his heart jumped and the color of his face changed.

改译 At this, his heart missed a beat and he became pale.

评析 原译拘泥于原句的形式，逐字翻译，不符合英语的表达习惯和方式。改译虽然在形式上与原句不一致，但地道而准确地表达出了原句的意思。

例 4 Size don't matter, chopping wood...

原译 说到劈柴，个头并不重要……

改译 个头没啥关系，劈柴嘛……

评析 原文说的是故事的叙述人想找一个人劈柴，见来了一个个头很小的孩子，便怀疑他是否能胜任，这个孩子便这样回答了。这个孩子文化程度不高，说的是不规范的英语（如主语 size 后应该用助动词 doesn't，而不是 don't；chopping wood 跟主句关系松散），而原译用的是较为规范的汉语，与原文的语体色彩不相符合。改译不仅准确地翻译出了原句的意思，而且再现了原文的语气和风格。

例 5 From there I could see the whole valley below, the fields, the river, and the village. It was all very beautiful, and the sight of it filled me with longing.

原译 从那里，我可以看见下面的整个山谷、田野、河流和村庄。这一切非常美丽，见到后使我心里充满了渴望。

改译 从这里望下去，整个山谷一览无遗，只见那田野、河流和村庄，全都美不胜收，真叫我心驰神往。

评析 原译追求的是字与字、结构与结构的机械对应，翻译腔比较重，特别是"使我心里充满了渴望"，既别扭又含混，不知道故事叙述者"渴望"什么。改译的效果就大不一样，表达自然流畅，非常好地传达了原文所表达的意境。

总之，翻译不是一种语言中的词语和语句结构到另一种语言的词语和语句结构的简单转换。德国翻译学家沃尔弗拉姆·维尔斯（Wolfram Wilss）在 *The Science of Translation*: *Problems & Methods* 一书中说："Translation is not simply a matter of seeking other words with similar meaning, but of finding appropriate ways of saying things in another language. Translating is always meaning-based, i. e. it is the transfer of meaning instead of form from the source language to the target language."（翻译不仅仅是在另一种语言中寻找意义相近的词语，而是寻找表达事物的恰当方式。翻译始终立足于语义，也就是说，它是语义而不是形式从源语到目的语的转换。）。这说明翻译是语义而不是语言形式的翻译，是运用另一种语言的恰当表述方式来表达一种语言所表达的内容。翻译必须跳出原文语言层面的束缚，必须着眼于传达原文的内容和意义。

翻译的基本方法

翻译的方法多种多样，翻译学界从不同的维度对翻译方法进行了不同的划分。直译、意译和音译是三种常用的基本翻译方法。此外，由于英汉两种语言在句法、词汇、修辞等方面均存在着很大的差异，因此在进行英汉互译时必然会遇到很多困难，需要有一定的翻译技巧作指导。常用的翻译技巧有增译法、减词法、合译法、分译法、调整语序、词性转换等。这些技巧将在后面各单元中结合具体实例分别介绍。

Ⅰ. 直译（Literal Translation）

直译指翻译时尽量保持原作的语言形式，包括用词、句子结构或修辞手法，从而达到与原文近似的语言效果，更好地体现原作的"异域色彩"，同时要求语言流畅易懂。直译不等于硬译。所谓硬译，也叫逐词翻译（word-for-word translation），力求目的语的每个词都能与源语的每个词对等，过于拘泥于原文的形式，一味追求形式对等，置翻译效果于不顾。由于不符合目的语的表达习惯，逐词翻译的译文往往晦涩难懂，甚至不知所云。直译和硬译的区别在于，直译是对译文进行必要的调整，因而比较符合目的语表达习惯，文字比较通顺，而且在大多数情况下，译文读者能够获得与原文读者大致相同的感受。例如：

hot line 热线
blind zone 盲区
black market 黑市
a laughing stock 笑柄
cold war 冷战
to fish in troubled waters 浑水摸鱼
to pour oil on the fire 火上浇油
Strike while the iron is hot. 趁热打铁。
Walls have ears. 隔墙有耳。
Rome was not built in a day. 罗马的建成非一日之功。
A rolling stone gathers no moss. 滚石不生苔。
香山 Fragrant Hill
芦笛岩 Reed Flute Cave
大雁塔 the Big/Great Wild Goose Pagoda
春节 Spring Festival
中秋节 Mid-autumn Festival
泼水节 Water-sprinkling Festival
火把节 Torch Festival
云计算 cloud computing
大数据 big data
物联网 the Internet of Things（IoT）
区块链 block chain
内卷 involution
现代制造业 modern manufacturing industry
经济特区 special economic zone
自由贸易试验区（自贸区）pilot free trade zones
数字化经济 digital economy
"一国两制" One Country，Two Systems
连锁反应 chain reaction
他是只纸老虎。He is a paper tiger.
别流鳄鱼泪。Don't shed crocodile tears.
必须弥合代沟。We must bridge the generation gap.
这事使他丢脸。This matter makes him lose face.

直译可以对号入座，字字翻译，但很多时候必须在句子的某些成分上进行词类、词序、句式等方面的调整或变动。

例1 Please identify the factors responsible for the increasing cost of living.
请指出引起生活费高涨的因素。

例 2 Here are some grammatical errors you have made in your composition.
这里是一些你在作文中所犯的语法错误。

例 3 Helen was born at 10 p. m. on March 3rd, 1990.
海伦出生于一九九〇年三月三日晚上十点。

例 4 Jack is mentally sound but physically weak.
杰克精神健全但身体虚弱。

例 5 A new syllabus has been drawn up.
已经拟定了一份新的教学大纲。

例 6 His failure to observe the traffic rules resulted in the road accident.
他没有遵守交通规则,导致了交通事故的发生。

例 7 With your permission, I will embark on the project as soon as possible.
如果你答应的话,我将尽快开展这个项目。

Ⅱ. 意译(Free Translation)

意译是指忠实于原文的内容而不拘泥于原文结构形式与修辞手法的翻译方法。由于不同民族在历史渊源、文化传统、风俗习惯、地理环境等诸多方面存在差异,源语与目的语往往不仅在词语结构上有所区别,在表达方式上也必然存在许多不同之处。汉英两种语言之间的种种差异就决定了翻译中不可能始终采用直译法,否则会使译文佶屈聱牙、生硬别扭,或者含糊不清、模棱两可,甚至背离原文。在这种情况下就需借助意译来摆脱原文结构和表达方式的束缚,在充分理解原文的基础上,根据目的语行文规范,重新遣词造句,把原文的意思通顺、地道地表达出来。但是,意译不等于胡译。所谓胡译,就是为了所谓"表达的顺畅",在没有真正理解原文的情况下,望文生义,对上下文进行随意的阐释,增添原文中并不存在的内容或删减、遗漏原文所包含的内容。此外,一味追求直译,则容易进入误区,造成误译。直译之所以会造成歧义,一方面是因为语言的形式与内容及句子的表层结构与深层意义有时不统一;另一方面,不同的文化和历史背景也造成了思维方式和语言表达形式的差异。例如:

bull's eye ×牛眼睛 √靶心
a black sheep ×黑羊 √害群之马
a white lie ×白色的谎言 √善意的谎言
the apple of one's eye ×眼睛里的苹果 √掌上明珠
That's all Greek to me. ×那对我来说全是希腊语。 √那个我可一窍不通。
Do you see any green in my eyes? ×你从我眼睛里看到绿色了吗? √你以为我是好欺负的吗?
经济作物 ×economic crops √cash crops
拳头产品 ×fist product √competitive product
向钱看 ×looking at money √money mad
寄人篱下 ×to live under one's fence √to live under one's roof
五湖四海 ×five lakes, four seas √all corners of the country
最美逆行者 ×the most beautiful going against the traffic √heroes in harm's way
直播带货 ×live broadcasting to sell the goods √live streaming E-commerce
此地无银三百两。The more is concealed, the more is revealed.

目不识丁 totally illiterate / Don't know one's ABC.

Do not cross a bridge before you come to it. 不要杞人忧天。

Give a dog a bad name and hang him. 欲加之罪，何患无辞。

He that lives with cripples learns to limp. 近朱者赤，近墨者黑。

Diamond cuts diamond. 棋逢对手。

总而言之，直译和意译各有所长，两种方法也经常并用。有些惯用语的英译就要先直译后意译，这样才能兼顾译文的表层结构和原文的深层意思。例如：

不劳而获 reap without sowing — profit by others' toil

饮水思源 When you drink the water, think of its source. — Never forget where one's happiness comes from.

种瓜得瓜，种豆得豆 Plant melons and get melons; sow beans and get beans. — You reap what you have sown.

真金不怕火炼 True gold fears no fire. — A person of integrity can stand severe tests.

Ⅲ. 音译（Transliteration）

音译是指用目的语的文字符号再现源语词语的发音。音译一般用于人名、地名、重要建筑物等名称的翻译，还用于翻译在目的语中找不到对应或类似表达的词语。在音译的同时，为了使目的语读者更好地理解源语文化，可以同时添加注解对所译概念进行解释，以消除翻译空缺现象。此种翻译方法称作音译加注法，使用这种翻译方法既可以保留源语独特的文化特征，又可以使读者更好地了解不同的文化。例如：

老子 Lao Zi　　　　　　　　　　Elizabeth 伊丽莎白

孙子 Sun Zi　　　　　　　　　　Abraham 亚伯拉罕

北京 Beijing　　　　　　　　　　Shakespeare 莎士比亚

香港 Hong Kong　　　　　　　　New York 纽约

渤海 Bohai Sea　　　　　　　　　Buckingham Palace 白金汉宫

叩头 kowtow　　　　　　　　　　coffee 咖啡

阴阳 Yin & Yang　　　　　　　　soda 苏打

功夫 Kung Fu　　　　　　　　　 ruble 卢布

太极 Tai Ji　　　　　　　　　　　sardine 沙丁鱼

气功 qigong　　　　　　　　　　champagne 香槟

风水 Feng Shui　　　　　　　　　marathon 马拉松

麒麟 kylin　　　　　　　　　　　talk show 脱口秀

荔枝 lychee, litchi　　　　　　　　mosaic 马赛克

龙眼 longan　　　　　　　　　　logic 逻辑

饺子 jiaozi　　　　　　　　　　　hacker 黑客

云吞 wonton　　　　　　　　　　humor 幽默

点心 dim sum　　　　　　　　　 Olympics 奥林匹克运动会

豆腐 tofu（bean curd）　　　　　　gene 基因

拉面 ramen　　　　　　　　　　nylon 尼龙

炒面 chow mein

琵琶 pipa

二胡 erhu

麻将 mahjong

台风 typhoon

生旦净丑 sheng, dan, jing and chou (the four main roles in Chinese traditional operas, i. e. the male role, the female role, the painted-face role, and the comic role)

衙门 yamen (government office in feudal China)

OPEC (The Organization of the Petroleum Exporting Countries) 欧佩克（石油输出国组织）

文化与翻译

Ⅰ. 文化的定义

有关文化的定义有很多种，但总体而言可以从广义和狭义两个角度来理解文化。广义的文化指人类社会历史实践过程中所创造的物质财富和精神财富的总和；狭义的文化指社会的意识形态，以及与之相适应的制度和组织机构。根据文化人类学的分类，文化有四大系统：①技术经济系统（包括生态、生产、交换和分配方式、科学技术、人工制品等）；②社会系统（包括阶级、群体、亲属制度、政治、法律、教育、风俗习惯、通史等）；③观念系统（包括宇宙观、民间信仰、艺术创造和意象、价值观、认识和思想方式等）；④语言系统（包括音位学、字位学、语法和语义学）。

从文化的定义可以看出，文化是一个非常宽泛的概念，包括历史、地理、风俗习惯、思想方式、价值观念、文学艺术、宗教信仰、政治制度等。

Ⅱ. 语言与文化的关系

语言与文化有着十分密切的关系。语言是一面镜子，它反映着一个民族的文化，揭示该民族文化的内容。文化具有鲜明的民族性和独特性，是民族差异的标志。各个民族由于地域、生态环境、社会制度、历史背景、风俗习惯、价值观念、行为模式等的不同，其文化也具有各自的特点。透过一个民族的语言，人们可以了解到该民族文化的独特性。

语言作为交际工具并不是独立存在的，它与文化是一个整体。要掌握一种语言就要熟悉其背后的文化特殊性，而翻译则需要译者洞察本族文化与其他民族文化的差异。

Ⅲ. 翻译中的文化意识

翻译中，对文化因素的处理是十分重要的任务。翻译不只是两种语言的语法、句式、语义系统之间的转换，更是两种文化的交流。了解汉英两种语言在思维方式和文化方面的差异，对于做好翻译工作是非常重要的。中国文化里的一些事物或行为也存在于其他国家和文化里，而且有相对应的表达，但含义大不相同。此外还有"文化空缺"现象，即有些说法无法在目的语文化中找到对应的表述，例如，汉语中的"唱红脸""跑龙套""阴阳""老油条""孔夫子搬家——净是书（输）"等；英语中的 a skeleton in the cupboard、a green eye、as poor as a church mouse、Trojan Horse、take the French leave 等。语言文化差异给翻译工作和活动带来许多困难，因此翻译时需透彻地理解原文中所涉及的文化现象和因素，这样才能产出最自然的、最为读者所接受的译文，并再现原文所表达的思想情感、异国情调及所蕴藏的文化内涵。

总之，翻译绝不能只着眼于语言转换，而应透过语言表层，理解其深层含义。在翻译过程中，要充分考虑源语和目的语存在的文化差异，适当地对文化差异进行处理，避免死译和硬译。

翻译的可译性与不可译性

在人类的历史进程中，翻译为不同文明的交流作出了不可磨灭的贡献。翻译的实践历史证明，各种语言、文化之间的共性使语言之间的互译成为可能，但同时因为各种语言、文化有其独特性，这种互译又存在着局限。英语属于印欧语系，而汉语属于汉藏语系，两种语言在语音系统、文字结构和修辞方法等方面存在很大差异，致使在英汉互译过程中，有时无法将源语翻译成目的语，从而造成一定程度上意义的损失，这就是翻译的"不可译性"。这种"不可译性"包括"语言层次上的不可译性"和"文化层次上的不可译性"。

Ⅰ. 语言层次上的不可译性

1. 语音方面

例1 Cat, cat, cat, catch the fat rat fast!

在汉译此句时，很难将英语中语音所表达出的急促而又朗朗上口的效果表达出来。

例2 Trick or treat.

Trick or treat 也是英语文化中的特有表达，常译为"不给糖就捣蛋"，而 trick 和 treat 这两个谐音词是不可译的。

2. 字（词）方面

例1 A：What makes a road broad? B：The letter "B."

这则英文谜语也具有不可译性，因为在汉语中"公路"与"宽阔"在词的构成方面没有任何联系。

例2 水有虫则浊，水有鱼则渔，水水水，江河湖淼淼。

木之下为本，木之上为末，木木木，松柏樟森森。

汉语中有拆字的写作技巧，这种技巧基于汉字的字形特征，基本上无法转译。这则对联的不可译性就在于对汉字结构特点的巧妙利用。对联采用了对仗的修辞手法，将汉字拆开表达，并具有一定意义，不论采取何种翻译技巧，原作的修辞效果和语义很难同时保留。

例3 小葱拌豆腐——一清（青）二白

歇后语是汉语的一种特殊语言形式，常运用双关、回文、拆字、对偶、顶真等修辞手法。译成英语时往往无法保留原文的修辞效果。

例4 Able was I ere I saw Elba.

此句很特别，以字母 r 为中心，向两侧展开，每一个字母都是对称的。英语中的回文无论是以单词形式还是以句子形式出现，在汉语中都很难体现或表达。

3. 诗歌方面

诗歌翻译中不可避免会存在一些不可译现象。汉语和英语的诗歌都具有意美、形美、音美的特点，翻译时往往只能注重原诗的意美，形美和音美很难完全保留。

例1 路漫漫其修远兮，吾将上下而求索。

The way ahead's a long, long one, oh!

I'll seek my Beauty high and low.

例 2　白日依山尽，黄河入海流。

　　　The sun beyond the mountain glows.

　　　The Yellow River seawards flows.

例 3　寻寻觅觅，冷冷清清，凄凄惨惨戚戚。……梧桐更兼细雨，到黄昏，点点滴滴。

　　　I look for what I miss.

　　　I know not what it is.

　　　I feel so sad, so drear.

　　　So lonely, without cheer.

　　　…

　　　Upon the plane—trees a fine rain drizzles

　　　As twilight grizzles.

Ⅱ. 文化层次上的不可译性

翻译中的文化不可译性指的是在翻译过程中，源语中的文化特色无法完全准确地翻译到目的语中，因为这些文化特色为源语文化所独有，目的语中可能不存在或不具有相同的文化内涵。例如，中国象棋中的"马走日"和"象走田"是"马"和"象"两个棋子的基本走法。此处"日"字不代表"太阳"(sun)，"田"字也不代表"田地"(field)，而是表示棋子"马"和"象"只能在棋盘的日形格和田形格中呈对角线方向移动。"他只会马走日，象走田"一句便生动形象地说明"他"只会中国象棋的基本走法，不懂下象棋的策略和布局，此句在译成英语时可采用意译策略，译成"He only knows the basic moves of the Chinese chess."，原文的文化内涵很难再现。又如，"龙"的形象在汉语和英语文化中的寓意大相径庭。中国文化中龙是上古时期图腾的产物，象征着尊贵、威严与权力，而在西方文化中则多象征邪恶。

当不可译现象发生时，可以采取相应的策略使不可译性向可译性转化。归化(domestication)和异化(foreignization)是常用的策略。归化译法指沿用目的语固有的表达形式，包括语义归化译法和修辞归化译法；异化译法指的是在目的语中引入源语的表达形式，包括异化直译法和异化直译加注法。

1. 归化译法

语义归化译法指沿用目的语固有的表达形式。例如：

原文　济公劫富济贫，深受穷苦人民爱戴。

译文　Jigong, Robin Hood in China, robbed the rich and helped the poor.

评析　译文采用的是语义归化，把济公比作英美文学中的罗宾汉，西方读者会感到熟悉和亲切，更容易理解原文的内涵。

以下译例也都运用了语义归化的方法：

狐假虎威 like a donkey in a lion's hide

势如破竹 like a hot knife cutting through the butter

谋事在人，成事在天。Man proposes, God disposes.

别多管闲事。Stop being a backseat driver!

新官上任三把火。A new broom sweeps clean.

Love me, love my dog. 爱屋及乌

Cry up wine and sell vinegar. 挂羊头，卖狗肉。

修辞归化译法指的是原文本身运用了某种修辞手法，翻译成目的语时，译者不但要准确地表达出原文的意义，还要保持原文的修辞效果。例如：

原文 A：Why is the river rich?

B：Because it has two banks.

译文 A：为什么说河水富有？

B：因为它年年有鱼呀。

评析 如果按字面意思翻译，原文的幽默诙谐就无法再现。译者采用修辞归化法，利用"鱼"和"余"谐音双关来表达原文的意义和修辞效果，形式上不同于原文的一词多义，但在修辞效果上是一致的，可以说是"形"异而"神"似。

2. 异化译法

异化直译法是指在符合目的语语言规范的基础上，在不引起错误的联想或误解的前提下，在译文中保留原文习语的比喻形象、民族色彩和语言风格。异化直译法既能保持原文语言的文化现象，又可以丰富译文语言，帮助读者扩大文化视野，体验不同文化的魅力。

对于英汉语言中意义和形式基本对应的习语，可以采用直译法。例如 blood is thicker than water（血浓于水）、like walking on thin ice（如履薄冰）等。汉语中也有一些习语被英语吸纳，如丢面子（to lose face）、纸老虎（paper tiger）等。

异化直译加注法是直译法的扩展，译者既用直译保留源语文化形象，又加上注解便于目的语读者理解，这样不仅可以使目的语读者了解源语语言中的相关文化知识，还有助于将全新的文化概念引入目的语文化。例如，把 to carry coals to Newcastle 译为"运煤到纽卡斯尔（多此一举）"是不够的，应加注说明纽卡斯尔是英格兰北部泰恩河畔的一个港口城市，以产煤著称，从别处再运煤到纽卡斯尔自然是多此一举。又如：

原文 嘴里天天说"唤起民众"，民众起来了又害怕得要死，这和叶公好龙有什么两样？

译文 If one shouts every day about "arousing the masses of the people," but is scared to death when the people do rise. What is the difference between that and *Lord Ye's love of dragons*?

Note：*Lord Ye's love of dragons* (*Ye was so fond of dragons that he adorned his whole palace with drawings and carvings of them, but when a real dragon heard of his infatuation and paid him a visit, he was frightened out of his wits.*)

总之，虽然语言和文化方面的差异给翻译带来许多很难解决的问题，但是不可译性并非绝对。在一定条件下，通过译者的创造性劳动，不可译性可以向可译性转化。只要译者对两种语言和文化具有深刻的造诣，并抱有严肃认真的治学态度，许多翻译难题都可以找到比较满意的解决方法。

译者的素养

翻译就是把一种语言文字的意义用另一种语言文字表达出来，译文既要忠实于原文，又要通顺流畅，这绝非易事。要做好翻译工作，译者必须具备一定的素养。对于初学者来说，要在以下几个方面多下功夫。

Ⅰ. 扎实的语言功底

语言功底包括源语和目的语的语言功底。翻译是对源语文字进行深刻剖析，得其义，悟其神，然后用畅达的目的语文字将其表达出来。没有良好的源语和目的语功底，便无法透彻理解原文，也就无法翻译出高质量的译文。

Ⅱ. 广博的知识

翻译是一种跨语言、跨文化、跨社会的交流手段，译者除了要具备扎实的语言功底，还应掌握广博的文化知识。文化知识主要包括两个方面：一是文化背景知识，涉及政治、经济、军事、外交、历史、地理、风土人情、民族心理、自然风貌、文学、艺术、文化传统等，以及两种语言所反映的文化差异；二是翻译工作所涉及的相关领域的专业知识。为了做好翻译工作，译者必须是一个杂家，一部活的百科全书。这当然是一个理想化的目标，但每个译者都应该向这个目标努力。

Ⅲ. 敏锐的感受能力

对于文化背景差异较大的两种语言，译者需敏锐地感受作者的思想意识、表达习惯以及作品的场景情调，体会源语文化与目的语文化之间的差异，这对于忠实传达原文内容至关重要。译者需要有良好的艺术感受能力，要准确理解原文，用精确恰当的语言表达原文的内容和精神实质。

Ⅳ. 严谨认真的态度和作风

翻译工作作为中外文化交流的桥梁，肩负着传播先进文化、促进世界文明发展的使命。因此，凡有志于从事翻译工作的人，必须具有一丝不苟、严谨认真的态度和作风。

Exercises

1. There are 10 English sentences below, each of which has two different Chinese versions. Compare the different Chinese versions with the original English and then comment on them in terms of the translation methods and the criteria of translation.

    1) "Since she left, I have done the cooking and baked the cakes, but mine are never as good as hers."

    "Nonsense, my dear; I don't think Lissie's cakes were any better than yours." said Mr. Priestly loyally.

    译文 A "自从她走后，我就自己做饭菜，烤蛋糕，但我做的从没有她做的那样好吃。"

    "胡说八道，亲爱的，我觉得你做的饼和莉茜做的一样好吃。"普里斯特先生诚心地说。

    译文 B "自从她走后，我就自己做饭菜，烤蛋糕，但我做的从没有她做的那样好吃。"

    "哪儿的话，亲爱的，我觉得你做的饼和莉茜做的一样好吃。"普里斯特先生诚心地说。

    2) Certainly I don't teach because teaching is easy for me. Teaching is the most difficult of the various ways I have attempted to earn my living… Why, then, do I teach? I teach because I like the pace of the academic calendar… I teach because teaching is a profession built on change…

    译文 A 当然，我不教书是因为我觉得教书轻松。我曾做过多种工作来赚钱谋生，而教书是其中最难的……那么，我为什么还要教书呢？我教书是因为我喜欢教学日历的节奏……我教书是因为教书是一种以变化为基础的职业……

    译文 B 当然，我教书并不是因为我觉得教书轻松。我曾做过多种工作来赚钱谋生，而教书是其中最难的……那么，我为什么还要教书呢？我教书是因为我喜欢教学日历的节奏……我教书是因为教书是一种以变化为基础的职业……

3) They ran as fast as their legs could carry them.

    译文 A 他们跑得像他们的腿所能载动他们的那样快。

    译文 B 他们拼命地跑，能跑多快就跑多快。

4) She was vexed by the persistent ringing of the phone.

    译文 A 她被执着的电话铃声搞得心烦意乱。

    译文 B 她被没完没了的电话铃声搞得心烦意乱。

5) All the inventors have a restless mind.

    译文 A 所有的发明家都生性好动。

    译文 B 所有的发明家都有一个思想活跃的头脑。

6) In private firms, green hands need special training.

    译文 A 在私人公司里，绿色的手都要接受特殊的培训。

    译文 B 在私营公司里，新手都要接受培训。

7) All the candidates cannot be employed.

    译文 A 所有的申请者都不能被录用。

    译文 B 并不是所有的申请者都可以被录用。

8) I can't thank you more.

    译文 A 我不能更多地感谢您。

    译文 B 我对您真是感激不尽。

9) She wears her years well.

    译文 A 她年年穿得都挺好。

    译文 B 她一点儿也不显老。

10) She tried hard to perform well, but the costume was not cooperating.

    译文 A 她努力想要表演好，但是服装不合作。

    译文 B 她努力想要表演好，但服装影响了她的发挥。

2 Compare the different Chinese/English versions with the original English/Chinese and then comment on them.

1) 不见黄河不死心。

    译文 A not stop until one reaches the Yellow River

    译文 B not stop until one reaches one's goal

    译文 C not stop until one reaches the Yellow River — not stop until one reaches one's goal

2) Kill two birds with one stone.

    译文 A 一石二鸟

    译文 B 一举两得

    译文 C 一箭双雕

3) All roads lead to Rome.

    译文 A 条条大路通罗马。

    译文 B 殊途同归

4)《水浒传》

  译文A *Water Margin*

  译文B *Outlaws of the Marsh*

  译文C *All Men Are Brothers*

5)Rome was not built in a day.

  译文A 罗马不是一天建成的。

  译文B 冰冻三尺，非一日之寒。

6)Two's company, three's a crowd.

  译文A 两人是伴，三人是患。

  译文B 两个和尚抬水吃，三个和尚没水吃。

7)God gives every bird its food, but He doesn't throw it into its nest.

  译文A 上帝给了鸟儿食物，但他没有将食物扔到它的巢里。

  译文B 授之以鱼，不如授之以渔。

8)My uncle Cassidy gives me money! Pigs might fly if they had wings!

  译文A 我的卡西迪叔叔会给我钱？那猪也会长翅膀飞上天啦！

  译文B 我的卡西迪叔叔会给我钱？除非太阳从西边出来！

9)人都是这山望着那山高，对自己的现状没有满意的时候。

  译文A Almost all people think that the other mountain is higher than the one he's standing on. They never feel satisfied with what they've already got.

  译文B Almost all people think that the grass is greener on the other hill. They never feel satisfied with what they have already got.

10)天有不测风云，人有旦夕祸福。

  译文A Storms gather without warning in nature, and bad luck befalls men overnight.

  译文B The weather and human life are both unpredictable.

3 Please translate the following sayings and proverbs from Chinese into English by using appropriate methods of translation.

1)知足常乐

2)时不我待

3)良药苦口

4)本性难移

5)本末倒置

6)眼见为实

7)诚实是上策

8)好书如挚友

9)患难见真情

10)三思而后行

11)善始才能善终

12)身教重于言教

13)英雄所见略同

14) 一花独放不是春

15) 人生得一知己难

16) 有其父，必有其子

17) 物以类聚，人以群分

18) 水能载舟，亦能覆舟

19) 不入虎穴，焉得虎子

20) 天网恢恢，疏而不漏

21) 智者千虑，必有一失

22) 己所不欲，勿施于人

23) 人民至上，生命至上

24) 坚持到底，就是胜利

25) 少壮不努力，老大徒伤悲

拓展阅读

Confidence in Chinese Culture
November 30, 2016
By Xi Jinping

I hope we all have full confidence in our culture and work to lift our national spirit with literary and art works. The realization of national rejuvenation requires us to have confidence in the path, theories, system and culture of socialism with Chinese characteristics. A good understanding of and a strong confidence in China's profound culture are the prerequisites for the creation of excellent works with distinct national features and unique personal style. Writers and artists should excel in learning from the best of the country's cultural heritage and siphon energy from it. They should have full confidence in the aspirations, values, vitality and creativity of their own culture, and produce works of art that give strength to the Chinese people on their march towards the future.

Culture is the soul of both a country and a nation. History and reality have proven that a nation which abandons or betrays its own history and culture cannot prosper and is likely to end in tragedy. Confidence in culture is basic, deep-rooted, and reaches far and wide; it is a force that is more fundamental, stable and persistent. Increasing confidence in our own culture is critical to the prospects of our country, to our cultural security, and to the independence of our national character. Without confidence in culture, there's no way to create works that are hard-hitting, unique and charming.

Human history tells us that all nations across the globe, without exception, are deeply influenced by excellent art and literature as well as by gifted writers and artists in each and every phase of their historical development. The spirit of the Chinese nation is embodied in the striving of the Chinese people and their achievements, in the cultural life of the Chinese people, in all the marvelous works created by the Chinese nation over thousands of years, and also in the fantastic creative activities of all Chinese writers and artists.

The Chinese nation has created numerous brilliant works at every step of its historical course, such as *Book of Songs*, *Songs of Chu*, *fu* poetry of Han Dynasty (206 BC – AD 220), poems of the Tang (618 –

907) and Song (960 – 1279) dynasties, operas of the Yuan Dynasty (1206 – 1368), and novels of the Ming (1368 – 1644) and Qing (1616 – 1911) dynasties, that give birth to the splendid history of Chinese art and literature. It is the prolific literary and artistic creativity of the Chinese nation, our marvelous achievements, and confidence in culture that make us so proud.

Each era has its unique art and literature as well as its unique spirit. Classical art and literature in any era epitomize the social life and spirit of that era with coincident traces and features. Only when the arts of an era are closely related to the nation and share weal and woe with its people, can they air resonant voices. Writers and artists should follow the path of the times, respond to the call of the times, listen to the voice of the times, and brave the challenges of the times.

There is a universally applicable law across the whole world throughout history: Art and literature rise and prosper at the beginning of a new era; they change as the momentum changes, march along with their time, and synchronize with their time in rhythm and wavelength. At every critical juncture of human development, art and literature are the harbinger of social progress, heralding periodic change and social transformation. Aloof from booming life and the zeitgeist, those writers and artists who indulge in self-admiration are bound to be marginalized by society.

The significance of any work of art and literature lies in the idea and values contained in it. All forms of expression are but a means to transmit the ideas and values. A work devoid of ideas and values is worthless no matter what dazzling forms of expression are adopted. Our core socialist values fully represent the spirit of contemporary China and serve as the cultural and ethical cornerstone that coalesces China's strength. Our writers and artists should undertake the principal task of developing and promoting the core socialist values and create excellent works carrying the distinct brand and style of China by following the Chinese ways of thinking, expression of emotions and aesthetical preferences.

Since our motherland gives us the strongest support while our heroes best represent our nation, singing the praises of our motherland and our heroes is the eternal theme and the most touching chapter of our literary and artistic creations. To ignite the sense of national pride and honor of all Chinese people, we should follow this patriotic theme, describe a beautiful China, and tell the best stories of our nation through striking language and vivid images. We must hold our heroes in great respect, present them and their stories in a respectful way, promote them in our art and literature, and help our people develop positive viewpoints on history, nation, state, and culture. Our art and literature should exhibit energetic efforts on behalf of reform and opening up, socialist modernization, and a fruitful, progressive and united China, to encourage all our people to march towards a promising future.

Strengthening cultural confidence is nothing but empty talk without perceiving and applying the history of the Chinese nation. History is a mirror, through which we can better see the world and life and understand ourselves; History is also a sage whose admonition can help us better understand the past, grasp the present, and face the future. There is a Chinese verse: "Our imagination expressed in literary and artistic creation can reach any point in time throughout history, and every corner of the whole world in a blink of an eye." Writers and artists struggling in search of inspiration and profound ideas should seek them in historical materials.

Our cultural legacy has provided writers and artists with abundant nourishment and sent their imagination flying. But writers and artists must not portray past events or persons merely through their unbridled imagination or by resorting to historical nihilism. No writers or artists can accurately reconstruct what has happened in the past, but they have the duty to tell the truth about our history and let the people know what are the most valuable in our tradition. Literary and artistic works that make travesty of history indicate that the author is not serious about history, that he's not serious about his own creations. Such works will not have a place in the literary and artistic pantheon. Only if we develop a sound outlook on history, show respect for our tradition and present the past through proper artistic means can our works stand the test of time, find their proper place in our time and pass on to prosperity.

The Chinese culture is both historical and contemporary belonging both to the Chinese nation and the whole world. Art and literature must take root in the land where they were born and grew up to reflect reality, strengthen confidence and absorb energy, if they are to hold against the impact of other cultures. These echoes with a Chinese poem which goes, "When we eat the fruit, we think of the tree that bore it; when we drink water, we think of its source."

We have to bear in mind the essence of Chinese culture, learn from foreign cultures, and look to the future. We need to complete a creative transformation in cultural inheritance, and try to surpass those from whom we learn. We hope to create excellent works that embody the essence of the Chinese culture, reflect the Chinese people's aesthetic pursuits, spread the values of contemporary China, and are in line with the world's progressive trends. We have to present our literature and art in the international arena with distinct Chinese features, in a distinctive Chinese style and Chinese ethos.

Exercises

 Translate the following expressions and sentences into English.

1) 文化自信

2) 文化遗产

3) 民族精神

4) 民族复兴

5) 文艺作品

6) 文化道德基石

7) 中国特色社会主义

8) 树立正确的历史观

9) 激发每一个中国人的民族自豪感和国家荣誉感

10) 任何一个时代的经典文艺作品,都是那个时代社会生活和精神的写照。

Unit 2

汉英语言及文化差异对比

Unit Goals

In this unit, you are going to
- acquire knowledge about the language characteristics of Chinese and English;
- develop an awareness of language differences between Chinese and English;
- know the strategies of translation from Chinese to English and from English to Chinese;
- become aware of the cultural differences between Chinese and English.

世界各民族和地域都有自己的语言和文化。文化是语言的土壤，语言是文化的组成部分，是传承文化的重要载体。翻译是通过语言来促进不同文化之间交流的有效方式。我们学习中国文化翻译理论和技巧是为了更好地传播中国文化，使更多的人了解它的博大精深。汉英两种语言和文化之间的差异为汉英互译增添了许多困难，要克服这些困难，译者需要深入了解这两种语言的异同，包括语言体系、语言类型、词法和句法、思维方式以及文化差异等。

汉英语言体系差异

汉语属于汉藏语系(Sino-Tibetan language family)中的汉语语族。汉字(Chinese character)是世界上最古老的文字之一，是集发音、词义、形象和韵律为一体的方块字，是一种表意文字(ideographic script)。表意文字的汉字由不同的笔画在一定的平面上展开并组合而成，这些不同的结构形式和汉字笔画的组合顺序一起构成了汉字的结构形式之美。汉语以文字为中心，现代汉语以普通话为发音标准，是一种声调语言(tone language)。汉字的发音由声母、韵母和声调(tone)构成。声调赋予汉语抑扬顿挫、高昂洪亮、优美动听的音乐之美。如果汉字的声母和韵母一样，但声调不同，那么它们所表达的意思往往也会不同，例如：帆、凡、反、饭；妈、麻、马、骂。汉字是迄今为止连续使用时间最长的文字。相较于英语而言，汉语词量小而义宽，字与字可以组合成不同的词，因此可以表达出非常丰富的意义。

英语属于印欧语系(Indo-European language family)中的日耳曼语族，是一种拼音文字(alphabetic script)。拼音文字是通过拼音字母线性排列而成的线性文字(有音、义，但无形)，虽然组合顺序有一定规律，但和汉字丰富的结构变化相比相对单调，英语单词没有声调，但是句子根据不同类型有不同语调(intonation)。英语是一种语调语言(intonation language)，英语语调有语法作用，能区分陈述句、一般疑问句和反义疑问句，也可起到表意和表情的作用，不同语调表示不同的态度、口气和思想感情。英语由多种语言融合而成，因此受外来语影响比较大，词汇独立性比较强且词汇量大，是目前世界上词汇量最大的语言。

汉英语言类型差异

目前世界上的语言从语言形态学角度可分为综合型语言(synthetic language)和分析型语言(analytic language)两大类。综合型语言主要通过词汇本身的形态变化(inflected forms)来表达语法意义，如性、数、格、语态等。分析型语言并非通过词汇本身的形态变化来表达语法意义，而是通过运用虚词和词序(word order)调整等手段。

古英语属于典型的综合型语言，现代英语由于受外来语的影响也具有了一些分析型语言的特点，因此现代英语属于综合-分析语(synthetic-analytic language)，英语中词的构词形态和构形形态变化丰富多样，词序相对固定。英语中起构词作用的词缀变化(affixation)数量众多。另外，为了表达语法意义，英语词语分为各种词性(part of speech)，名词有单、复数之别(number)，代词有格(case)，动词有各种时态变化(tense)、主动和被动语态(voice)、虚拟语气和真实语气(mood)，形容词和副词有原级、比较级和最高级(degree of comparison)。英语中的各种词性会随着时态、语态、语气、数、格、人称的变化而使词的构形形态发生变化。例如：英语用 student 表示"学生"的单数，用 students 表示复数；英语陈述句的一般现在时态第三人称单数，动词要加 s 或 es；英语中的形容词和副词表示比较级和最高级时要加 er 和 est，如 tall、taller、tallest。

例 1　原文　I am working.
　　　译文　我正在工作。
例 2　原文　I worked a whole day yesterday.
　　　译文　我昨天工作了一整天。
例 3　原文　I have worked for a week.
　　　译文　我已经工作一周了。

以上例子中，work 一词的词形随着时态的变化而变化，而汉语译文中的"工作"一词却没有任何词形上的改变。

汉语属于典型的分析型语言。汉语没有任何词的形态变化，要表示各种不同的语法关系或构成各种不同的句式，必须借助虚词和词序的变化和调整，虚词包括"着、了、过""的、地、得"等。汉语语法的主要特点是词序固定，虚词传神，词义往往要通过词在句中的词序或位置加以判别。例如：

①A. 他什么都懂。（他很博学）　　B. 他都懂什么。（他很无知）
②A. 一会儿再说。（还未说）　　　B. 再说一会儿。（已经说了）

在这两组例子中，字词没有增减，只是在句中的顺序发生了变化，句子的意思也随之完全改变。词语的顺序排列是汉语表达语法和语义的重要手段之一。

汉英词法差异

词汇是构成语言的基本要素，是整个语言系统的支柱。作为可以独立运用的最小语言单位，词具有书写形式、读音和意义。在翻译中，词的意义选择是译者需重点关注的问题。汉英词语之间存在很大差异，了解这些差异对于更好地进行汉英互译非常重要。下文将从词义对应关系、词类划分及构词法方面对汉英两种语言进行分析和对比。

Ⅰ. 汉英词语指称意义对应关系

一般情况下，汉英词汇在词义方面有五种对应关系。

1. 一一对应关系

汉语和英语中完全一一对应的词比较少,主要是一些专有名词和专业术语。例如:

Marxism—马克思主义

DNA—脱氧核糖核酸

ICU—重症监护病房

socialism—社会主义

北京—Beijing

联合国—United Nations

太平洋—Pacific Ocean

生物技术—biotechnology

这类对应关系的词含有较少的特定文化意义,在翻译的时候采用直译的方法即可。

2. 多词同义关系

有时一个英语或者汉语词语对应多个汉语或者英语词语,不同的词语有着相同的意义,例如:

wife—妻子、老婆、媳妇、老伴、爱人、夫人、堂客、内人……

potato—土豆、马铃薯、洋芋……

人—people, human being, person, man…

学生—pupil, student, disciple…

针对这种对应关系,翻译的时候可以根据语境和目的语的表达习惯选取恰当的词义。

3. 一词多义关系

有时一个英语或者汉语词语对应多个汉语或者英语词语,但是这些词有着不同的意义,例如:

school—学校、院系、学派、研究所、锻炼、上学、教育、训练……

president—主席、总裁、总统、会长、校长、董事长、议长……

车—car、truck、motorcycle、jeep…

羊—sheep、goat、ram、ewe、lamb…

4. 词义交织关系

有时不同的上下文语境中一个英语词语有多个汉语词义,反之亦然,汉英词义交织在一起。例如:

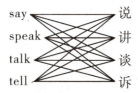

英语中的 say、speak、talk、tell 都有"说、讲、谈、诉"的意思,英译汉时可以根据上下文和汉语的表达习惯选择其中恰当的词,反之亦然。汉英互译中词义交织的情况增加了翻译中选词的难度和复杂性。

5. 词义无对应关系

由于自然环境、历史文化、民族风俗等差异,汉语中许多具有文化特色的词语在译入语中找不到相对应的词,例如:

阴 yin (in Chinese thought) the soft inactive female principle or force in the world

阳 yang (in Chinese thought) the strong active male principle or force in the world

目不识丁 not know one's ABC

奔小康 strive for a relatively comfortable life

科教兴国战略 the strategy for invigorating China through science and education

英语中也有一些与特有文化相关的词语在汉语中很难找到相对应的词。例如：

teenager 13 岁至 19 岁的青少年

clock-watcher 不停地盯着钟表等着下班的人

DINK 丁克家庭（double income，no kids）

cyber slacker 利用工作时间在公司上网、做与工作无关事情的雇员

英汉互译中常见的现象是一词多义。为了确定正确的词义，必须考虑语境，包括内部语境和外部语境。内部语境指上下文提供的相关信息，外部语境即所谓的背景知识。如果在翻译时不考虑语境而生搬硬套词典中的解释，会导致译文死板生硬，不能准确表达原文的意思。因此，正确选择词义是保证译文质量的关键环节。对于有多个释义和搭配的普通词语，翻译时，需要注重词的广义、狭义、所处的语境、词义的褒贬和感情色彩。如果遇到没有对应词语的情况，翻译的基本策略是采用音译、直译或意译加解释的方法来解决。

Ⅱ. 汉英词类差异对比

汉语和英语都有实词和虚词之分。英语的一大特点就是大量使用冠词。由于英语有冠词而汉语无冠词，英译汉时，冠词常被省略。有时英语中的一个冠词之差会使汉语意思大相径庭，翻译时需特别注意。

例 1　A. out of question 毫无疑问

B. out of the question 根本不可能的

例 2　A. take the chair 主持会议

B. take a chair 坐下，就座

例 3　A. a hundred and one 许许多多

B. one hundred and one 一百零一

例 4　A. She was with a child. 她带着一个孩子。

B. She was with child. 她怀孕了。

例 5　A. They are students of our school. 他们是我们学校的学生。

B. They are the students of our school. 他们是我们学校的全体学生。

汉语有量词和助词，而英语没有这两种词类。英语中有关系词和反身代词，汉语中则没有。汉语频繁使用动词，属于动态语言；英语频繁使用名词，属于静态语言。英语比汉语更多地使用连词和介词。由于词类性质的差异，各种词类相互转换也是英汉互译中常见的翻译策略和技巧。

英语的连词使用频率远高于汉语连词。英语是形合语言，注重句子形态结构的严谨和连贯，而汉语是意合语言，更注重语义的内在联系。因此在英译汉时，不少英语句子中的连词可省略不译。

例 6　Write to me when you have time.

有时间就给我写信。

例 7　They were so excited that tears came to their eyes.

他们激动得热泪盈眶。

例 6 和例 7 分别用了表示时间的连词和表示结果的连词，这是英语表达的需要，翻译成汉语后省略了这些连词，句意依然准确且符合汉语表达的习惯。

英语常用介词，汉语则少用介词。英语介词数量多，使用广泛并且意义变化大；而汉语中用介

词的情况比较少，介词使用面窄，意义比较固定。汉语的介词大多是从动词"借"来的，英译汉时，许多英语中含有动作意味的介词常译为汉语的动词，有些表示时间和地点的介词可以省略不译。

例 8　She has intelligence beyond the ordinary.
　　　　她的智力超过常人。

例 9　His work at school is below the average.
　　　　他的学习成绩达不到一般水平。

汉语有丰富多彩的助词，这是汉语语言的一大特点。助词可分为动态助词（"着""了""过"等）、结构助词（"的""地""得"等）和语气助词（"呢""吗""啊""吧""呀"等）。这些助词有表示时态变化的作用，也有表达语气的作用。

例 10　我已经吃过晚饭了。（表时态，指动作已经发生）
　　　　I have had my supper.

例 11　他真来啦？（表疑问语气）
　　　　Has he really come?

例 12　你好好想想吧。（表提议语气）
　　　　Just think it over.

英语中常使用关系代词、物主代词和反身代词，这些代词在英译汉时常常省去不译。

例 13　He covered his eyes with his hands.
　　　　他用手捂住眼睛。

例 14　One should help those who are in difficulty.
　　　　应该帮助有困难的人。

例 15　She must be very proud of herself.
　　　　她一定非常自豪。

Ⅲ．汉英构词法的对比

汉语和英语的词都使用了派生、合成、转化、缩略等构词手段，除此之外汉语还经常使用重叠构词法。派生主要指在单词前后加上词缀。加在单词前面的为前缀，加在单词后面的为后缀。英语的词缀很丰富，而汉语的词缀在数量上相对较少，应用范围也没有英语广泛。英语词缀可表示人、事物、形状等，可构成名词、动词、形容词等。汉语词缀则主要是表示人。汉语后缀要比前缀丰富一些，且多数后缀是名词性的。

1. 前缀

英语："dis-""un-""in-""im-""anti-""mis-"等

例如：disagree、discover、unable、unhappy、inevitable、impolite、antiwar、misunderstand

汉语："老""小""阿""可"等

例如：老板、老师、老王、小伙、阿爸、阿姨、阿公、可爱、可怜、可口

2. 后缀

英语："-or""-er""-ist""-tion""-age""-ly""-ment"等

例如：actor、writer、scientist、creation、percentage、clearly、treatment

汉语："们""者""化""家""员""子""手"等

例如：我们、你们、作者、记者、工业化、社会化、音乐家、歌唱家、伤员、办事员、儿子、女孩子、选手、投手

合成是指由两个或两个以上的词合成一个新词。英语中有的合成词中间可以用连字符连接，例如 birth-control、take-off、man-made、good-looking、self-esteem、white-haired 等；有的则不用连字符连接，例如 washroom、dustbin、himself、outside、easygoing、widespread 等。汉语中的合成词不用连字符，如矛盾、价值、书架、骨肉、动静、风浪、教育、演讲等。

转化是指一种词类转化为另一种词类。转化后的词义与原词类有密切的关系。例如：

good	*adj.* 好的	*n.* 益处
eye	*n.* 眼睛	*v.* 看，目击
water	*n.* 水	*v.* 浇水
drink	*v.* 喝	*n.* 饮料
slow	*adj.* 缓慢的	*v.* (使)放慢速度

英语<u>学习</u>(*n.* 名词)　　<u>学习</u>英语(*v.* 动词)
努力<u>工作</u>(*v.* 动词)　　教学<u>工作</u>(*n.* 名词)

英语和汉语中都有缩略构词法。英语中的缩略语通常采用合并法，例如：

interpol ＝ international police 国际警察
heliport ＝ helicopter airport 直升机场
medicare ＝ medical care 医疗保健
copytron ＝ copy electron 电子复写技术
nanotech ＝ nanometer technology 纳米技术
blog ＝ web log 博客

此外还有首字母缩写法。例如：

UFO　Unidentified Flying Object 不明飞行物
WHO　World Health Organization (联合国)世界卫生组织
AIDS　Acquired Immune Deficiency Syndrome 艾滋病
RAM　Random Access Memory 随机存取存储器
CAT　Computer-Aided Translation 计算机辅助翻译

汉语中的缩略词也常由合并法构成，例如地铁(地下铁路)、科研(科学研究)、高校(高等学校)、投产(投入生产)、全会(全体会议)、彩电(彩色电视机)、高考(普通高等学校招生全国统一考试)、立交桥(立体交叉交通用桥)、亚运会(亚洲运动会)、博士生(攻读博士学位的研究生)等。

重叠是汉语构词法的一大特色。汉语中名词、动词、形容词、量词等不同词类的词中都有一部分可以重叠。例如：岁岁年年、蹦蹦跳跳、条条道路、干干净净、走走瞧瞧、一排排房子、一座座山、喜盈盈、栩栩如生、翩翩起舞、源源不断、忙忙碌碌等。

汉英句法差异

句子是语言中比词语更高一级的语法单位，能够独立表达完整意思、单独完成一个交际任务。现代翻译理论认为，句子是最重要的翻译单位之一。翻译者要了解并掌握汉英语言中句法的差异，并运用符合目的语规范的语言来表达源语，这对翻译质量至关重要。

Ⅰ. 英语重形合，汉语重意合

英语和汉语两种语言在句子结构上表现出两种截然不同的形态特点，即英语注重形合(hypotaxis)，汉语注重意合(parataxis)。所谓形合，是指语言使用诸如关联词等形式手段来连接词语和分句，从而表达语法意义和逻辑关系。而意合则指词语或分句之间不需要形式手段即可表达语法意义和逻辑关系，句子结构并不需要借助关联词，而是通过词语和句子本身的连贯和逻辑顺序来实现连接。

英语句子注重形合，因而更注重句子结构的完整性和规范性。在句式上，英语属于"聚集型"，即运用形合手段和连接词语来明确各成分之间的关系，注重显性接应。句子结构紧凑严密，以形式来表现其意义。此外，英语句子中的成分或词语之间必须保持协调一致的关系，包括人称、数、性以及意义等方面的一致性。

相比之下，汉语句子更注重意合，很少使用甚至不使用形合手段。汉语句子更加注重隐性的连贯，注重逻辑事理的顺序、功能和意义，即以意义统领形式。汉语中没有像英语那样常用的关系代词、关系副词等，因此在翻译时，并列连词、从属连词和关联副词常常可以省略不译。汉语主要通过调整语序以及词语的意义来表达句子的意思。

例 1　原文　Because he is not honest, I can't trust him.
　　　译文　（因为）他不老实，我不能信任他。
　　　评析　英语句子中有引导原因状语从句的关联词 because，译成汉语时可以省去关联词"因为"，意思同样清楚明了。

例 2　原文　If winter comes, can spring be far behind?
　　　译文　冬天来了，春天还会远吗？
　　　评析　英语句子中有引导条件状语从句的关联词 if，译成汉语时省去关联词"如果"，意思同样明晰，读起来也朗朗上口、富有意蕴。

例 3　原文　If he won't come here, I'll not go there.
　　　译文　他不来，我不去。
　　　评析　此句译成汉语时省去关联词"如果"，能在保留原意的基础上使句式整齐，简短明快。

例 4　原文　If you have never tasted the bitterness of gall, how can you know the sweetness of honey?
　　　译文　不知苦中苦，哪知甜中甜？
　　　评析　此句译成汉语时同样省去了关联词"如果"，此外，译者还采取意译的策略处理原句中的一些词语，译文句式更加紧凑简约。

Ⅱ. 英语多长句，汉语多短句

英语注重形合，句子结构严谨，主谓结构明确，谓语动词是句子的核心。句子中的分句可通过丰富的词形变化转化为不同形式的附加结构，如介词短语、分词短语、状语从句和独立结构等。英语句子形态标记明确，语义层次分明，结构紧凑严谨，通常是主句中带有从句，从句中又套着从句，因此多长句是英语句子的主要特点之一。

汉语注重意合，句子注重意义连贯，不强求结构齐整，采用的是散点句法。汉语主谓结构相对复杂，表达复杂思想时往往借助动词，以时间为逻辑语序，横向铺叙，层层推进，归纳总结，形成"流水型"的句式结构。这种句式结构通常是用节节短句逐点交代，将问题层层展开。因此，汉语句子大都简短明快，很少出现长句。例如：

原文　Don't let the sadness of your past and the fear of your future ruin the happiness of your present.
译文　别让过去的悲伤和未来的忧虑，毁掉自己当下的快乐。

Ⅲ. 汉英句子语序的差异

汉英两种语言在句子语序方面有截然不同的思路。在叙述事物发展过程的句子中,汉语常常按照由先到后、由因到果、由假设到推论、由事实到结论这样的顺序来排列逻辑关系;英语一般则采取相反的顺序,往往是先表示说话人个人的感受、态度或是首先就事情本身进行评价,然后再叙述事情的细节、原委,形成句式上先短后长、头轻脚重的语言现象。如果一个句子既有叙事部分,又有表态部分,汉语的表达习惯往往是叙事在前,表态在后。英语句子则往往表态在前,叙事在后。例如:

原文 现在,中国人民正满怀信心地在改革开放和现代化的道路上阔步前进,这是令人欣慰和自豪的。

译文 It is gratified and proud that the Chinese people, now, filled with confidence, are advancing in giant strides along the road of reform, opening-up and modernization.

Ⅳ. 英语多"物称"表达,汉语多"人称"表达

英汉句子主语的选择与思维方式有关,表现为"人称"和"物称"的差异。英语句子常用"物称表达"法,即用无生命的事物作为主语,以呈现出客观状态,表达客观的叙述语气。相反,在汉语中,主体意识较为强烈,强调"事在人为",因此在表达时通常采用"人称表达"法,即用人或有生命的事物作为句子的主语。如果没有人称可用,则使用泛称,例如"有人""人们""大家""人家"等。此外,汉语也常采用无主语句,即在句中隐含或省略人称。

例1 原文 An idea suddenly struck me.

译文 我突然想到了一个主意。

例2 原文 The thick carpet killed the sound of my footsteps.

译文 我走在厚厚的地毯上,一点声音也没有。

例3 原文 It never occurred to me that she was so dishonest.

译文 我从来也没有想到她这么不老实。

例4 原文 The truth finally dawned on her.

译文 她最终明白了真相。

Ⅴ. 英语多用被动句,汉语多用主动句

为了客观、间接或委婉地表达观点,英语句子常使用被动语态。在科技英语中,被动句更为常见,这是因为英语思维方式强调事件本身,而非事件的发出者。相反,汉语更强调动作的发出者,因此更多地使用主动语态,并采用人称、泛称或隐称表达法来代替被动语态。

例1 原文 Rubber is found a good isolating material.

译文 人们发现橡胶是一种良好的绝缘材料。

例2 原文 It is well known that smoking is harmful to the health.

译文 众所周知,吸烟有害健康。

以下是英语常用被动句型的汉语表达:

It must be pointed out that…	必须指出……
It must be admitted that…	必须承认……
It is imagined that…	可以想象……
It cannot be denied that…	不可否认……

It will be seen from this that...	由此可知……
It should be realized that...	必须认识到……
It is stressed that...	人们强调……
It may be said without fear of exaggeration that...	可以毫不夸张地说……

在英汉互译过程中，译者应根据英汉句子主语表达习惯的差异，在准确理解原文的基础上，对译文的主语进行重新选择。英译汉时，可将原文的物称主语转换为汉语的人称主语；汉译英时，要根据汉语意义，或转换或添加适当的主语，以符合英语的语言表达习惯和规范。

汉英思维差异

语言是人类最重要的交际工具，而思维则是人脑对客观事物的间接和概括反映。语言和思维之间关系密切，语言是思维的工具和材料，思维则借助语言对客观事物进行分析和认知。因地理环境、生活条件、风俗习惯等因素的影响，不同民族往往有着不同的思维方式。这种思维差异在翻译过程中产生了重要的影响。翻译不仅是一种语言活动，还是一种思维活动。

汉英文化的思维方式差异体现在语言的多个方面。在表达方式上，汉语习惯先讲细节，然后再归纳总结要点；英语则习惯先讲要点，再进一步说明细节。在语言结构和形态方面，当涉及行为主体时，汉语通常使用表示人或生物的词作为主语；英语则更常用物或事作为主语。在词法和句法层面，受综合性思维方式影响的汉语没有词形变化，语法形式主要依赖词汇手段表达，并根据语义逻辑和动作发生的时间先后来决定词语和分句的排列顺序，从而表现出整体的意合特征；受分析性思维方式影响的英语则有明显的词形变化、多样的语法形式和灵活的语序结构，句子各部分逻辑关系较明显。

Ⅰ. 主体意识思维和个体意识思维

中式思维主张主体意识和客体意识的统一，即心物一体。这种思维常以"我"为视角，以"我"的情感、态度、观念为依据进行价值判断，注重主体的参与，主客体在思维上没有明显的区分。因此，汉语注重人称，在表达主体与叙述事物之间的关系时常以"人"（主体）为中心，并使用表"人"的词、词组、短语作主语，主动句和省略句使用较多，被动句使用较少。

相比之下，西方思维模式更强调主体意识和客体意识的对立，主张心物二分，注重理性分析，强调客观事物对人的作用和影响，以"事物"为中心。因此，英语中常使用物称主语，被动句使用较多。

Ⅱ. 综合性思维和分析性思维

中国传统哲学强调整体性思维，这在一定程度上也影响了中国人思考问题的方式，即通常从整体出发，全面观察事物，发现各方面的对应关系。这种强调整体的思维方式对汉语也产生了重要影响。汉语句子中虽然连词使用较少，从外形上看比较松散自由，但各部分内在关系紧密，体现了中式思维的综合性和整体性。

相比之下，西方思维模式更偏分析性，即将事物分离出来，对事物的本质特性进行逻辑分析。因此，英语注重形式连接手段，重视语法形式，常用各种连接词、介词、定语从句和独立主格结构等表达成分之间的各种语法关系，严格受逻辑形式支配，表现形式相对严谨。

针对汉语意合和英语形合的不同特点，在英译汉时，许多英语中的连接词可以省略不译，介词短语、定语从句和独立主格结构在多数情况下可以转译为短语式分句。在汉译英时，首先要处理好句子的内在关系，增添连接词，将语句中的各种关系（如因果关系、条件关系、递进关系等）体现出来，其次要善于将汉语的分句转换为英语的名词、分词短语、定语从句和独立主格结构等。

Ⅲ. 形象思维和抽象思维

形象思维是一种用直观形象和表象来解决问题的思维方式。中国文化强调形象思维，习惯使用直觉和意象等形象的表达方式来表达抽象的概念和意义。大多数汉语成语、比喻、谚语和歇后语都采用形象表达法来描述抽象事物。

西方思维方式偏抽象，因此英语中常常使用含义概括、指称笼统的抽象名词来表达复杂的理性概念和微妙的情感。英语中广泛使用的笼统概括的抽象名词常难以在汉语中找到对应的翻译。在英译汉的过程中，常需要将抽象概念具体化；在汉译英的过程中，常需要将具体事物抽象化。例如：

disintegration 土崩瓦解

ardent 热心的；热情的

loyalty 赤胆忠心

total exhaustion 筋疲力尽

far-sightedness 远见卓识

carefully deliberate；think and contemplate thoroughly 深思熟虑

水乳交融 in complete harmony

画饼充饥；望梅止渴 feed on fancies；feed on illusions

如饥似渴 with great eagerness

三天打鱼，两天晒网 lack of perseverance

添砖加瓦 make a little contribution

危在旦夕 on the verge of destruction

汉英文化差异

语言承载着丰富的文化内涵。因此在翻译时，译者不仅要具备语言能力，还需要了解不同文化的知识。不同的历史文化、地域文化、风俗文化都会对翻译产生影响。

Ⅰ. 历史文化差异

由于各个民族和国家的历史发展不同，在其漫长的历史长河中所积淀形成的历史文化也各不相同。在语言的发展过程中，历史文化的痕迹主要表现在习语和成语中，这些与历史文化相关的习语和成语都会对理解和翻译造成一定困难。

例如，对中国人来说，"卧薪尝胆"这一汉语成语典故很好理解，但是如果将这个成语简单地翻译为 Sleep on the brushwood and taste the gall，对于不了解中国历史文化的人来说就难以理解。比较好的翻译策略是采用直译加注解的方法，译为"Sleep on the brushwood and taste the gall: After being defeated by the state of Wu, Gou Jian, the king of Yue, lay on brushwood and tasted the gall to remind himself not to forget the humiliation and endure hardships to accomplish his ambition."。通过注解的方式就能清楚地表达和再现原典故的含义，目的语读者也能了解这一成语的真正内涵。

西方文化中也有大量的成语和典故具有历史文化内涵。大不列颠岛曾被罗马人征服和统治了很长时间，英语中 do in Rome as the Romans do（入乡随俗）、Rome was not built in a day（伟业非一日之功)、all roads lead to Rome(条条大路通罗马)等习语就是这段历史文化在语言中的反映。

在翻译中，译者如果对两种语言的历史文化背景不熟悉，就容易出现困惑。因此，译者要学习和掌握汉英两种语言背后的历史文化知识，注重历史文化之间的差异，这样才能在理解典故含义的基础上进行准确恰当的翻译。

Ⅱ. 地域文化差异

"地域文化"作为一个科学概念，至今学术界对此仍然众说纷纭、莫衷一是。有学者认为地域文化是不同区域范围内物质财富和精神财富的总和。由于地域文化不同，不同民族对同一事物的认识往往存在差异。在中国文化中，"东风"(east wind)象征春天和温暖，使万物复苏，因此有"东风报春"的说法。"西风"(west wind)则给人一种寒冷刺骨的感觉，马致远的诗句"古道西风瘦马"便是很好的例证。而英国的气候状况与中国截然相反，英国的"东风"从欧洲大陆吹来，寒冷而刺骨，给人们带来不愉快的感受，而"西风"从大西洋吹来，温暖宜人。

Ⅲ. 风俗文化差异

风俗文化是在各民族日常生活和交际活动中形成的文化，由各种风俗习惯构成。中国和西方社会在风俗习惯方面存在许多差异，这些差异会对翻译产生影响。不同的民族在打招呼、称谓、道谢、恭维、致歉、告别、打电话等方面表现出不同的文化习俗。例如，中国人在见面时常用"你去哪儿？""你要干什么？""你吃过饭了吗？"等客套话来表示礼节性的问候，而在西方，这些话题可能被视为隐私话题，要避免谈论。因此，翻译时适当进行文化转换是非常必要的。

再如，中国人认为红色是吉祥如意的颜色，代表顺利和成功，因此在庆祝喜庆场合时常用"满堂红""开门红""大红大紫""红利""红红火火"等词语来表达喜庆的情绪。而在西方文化中，红色通常被视为"火"和"血"的象征，代表着残暴、流血、危险和暴力，例如 a red battle(血战)、red alert(红色预警)等。这些文化差异在跨文化交际中也需要注意，以避免文化差异带来的误解和冲突。

Exercises

 Please answer the following questions.

1) Which language family does Chinese belong to? Which language family does English belong to?

2) What are the differences between synthetic language and analytic language?

 Please translate the following sentences and pay attention to the meaning of those underlined words.

1) The lathe should be set on a firm base.

2) A base reacts with an acid to form a salt and water.

3) A transistor has three electrodes, the emitter, the base and the collector.

4) Line AB is the base of the triangle ABC.

5) The weary troops marched back to the base.

6) He is on the second base.

7) It is a skyscraper built on a base of solid rock.

8) The base of the thumb is where it joins the hand.

9) That company has offices all over the world, but their base is in Paris.

10) Ordinary numbers use base 10, but many computers work to base 2.

11) He ran cross the road.
12) I'll run the car into town.
13) He ran his eyes down the list.
14) The car ran down the hill.
15) The engine runs well.
16) The story runs like this.
17) He ran for president.
18) The buses run every ten minutes.
19) Most of motor vehicles run on petrol.
20) Your nose is running.
21) The river has run dry.
22) The butter will run if you put it near the fire.
23) The road runs beside the river.
24) The insurance runs for another month.
25) The coal industry is being run down.
26) Is everything running well in your office?
27) A young man came to the police office with a story.
28) Once the story got abroad, I would never hear the last of it.
29) I don't buy your story.
30) Her story is one of the saddest one.
31) I don't want you to get a wrong idea of me from all these stories that you hear.
32) You put me on the spot. I'll have to cook up a story this time.
33) It was reported that the general was dead, but officials refused to confirm the story.

 Please add a prefix or a suffix to each of the following words and translate them into Chinese.

advantage, agree, able, acceptable, biotic, war, adventure, apply, moral, polite, complete, formal, write, adjust, rich, able, president, wife, western, appraisal, assertive, teach, read, train, interview, edit, act, person, cover, create, dictate, ill, fond, friend, leader, treat, manage, west, east, use, meaning, fool, girl, love, clear, modern, industrial, deep, wide, sun, wind

Unit 3

历史地理

> **Unit Goals**
>
> In this unit, you are going to
> - grasp words and expressions concerning Chinese history and geography;
> - acquire knowledge about Chinese history and geography;
> - know how to translate sentences by applying amplification;
> - grasp translation skills of paragraphs on Chinese history and geography.

Related Words and Expressions

原始的，早期的 primeval*
旧石器时代 the Paleolithic Age
新石器时代 the Neolithic Age
石器时代 the Stone Age
青铜器时代 the Bronze Age
铁器时代 the Iron Age
母系氏族社会 matriarchal clan society
父系氏族社会 patrilineal clan society
封建的 feudal
中华文明 Chinese civilization
华夏祖先 the Chinese ancestors
秦始皇统一中国 unification of the country by Emperor Qinshihuang
春秋时期 The Spring and Autumn Period
战国时期 The Warring States Period
明清两代 Ming and Qing dynasties
祖先；祖宗 ancestor; forefather
皇帝，君主 emperor; monarch
丞相 prime minister (in ancient China)
家系，宗谱 genealogy
祭祀 offer sacrifices to gods or ancestors
考古学 archaeology
历史文物和遗迹 historical relics and sites

---

* 黑体为必须掌握的表达

文物 cultural relics

青铜器 bronze ware

文人雅士 refined scholars

年代学的，按年代顺序的 chronological

传记的，传记体的 biographical

种族的 racial

族群的，族裔的 ethnic

发掘 excavation

地质学 geology

地理学 geography

史诗，叙事诗 epic

游牧的，游牧民族的 nomadic

中国地形 Chinese topography

流域，山谷 valley

高原 plateau

绿洲 oasis

半岛 peninsula

海峡 strait

山峰 peak

盆地 basin

峭壁 cliff；crag

峡谷 gorge；canyon

黄土高原 loess plateau

水循环 hydrologic cycle

荒漠化 desertification

自然保护区 nature reserve

自然景观 natural landscape

海拔（高度）altitude；height above sea level

气候资源 climate resources

气候带 climatic zone

季风 monsoon

台风 typhoon

气候灾害 climate damage

热带 tropical zone

温带 temperate zone

寒带 cold zone

亚热带 sub-tropical zone

湿润气候 humid climate

干燥气候 arid climate

赤道的 equatorial

大陆性气候 continental climate

海洋性气候 maritime climate
地理大发现 The Great Geographical Discoveries
国土规划 territorial planning
经济发展战略 strategy of economic development
流域规划 river basin planning
区域开发 regional development
资源优势 resources superiority

Lead-in Activities

1 **Answer the following questions.**

1) When can the primeval human beings in China be traced back?
2) Do you know the differences between the Paleolithic Age and the Neolithic Age?
3) Can you name the major mountains and rivers in China?

2 **Listen to a brief introduction to the Loess Plateau and fill in the blanks with the words you hear.**

The Earth is a place of endless wonder where landscapes are often created from mere dust. The Loess Plateau is such a place. It is located in _____ and contains seventy percent of the loess on the planet. It is hard to imagine a time when it did not exist. But this yellow land was _____.

The entire plateau covers a total area of six hundred and forty thousand square kilometers. Even seen from above, it's hard to comprehend the _____ of it. The loess dunes are dozens of meters high, and three hundred meters _____.

Eight million years ago, super strong winds blew sand and dust here. The entire process of dust _____ took more than 2.6 million years. Scientists can _____ of the loess. Because _____ are carried the furthest, they came to rest in the southeastern-most part of the plateau.

The sand in the northwest part of the plateau is much rougher. Where a river crossed the plateau, an alluvial plain formed from the deposits of sediment. People gradually started to _____ _____. They farmed in the valley and built roads between the ravines. In this way, they made this ancient land their home and _____.

3 **Read the following passage and then do the exercises.**

Early History and Early Culture

Yuanmou People

In 1965, Chinese scientists found two teeth and some coarse stone tools in Yuanmou County, Yunnan Province. Scientists determined that these are leftovers from primeval humankind, about 1.7 million years ago. They are called "Yuanmou People." They were the ever-known earliest humankind that lived in China.

Lantian People, Peking People

For more than 50 years, primeval relics of humankind had been found in more than 20 places on Chinese mainland, from the Liao He in the north to the Pearl River in the south, most of them were found in the Yellow River and the Chang Jiang River valley. The "Lantian People" found in Shaanxi Province and the famous "Peking People" (Beijing People) are among them. China is the country in the world where most relics of primeval humankind were found.

During the early 20th century, at the cave in Longgu Hill (龙骨山), Zhou Koudian, southwest of Beijing, bones of primeval humankind were found. They lived 500 to 200 thousand years ago. The "Peking People" retained the features of apes, but they could use tools. They were humans. They used stones to strike and make coarse stone tools. The era when such stone tools were used is called "Old Stone Age." They also cut down branches to make bat. Stone tools and bats were the earliest tools that humankind used in labor, and to be able to make tools is the fundamental factor for distinguishing humankind from animals.

The "Peking People" used natural fire. They used fire to bake foodstuff, and to make light and keep warmth, also to scare away beasts. The use of fire strengthened their ability to conquer nature, and was a great progress in the evolution of humankind.

The "Peking People" lived in a hostile environment and used simple and coarse tools. Individuals could not survive by their own efforts. They worked together in groups of several persons, and shared fruits of labor—they lived in groups, but it was hard. This is also one of the characteristics of the early human society in primeval time.

During the long period of several hundred thousand years that followed, our ancestors struggled hard with nature and got progress step by step.

Upper Cave People

About 30,000 years ago, in the same region of the "Peking People," there also lived primeval humankind. Their outlook was almost alike to the modern men. Their bones were found in a cave on top of the Longgu Hill; that's why they are called the "Upper Cave People."

The "Upper Cave People" still used ground stone tools, but they knew how to polish and drill holes on stone, and they also knew how to make bone needles and the other similar instruments. They also made ornaments. The "Upper Cave People" knew how to make fire by hand. Fishing, hunting and collecting were their major productive labor.

The social unit where the "Upper Cave People" lived was a "clan" linked by genealogy. One clan had only several dozen persons descended from a common ancestor. They used common tools in collective labor, shared foods among the members and they lived together. Such a living unit is called "clan commune." Members of the clan relied on collective efforts to struggle against nature. Human society was, by that time, in "clan commune" stage of primitive society.

Yangshao Culture

In the Middle and Lower Yellow River Valley is Yangshao Culture. Here agriculture was practiced. Pottery was made with geometric patterns and baked at 1,000 – 1,500 degrees centigrade. The first evidence of a Neolithic culture in China was discovered at Yangshao, in Henan Province, in 1921. In 1953, at Banpo, near the city of Xi'an in Shaanxi Province, a Neolithic village belonging to the Yangshao Culture was accidentally uncovered. This village covered an area of two and a half acres. Careful excavation revealed the presence of 45 houses, more than 200 storage pits, about 10,000 needles, tools, arrowheads, fishhooks and six kilns. There were also many adults' and children's graves. The Neolithic people of Banpo hunted, fished, cultivated millet, cooked their food and raised pigs as domestic animals.

Especially noteworthy thing was their gray or red pottery. The red pottery was painted with black geometrical designs and occasionally with pictures of fish or human faces. Because the potter's wheel was unknown at that time, the vessels were probably fashioned with strips of clay.

Longshan Culture

In the Middle and Lower Yellow River Valley is Longshan Culture. In 1928, another Neolithic culture was discovered at Longshan, in Shandong Province. The Longshan Culture was more advanced than the Yangshao Culture and probably flourished between 2500 BC and 2000 BC. People of the Longshan Culture also hunted, fished and planted grain. They probably domesticated the pig, dog and ox. They made stone tools such as axes and knives as well as bone necklaces and bracelets. They also made an exquisite black pottery, probably with the potter's wheel. Their pottery was not painted but was decorated with rings, either raised or grooved.

The Longshan Culture, because of its distinguished pottery, has been called the "Black Pottery" Culture. It was probably the predecessor of the Xia and Shang dynasties.

Recent research has persuaded some authorities that the Yangshao and Longshan Cultures were not separate and distinct. These scholars now believe that the Longshan Culture was in fact a later development of the Yangshao Culture.

1) Answer the following questions.
   (1) According to the scientific research, who are known as the earliest humans that lived in China?
   (2) When and where did the "Peking people" live? What are the characteristics of the "Peking people"?
   (3) What are the differences between the "Peking People" and the "Upper Cave People"?
   (4) Where was the first evidence of a Neolithic culture in China discovered? What was specially noted in Neolithic period?
   (5) Which culture does the "Black Pottery" Culture refer to? Who was the possible predecessor of the Xia and Shang dynasties?

2) Translate the following sentences into English.
   (1) 石器和木棒是人类最早使用的劳动工具，能够制作劳动工具是人类和动物最根本的区别。
   (2) 北京人生活在恶劣的环境中，使用简陋而粗糙的工具。个人仅靠自己的努力根本无法生存。他们几个人为一组一起劳作并分享劳动成果。
   (3) 在接下来的几十万年，我们的祖先和大自然不断进行斗争，一步一步向前迈进。
   (4) 龙山文化比仰韶文化更加先进，大致在公元前2500年到公元前2000年间开始蓬勃发展。

翻译技巧：增译法（Amplification）

在翻译中，译者应该忠实于原文，不应对原文内容进行随意的添加和删减。但是由于汉英两种语言在许多方面存在差异，在翻译实践中实现字词上的完全对等非常困难，为了准确表达出原文的信息，译者有时需要在原文基础上增加原文中虽无其词却有其意的内容，从而使译文更加准确流畅，把原文中蕴含的信息充分表达出来。这种翻译方法就是增译法。增译法的原则是增词不增义，即虽然增加了原文中没有的词或者句子成分，但是原文的内容和意思并没有改变，增译的部分反而使读者对原文内容有更好的理解。

Ⅰ. 英译汉

1. 增补量词

量词在汉语中除了具有与数词构成数量词组的组合功能之外，还有表意和概括的功能。"磅""千克""元""千米"等作为计量单位的量词，在英语里都是名词，英译汉时把它们直接转换成相应的汉语词语即可。而"个""只""件""条""根"等量词在英语中不存在对应的词，在英译汉时就需要根据汉语名词的形状、特征或材料内容增添相应的量词。

例1　A full moon is rising from the east.
　　　一轮满月从东方升起。

例2　A stream was winding its way through the valley into the river.
　　　一湾溪水蜿蜒流过山谷，汇入了那条河。

2. 增补语气助词

汉语中有许多语气助词，如"啊""嘛""吧""吗""呢""啦"等，分别表示不同的语气色彩。英语中没有此类词语，在英译汉时，为了完整地再现原文的语气，在翻译中有时需要适当增加此类语气助词。

例1　Don't take it seriously. I'm just joking.
　　　别当真嘛，我不过是开个玩笑罢了。

例2　How beautiful the scenery here is!
　　　这里的风景多美啊！

3. 增补表示时态和复数概念的词

在英语中，动词时态和名词的复数含义往往表现在词语本身的曲折变化上，而汉语则没有这种变化，因此英译汉时需要用增译法，增加能表达时间和复数概念的词。

例1　I treated you as my brother, but not now.
　　　我曾经把你当成兄弟，但现在不了。

例2　The jet planes are flying over the sky.
　　　一架架喷气式飞机掠过天空。

例3　The lion is the king of animals.
　　　狮子是百兽之王。

例4　The mountains began to throw their long blue shadows over the valley.
　　　群山开始向山谷投下一道道蔚蓝色的长影。

4. 增补动词、名词、形容词或者副词

出于对语言结构和汉语搭配习惯的考虑，有时为了使译文的语言结构更加完整、通顺，在英译

汉过程中需要通过增译法增加一些动词、名词、形容词或者副词。

例 1　After the football match, he's got an important meeting.
　　　在观看足球比赛之后，他得参加一个重要会议。（增加动词）

例 2　My work, my family, my friends were more than enough to fill my time.
　　　我干工作，做家务，有朋友往来，这些占用了我全部的时间。（增加动词）

例 3　He wanted to learn, to know, to teach.
　　　他想学习，增长知识，也愿意把自己的知识教给别人。（增加名词）

例 4　As he sat down and began talking, words poured out.
　　　他一坐下来就讲开了，滔滔不绝地讲个没完。（增加副词）

例 5　He doubtlessly expected hugs, tears and laughter.
　　　毫无疑问，他期待会有热情的拥抱、激动的泪水和欢乐的笑声。（增加形容词）

5. 补足原文中的省略部分

在英语表达中，有些词语为了避免重复而被省略掉，在英译汉时往往需要把省略的部分还原才能使所译语句的意思完整。

例 1　My brother majors in English, and I in physics.
　　　我兄弟的专业是英语，我的专业是物理。

例 2　We won't retreat, we never have and never will.
　　　我们不后退，我们从来没有后退过，我们将来也决不后退。

例 3　Matter can be changed into energy, and energy into matter.
　　　物质可以转化为能量，能量又可以转化为物质。

Ⅱ．汉译英

相较于英语，汉语缺少冠词，较少使用连词、介词和代词。因此，在汉译英时，应适当增添代词、冠词、连词和介词，使译文符合英语形合的语言特点和语法结构。

1. 增补代词

例 1　大作收到，十分高兴。
　　　I was very glad to have received your writing.

例 2　没有调查研究就没有发言权。
　　　He who makes no investigation and study has no right to speak.

例 3　大脑是神经系统的中枢。
　　　The brain is the center of our nervous system.

2. 增补冠词

例 1　我们对问题要进行全面的分析，才能解决得妥当。
　　　We must make a comprehensive analysis of a problem before it can be properly solved.

例 2　当老师的应该有耐心。
　　　A teacher should have patience in his work.

例 3　耳朵是用来听声音的器官。
　　　The ear is the organ which is used for hearing.

3. 增补连词

例 1　他在等我，我得走了。

He is waiting for me, so I must be off now.

例 2 虚心使人进步，骄傲使人落后。

Modesty helps one to go forward, whereas conceit makes one lag behind.

例 3 留得青山在，不怕没柴烧。

So long as green hills remain, there will never be a shortage of firewood.

4. 增补介词

例 1 这台机器状况良好。

This machine is in good condition.

例 2 咱们校门口见吧。

Let's meet at the school gate.

例 3 他始终低着头一言不发。

He remained silent with his head down all the time.

段落翻译

1. 黄河

黄河全长约 5,464 千米，是中国北方的一条重要河流，也是长度仅次于长江的中国第二大河。黄河是中华文明的摇篮。它发源于青海省巴颜喀拉山脉，流经 9 个省（自治区），最后流入渤海。黄河中上游以山地为主，中下游以平原、丘陵为主。黄河被称为世界上含沙量最大的河流，主要是由于黄河中游流经黄土高原，含沙量大，每年有约 12 亿吨泥沙流入大海，约 4 亿吨则淤积在黄河下游，形成利于耕种的冲积平原。黄河被中国人民称为"母亲河"。它是中华民族的象征，是中华民族的精神体现。

难点讲解：

1) 本段主要介绍了黄河的特点，文体属于说明文，汉译英时可以采用一般现在时来客观地表述内容。其中段落中包含的各种表达河流长度、地形特点的词语，汉译英时也应采用恰当的表述方式。

2) "黄河全长约 5,464 千米，是中国北方的一条重要河流，也是长度仅次于长江的中国第二大河"一句由 3 个并列分句组成，每个分句的主语都是"黄河"。翻译时可以采用分译法，适当添加主语。

3) "它发源于青海省巴颜喀拉山脉"可译为"It originates from Bayan Har Mountains in Qinghai Province."。注意英语中小地名位置在前，大地名位置在后。

4) "流经"可译为 run through 或 flow through。

5) "黄河中上游"可译为 the middle and upper reaches of the Yellow River，"黄河中下游"可译为 the middle and lower reaches of the Yellow River，其中 reach 在这里的意思是 a straight section of water between two bends on a river，意思是"河段"。

6) "含沙量最大的河流"可译为 the most sediment-laden river。

7) "12 亿吨"译为 1.2 billion tons，billion 意为"十亿"；"4 亿吨"译为 400 million tons，million 意为"百万"，此处需注意不同的英文表达方式。

8) "冲积平原"可译为 alluvial plain；"利于耕种的冲积平原"可译为 alluvial plain which is conducive to planting。

9) "母亲河"是黄河在中国文化中的代表性称谓，翻译时需要考虑文化背景差异，选择恰当的翻译策略。

2. 长江

长江，又名扬子江，全长约 6,300 千米，是中国最长的河流，也是世界第三大河流。长江发源于中国西部青海省唐古拉山脉，由西向东流经 11 个省、自治区和直辖市，最后注入东海。长江干流可分为 3 个区域，宜昌以上是长江上游，该河段是最具吸引力的区域，以其令人叹为观止的山脉、雄伟的峡谷、湍急的河流和迷人的景观而闻名；从湖北宜昌市至江西湖口县是中游地区；湖口至出海口为下游，以三角洲平原、纵横交错的运河和水道以及中国南方宁静的水边村庄为特色。该地区土地肥沃，人口众多，是中国经济最发达的地区之一，被称为长江三角洲。作为中国最大的水系，长江在历史、经济和文化方面具有重要意义，几千年来，长江一直被用于供水、灌溉、卫生、交通、工业和边界标记，长江流域也被誉为中华文明的发祥地。

难点讲解：

1) 本段主要介绍了长江的特点，属于说明文文体，时态可以采用一般现在时。汉译英时同样要注意段落中各种关于河流和地形特点的表达。

2) "长江，又名扬子江"，英文可译为 the Changjiang River or the Yangtze River。

3) "注入"可译为 empty into 或 pour into。

4) 翻译"以其令人叹为观止的山脉、雄伟的峡谷、湍急的河流和迷人的景观而闻名"时需注意形容词的翻译，此处可译为 famous for its breathtaking mountains, imposing ravines, rushing rapids and fascinating landscape。

5) "纵横交错的运河和水道"可译为 the crisscrossed canals and waterways。

6) "长江三角洲"可译为 the Yangtze River Delta。

3. 西安

古都西安是一座闪耀着古代文明和高科技之光的历史文化名城。西安，古称长安，是世界四大古都之一，有 13 个朝代在此定都，建都史长达一千多年。西安是联合国教科文组织确立的世界历史名城之一，拥有 6 处世界文化遗产。西安拥有中国最大的明代钟楼，还有大雁塔、小雁塔、收藏碑石最多的碑林博物馆以及有两千多年历史的秦兵马俑。历史文化的积淀造就了这座著名的旅游城市。西安是丝绸之路的起点，在最繁华的时候，它是东西方贸易的中心。西安还享有"通史博物馆"的美誉，这座古老的城市正在现代化的进程中飞速发展。

难点讲解：

1) "历史文化名城"可译为 a notable historic and cultural city。

2) "西安，古称长安，是世界四大古都之一，有 13 个朝代在此定都，建都史长达一千多年。"此句很长，在句中主语有变化，主语从"西安"转变为"13 个朝代"，因此可在主语变化处进行断句，采取分译的方法译为两句。

3) "联合国教科文组织"译为 UNESCO（United Nations Educational, Scientific and Cultural Organization）。

4) "世界文化遗产"可译为 world cultural heritage。

5) "明代钟楼""大雁塔""小雁塔""碑林博物馆""秦兵马俑"分别译为 Bell Tower of the Ming Dynasty、the Big Wild Goose Pagoda、the Little Wild Goose Pagoda、the Forest of Stone Steles Museum 和 the Terracotta Warriors。

6) "丝绸之路的起点"可译为 the starting point of the Silk Road。

7) "东西方贸易的中心"可译为 commercial center connecting the Orient and the West。

4. 长城

长城又称万里长城，是中国人用了两千多年的时间陆续修建的。明长城全长达 8,851.8 千米。中国古代人修建长城是为了防御和保护家园，自己也不去侵犯别人的领地。若有敌人进攻，烽火台会立即燃起狼烟，敌情便随着烽烟一站站地传向军事中心。长城是世界文化遗产之一，它不仅是中华文明的瑰宝，还是中国古代人民智慧的结晶，更是中华民族的象征。长城不只是一道墙，它是世界建筑的奇迹。长城在建筑上的价值，足以与它在历史和战略上的重要性相媲美。北京八达岭长城是著名的风景区，每年都会接待来自世界各地的游客。

难点讲解：

1)本段主要介绍了长城的建造历史、主要特点以及在中国历史上的地位和价值，属于说明文文体。在时态选择上，可以根据上下文采用过去式描述长城过去的历史，用一般现在时描述长城的客观状态。

2)本段第一句中时态和语态有变化，翻译时可用一个主语"The Great Wall"，前半句是客观事实，用一般现在时的主动语态，后半句用过去完成时的被动语态较为合适，这样可翻译成包含2个并列句的长句。

3)"烽火台会立即燃起狼烟"可译为 the beacon tower would immediately light a beacon-fire。"烽火台"可译为 beacon tower。

4)"敌情……传向……"可用"transmit ... to ..."结构来表达；"军事中心"可译为 military center。

5)"长城是世界文化遗产之一，它不仅是中华文明的瑰宝，还是中国古代人民智慧的结晶，更是中华民族的象征。"此句中表示并列关系的"不仅……还……"，可用"not only ... but also ..."来翻译，也可用 and 或 as well as 表示并列。"中华文明的瑰宝"可译为 the treasure of Chinese civilization。

6)"著名的风景区"可译为 famous scenic spot。

7)"长城在建筑上的价值，足以与它在历史和战略上的重要性相媲美"可译为"The Great Wall's architectural value is comparable to its historical and strategic importance"。"和……相媲美"可用"be comparable to ..."表示。

5. 兵马俑

公元前221年，秦始皇统一六国，建立了中国第一个统一的中央集权制封建王朝——秦朝。秦始皇去世后被葬于西安东边的骊山脚下。秦始皇陵和兵马俑是两千多年前由几十万人用了数十年时间修建而成的。兵马俑是独一无二的，雕像大多为士兵和马匹，也有战车、武器和其他物品。兵俑的外形与秦军士兵一样，五官、发纹均按照真人塑造而成，面部表情也各不相同，战车与战马也同实物一般大小。这支陶俑组成的军队气势恢宏，十分逼真。1987年，秦始皇陵和兵马俑被联合国教科文组织列为世界文化遗产。

难点讲解：

1)本段主要介绍了秦始皇陵和兵马俑的建造历史、主要特点及历史文化价值，属于说明文文体。

2)第一句中的"秦始皇"可用音译法译为 Emperor Qinshihuang；"中央集权制封建王朝"可译为 centralized feudal dynasty。

3)"秦始皇陵和兵马俑"可译为 Emperor Qinshihuang's Mausoleum Site and the Terracotta Warriors and Horses。

4)"独一无二的"可译为 unique。

5)"兵俑的外形与秦军士兵一样，五官、发纹均按照真人塑造而成，面部表情也各不相同，战车与战马也同实物一般大小"一句比较长，每句主语各不相同，因此可在主语变化处进行断句，采取分译法译为几个相对较短的句子。"五官""发纹""面部表情"可分别译为 facial feature、hair patterns、facial expressions；"和……一样大小"可译为"the same size as…"。

6)"这支陶俑组成的军队气势恢宏，十分逼真"可译为"The army made up of the terracotta figurines is magnificent and lifelike."。"陶俑"可译为 terracotta figurine。翻译此句时，可以选择一般现在时表示客观事实。

7)"被……列为世界文化遗产"可译为 be listed as the world cultural heritage。

6. 杭州西湖

在中国，以西湖命名的湖泊有不下 30 个，但是真正称得上是家喻户晓的只有杭州西湖。它位于中国东南沿海浙江省的省会杭州市，一座在国内被誉为人间天堂的城市。数千年前，西湖曾与大海相连，不远处的钱塘江正是这片水域的东部入口。江水带来的泥沙不断淤积，最终阻隔了西湖与大海，使西湖成为内陆湖泊。西湖美景在四季轮转中承载了许多的诗词、故事与传说。据不完全统计，仅关于西湖的传说就有 630 余个。2011 年，杭州西湖文化景观被列入世界遗产名录，慕名而来的国际游客络绎不绝，也许他们将为西湖续写更多的故事。

难点讲解：

1)本段介绍了杭州西湖的位置以及形成的原因，属于说明文文体。翻译时要注意和湖泊相关的表达。

2)原文首句可以用包含让步状语从句的复合句来表达，译为"Even though there are no less than thirty lakes named West Lake in China, the West Lake in Hangzhou is the best known to every household."。"家喻户晓"可用 be known to every household 来表达。

3)文中第二句可以用名词性短语和非限定性定语从句来修饰和说明"西湖"所在的城市"杭州"，此句可译为"It is located in Hangzhou, the capital of Zhejiang Province on the southeastern coast of China, which is known as the paradise of the world in China."。"人间天堂"可译为 paradise of the world 或 paradise on the earth。

4)"内陆湖"可译为 inland lake；"传说"可译为 legend。

5)"据不完全统计"可译为"It is roughly estimated that…"。

6)"杭州西湖文化景观被列入世界遗产名录"可译为"The West Lake Cultural Landscape of Hangzhou was included on the World Heritage List."。

7)"国际游客络绎不绝"可译为 an endless stream of international tourists。

7. 丝绸之路

丝绸之路是古代起始于中国并经古波斯国连接欧洲的通商道路，中国盛产丝绸，在这条道路上丝绸贸易占绝大部分，所以这条道路被称作丝绸之路。丝绸之路是最早、最重要的东西方文明交流的通道。广义上讲，丝绸之路又分为陆上丝绸之路和海上丝绸之路。陆上丝绸之路始于西汉，汉武帝派张骞出使西域，开辟了以首都长安（今西安）为起点，经甘肃、新疆，到中亚、西亚，并连接地中海各国的陆上通道。它的最初作用是运输产于中国的丝绸。海上丝绸之路是古代中国与外国进行交通贸易和文化交流的海上通道，该条路以南海为中心。海上丝绸之路形成于秦汉时期，发展于三国至隋朝时期，繁荣于唐宋时期，转变于明清时期，是已知的最为古老的海上航线。丝绸之路的开辟，有力地促进了东西方的经济文化交流，至今仍是中西方交往的重要通路。

难点讲解：

1) 本段介绍了丝绸之路的由来以及古往今来它在东西方文明交流中的重要作用和价值。文体为说明文文体。时态可采用一般现在时和一般过去时。

2) 此段首句较长，可以采用分译法进行处理。"丝绸之路"可译为 the Silk Road；"古波斯国"可译为 ancient Persia；"通商道路"可译为 trade road。整句可译为"The Silk Road was a trade road that started from China and connected Europe through the ancient Persia since ancient times. Because China was famous for producing silk which comprised a large proportion of the trade along the road, it was named the Silk Road."。

3) "东西方文明交流的通道"可译为 communication channel between the Eastern and Western civilizations；"陆上丝绸之路"可译为 Land Silk Road；"海上丝绸之路"可译为 Maritime Silk Road。

4) "陆上丝绸之路始于西汉"可译为 The Land Silk Road originated in the Western Han dynasty；"中亚、西亚"可译为 Central and West Asia；"地中海国家"可译为 Mediterranean countries。

5) "海上丝绸之路形成于秦汉时期，发展于三国至隋朝时期，繁荣于唐宋时期，转变于明清时期，是已知的最为古老的海上航线。"此句在翻译时可用几个并列句来描述海上丝绸之路的形成、发展、繁荣和转变。整句可译为"The Maritime Silk Road was formed in the Qin and Han dynasties, developed from the Three Kingdoms to the Sui Dynasty, prospered in the Tang and Song dynasties and changed in the Ming and Qing dynasties."。

6) "促进了东西方的经济文化交流"可译为 promote the economic and cultural exchanges between the East and the West。

拓展阅读

The Tang Dynasty

The Tang Dynasty ruled ancient China from 618 to 907. During the rule of the Tang Dynasty, China experienced a time of peace and prosperity that made it one of the most powerful nations in the world. This period is sometimes referred to as the Golden Age of Ancient China.

Considerable advancement in the areas of engineering and technology were made during the Tang Dynasty. Perhaps the most important was the invention of woodblock printing. Woodblock printing allowed books to be printed in mass production. This helped to increase literacy and to pass on knowledge throughout the empire. Another major invention of the time was gunpowder. Although it would continue to be perfected over hundreds of years, gunpowder was mostly used for fireworks during the Tang Dynasty. The people believed that fireworks could help to scare off evil spirits. Other inventions included a ceramic called porcelain, advances in mapmaking, cylinders for natural gas, advances in medicine, and advancements in clock making.

The arts flourished during the Tang Dynasty. It was during this time that poetry became an integral part of the Chinese culture. Poetry was a required study for those who wished to pass the civil service exams. Talented poets were well-respected and often recited their poetry as entertainment at parties. Some of the great poets in Chinese history lived during this time such as Li Bai, Du Fu, and Wang Wei. While the Tang Dynasty is most famous for its poetry, other arts also became popular during this time. Many forms of literature were written including short stories, encyclopedias, and histories. Also, painting was very popular and the era produced famous painters such as Wu Daozi, Wang Wei (also a famous poet), and Zhou Fang.

The Tang Dynasty ruled over a vast area. It took a very organized government to control all of this territory. The Tang established a detailed code of laws and administrative functions. They taxed the people based on their land and also required that farmers serve in the army for a period of time.

The capital city of the Tang Empire and center of the government was the city of Chang'an known as the modern city of Xi'an. It was here that the emperor lived and ruled over his vast empire. Government officials were assigned based on their scores on the civil service examinations. In an effort to get the best talent into the government, examinations were more open to men of the non-noble classes than with previous dynasties. There were even government-run schools to help educate more people.

Over time, the Tang Dynasty began to weaken due to government corruption and high taxes. A rebellion by the over-taxed people occurred in 874 where much of the city of Chang'an was destroyed. The Tang managed to halt the rebellion, but the government never fully recovered. In 907 the dynasty came to an end when a general named Zhu Wen removed the last Tang emperor and took power.

Exercises

1 Choose the best answer for the following questions.

1) What Chinese dynasty preceded the Tang Dynasty?

　　A) Ming.　　　　　B) Qin.　　　　　C) Sui.　　　　　D) Song.

2) Which statement below is sometimes used by historians to describe the Tang Dynasty?

　　A) The Spring and Autumn Period.　　　B) The Golden Age of Ancient China.

　　C) The Ten Kingdoms.　　　　　　　　D) The Religious Awakening.

3) Who was the first emperor of the Tang Dynasty?

　　A) Ying Zheng.　　B) Li Yuan.　　　C) Yellow Emperor.　D) Zheng He.

4) Which of the following was an important Chinese invention during this time period?

　　A) Woodblock printing.　B) Bronze.　　C) Iron casting.　　D) Silk.

5) What did the Chinese believe would help to scare off evil spirits?

　　A) Mechanical clocks.　B) Porcelain.　　C) Poetry.　　　D) Fireworks.

6) Why did government officials need to learn poetry?

　　A) Because most of the laws were written in poetry.

　　B) Because they used poetry for secret military codes.

　　C) Because it was part of the civil service test.

　　D) Because they could not be promoted if they didn't learn poetry.

7) Which of the following was a part of the Tang government system?

　　A) Taxes.　　　　　　　　　　　　　B) Farmers had to serve in the army.

　　C) A code of laws.　　　　　　　　　　D) All of the above.

8) Around what period of time did the Tang rule China?

　　A) From 200 BCE to 110 BCE.　　　　　B) From 618 CE to 907 CE.

C) From 340 CE to 540 CE.   D) From 22 BCE to 210 CE.

9) What was the capital city of the Tang Dynasty?

A) Chang'an.   B) Beijing.   C) Shanghai.   D) Chengdu.

10) Who overthrew the Tang Dynasty?

A) An Lushan.   B) Zhu Wen.   C) Huang Chao.   D) Li Mi.

翻译佳作赏析

登幽州台歌

陈子昂

前不见古人，

后不见来者。

念天地之悠悠，

独怆然而涕下。

译文：

Ascending the Youzhou Terrace

By Chen Zi'ang

Where are the great men of the past?

And where are those of future years?

The sky and earth forever last,

Here and now I alone shed tears.

（许渊冲　译）

赏析：

该译文是我国著名翻译家许渊冲的译作。前两句用 where 提出问题，问过去和问将来，形成强烈的对比，表达了诗人处于现在展望未来和回顾过去所感到的迷茫和疑惑。"古人"并不单纯指一般古代的人，而是指过去的有成就的人，因此许渊冲翻译为 the great men of the past，第二句中为了避免重复，用 those 来代替 the great men。许渊冲的译文讲究韵脚的对应，单数行诗句结尾处分别选取 past 和 last 这两个单词，双数行诗句结尾处分别选取 years 和 tears 这两个单词，韵脚对应工整，读起来朗朗上口。译文体现了许渊冲提倡的音美、意美、形美的翻译标准。

翻译练习

1. 泰山位于山东省泰安市中部，有"五岳之首""天下第一山"的美称，是中外闻名的游览胜地。泰山的主峰玉皇顶气势磅礴，雄伟壮观。泰山有四大奇观：泰山日出、云海玉盘、晚霞夕照、黄河金带。泰山以其壮观、雄伟、巍峨、宽广和厚重著称。自古以来，泰山被认为是中国的圣山，有"泰山安，四海皆安"的说法。几千年来，先后有十几位帝王到泰山拜祭封禅，形成了泰山在世界上独一无二的封禅祭祀文化。每个时代的皇帝、诗人和学者都曾在此留下大量的诗歌和石刻。泰山有大量的古树，如秦代的松树、汉代的柏树、唐代的槐树。这些自然景观与人文景观融为一体，是泰山风景的精华所在。泰山是中国首批文明风景旅游区示范点和中国 5A 级旅游景区之一，也被联合国教科文组织批准列为世界文化与自然双遗产，并因其独特的地质价值成为世界地质公园。

2. 中国季风性气候十分显著，大部分地区都受季风气候影响。温带季风性气候和亚热带季风性气候是中国主要的气候类型，海南和云南等少部分地区还受热带季风性气候影响。中国的西北地区由于地处内陆，属于温带大陆性气候。中国的大部分地区四季分明。通常每年九月至来年的四月，来自西伯利亚和蒙古国的干冷冬季季风到达中国后逐渐减弱，导致中国北方地区冬季寒冷干燥，温差很大。夏季季风一般从四月持续到九月。来自海洋的温暖湿润的夏季季风带来了高温和丰沛的降雨，南北温差不大。中国复杂多变的地形和气候形成了各种各样的温度带和干湿带。在温度方面，中国从南到北可分为赤道带、热带、亚热带、暖温带、中温带和寒温带；就湿度而言，从东南到西北可分为湿润区、半湿润区、半干旱区和干旱区。

3. 中国的耕地，主要分布在东北平原、华北平原、长江中下游平原、珠江三角洲平原和四川盆地。东北平原肥沃的黑土非常适合种植小麦、玉米、高粱、大豆、亚麻和甜菜。华北平原的褐色土适合种植小麦、玉米、谷子、高粱和棉花。长江中下游平原有许多湖泊和河流，特别适合种植水稻和养殖淡水鱼，因此被称为"鱼米之乡"。温暖湿润的四川盆地的紫色土壤四季都有适合种植的农作物，包括水稻、油菜籽和橘子，整片土地绿意盎然。

4. 青海湖是中国最大的湖泊，属内陆咸水湖，位于中国西部青藏高原东北部的青海省。青海湖的面积为4625.6平方千米，平均深度为21米，最大深度为32.8米，海拔为3,196米。有20多条河流和小溪汇入湖中。青海湖咸度是海水的2倍，但它仍然孕育了许多鱼类。湖上的鸟岛每年吸引大约10万只候鸟。迷人的青海湖也因为每年的环青海湖自行车赛而吸引着来自世界各地的职业自行车手。青海湖就像一颗巨大的蓝宝石在阳光下闪闪发光。青海湖在藏语里的意思是"青色的海"，以群山和蓝天为背景的湖泊展现出一种非凡的美丽。泛舟湖上，人们可能会以为自己身处浩瀚的蓝色海洋中。

5. 长白山位于中国东北吉林省吉林市。长白山是一座休眠火山，因常年积雪而得名。长白山拥有珍稀的动物、神奇的湖泊、令人叹为观止的温泉和绵延至地平线的森林。长白山主峰上有一个海拔超过2,100米的火山口湖，中文名为天池。天池是中国最大的火山湖，也是世界上最深的高山湖泊，平均水深204米，储存着超过20亿立方米的淡水。长白山的冬季有整整9个月。山顶常年积雪，积雪深度一般在50厘米。冬季登上长白山是一件极其困难的事，一般只有到盛夏时节冰封的天池才能融化。长白山是"中国十大名山"之一，是国家级自然保护区。

6. 莫高窟又称千佛洞，以精美的壁画和保存在洞穴中的各种雕塑而闻名。莫高窟拥有735个洞窟、45,000多平方米壁画和2,400多个不同大小的彩色雕塑，是世界上最伟大的佛教艺术宝库。从中可以一个朝代接一个朝代地追溯中国艺术绵长的发展历史。该遗址与龙门石窟和云冈石窟并称中国三大石窟。1987年，联合国教科文组织将莫高窟列入《世界遗产名录》。

7. 坚持人与自然和谐共生。建设生态文明是中华民族永续发展的千年大计，必须树立和践行绿水青山就是金山银山的理念，坚持节约资源和保护环境的基本国策，像对待生命一样对待生态环境，统筹山水林田湖草系统治理，实行最严格的生态环境保护制度，形成绿色发展方式和生活方式，坚定走生产发展、生活富裕、生态良好的文明发展道路，建设美丽中国，为人民创造良好生产生活环境，为全球生态安全作出贡献。

Unit 4

语言文字

Unit Goals

In this unit, you are going to
- acquire knowledge about Chinese language and calligraphy;
- know how to appreciate Chinese language and calligraphy from different perspectives;
- learn useful words and expressions that describe Chinese language and calligraphy;
- learn how to use the technique of "Omission" in English-Chinese and Chinese-English translation.

Related Words and Expressions

（母语不同的人共用的）通用语 lingua franca
母语 mother tongue; native language
普通话 putonghua (common speech of the Chinese language)
汉字 Chinese character
（古埃及所用的）象形文字 hieroglyph; pictograph
六书 six categories of Chinese characters
象形字 pictographs; pictographic characters
指事字 ideographs; ideographic characters; indicative characters
会意字 compound ideographs; associative compounds
形声字 phono-semantic compounds; phonograms
转注字 transformed cognates; mutually explanatory characters
假借字 phonetic loan character
同音字 homophonic characters
甲骨文 oracle bone script; inscriptions on oracle bones
金文 bronze inscriptions; bronzeware script
大篆 large seal script
小篆 small seal script
隶书 clerical script; official script
楷书 regular script
行书 running script

草书 cursive script

繁体字 traditional /unsimplified Chinese character

简体字 simplified Chinese character

偏旁 radicals

部首 components

笔画 stroke

笔顺 stroke order

点 dot

横 horizontal stroke

竖 vertical stroke

撇 left-falling stroke

捺 right-falling stroke

提 rising stroke

钩 hook

声调 tone

语调 intonation

阴平 high and level tone

阳平 rising tone

上声 falling-rising tone

去声 falling tone

轻声 light tone; neutral tone

声母 initial of a Chinese syllable

韵母 simple or compound vowel (of a Chinese syllable)

威妥玛式拼音法 Wade-Giles romanization

中国书法 Chinese calligraphy

文房四宝 Four Treasures of the Study

笔 writing brush

墨 ink stick

纸 paper

砚 inkstone; inkslab

Lead-in Activities

 Answer the following questions.

1) As we know, there are different styles (like Gothic and Italian) in English writing. How many writing styles can you name in Chinese calligraphy?

2) The so-called "Four Treasures of the Study" refer to _____, _____, _____, and _____.

3) Can you say something about Chinese dialects?

2 **Listen to a brief introduction to the Chinese language and dialects, and fill in the blanks with the words you hear.**

As one of the six official languages used by the UN (United Nations), Chinese has now ____ _____ in the World. The official language of China is Putonghua, otherwise known as Hanyu, which belongs to the _____.

Putonghua is based on _____ and other dialects spoken in the northern areas of China. Students are often taught Putonghua in their schools. It is _____ that Putonghua is used as a _____ by more people than any other language, accounting for about _____ of the world's population. In the past, the Chinese language and writing system had a strong influence on those of neighboring countries, such as Japanese, Korean and Vietnamese.

With a _____ and huge population, China has many different dialects which are _____. Due to the differences between each of the dialects, there are obvious obstacles to people speaking their own dialects and communicating with each other.

The Chinese character has more than 3,000 years of history. It is a kind of hieroglyphic which _____ oracle bone script in the Shang Dynasty. It then developed into different forms of _____ including large seal script, small seal script, official script, regular script, _____ and running script.

There are altogether approximately 80,000 Chinese words that originate from ancient times; however, only about 3,000 characters are generally needed for daily use in expressing over 99% of the information in _____ because a Chinese character contains many different meanings. There are now two kinds of characters—simplified Chinese and traditional Chinese.

3 **Read the following passages and do the exercises.**

Passage One

The Formation of Chinese Characters

Chinese characters originated from drawings, with the earliest Chinese characters being only paintings of the things that people saw in front of them. However, the total number of Chinese characters now has exceeded 100,000. It is, of course, entirely impossible to form so many characters just using drawings. In fact, the resourceful people of ancient China learned to create Chinese characters by using four methods. They created Chinese characters pictographically, by indication, as associative compounds, and as phonograms.

The Development of the "Six Categories"

Shuowen Jiezi is a famous study of ancient characters, written during the Eastern Han Dynasty (25—220). It is one of the oldest dictionaries in the world and laid the foundations for our understanding of how Chinese characters are formed.

The Creation of *Shuowen Jiezi*

In the Western Han Dynasty (206 BCE—25 CE), Emperor Wudi adopted the thoughts of Confucius and Mencius as the basis of his feudalist approach to government. He also promoted Confucian philosophy to strengthen the unification of the state. As a result, the study of the Confucian classics became popular.

To support the study of Confucian thought, the emperor established the Taixue Imperial College in his capital Chang'an (present-day Xi'an, Shaanxi). He also appointed "five-classics court academicians" (equivalent to modern-day professors) to teach the five Confucian classics, namely *Book of Songs*, *Book of History*, *Book of Rites*, *Book of Changes* and *Spring and Autumn Annals*.

At that time, the classics were written in the popular Lishu style, which belongs to the school of "modern characters." As a result, these classics were called "modern-character classics." However, at the end of the reign of Emperor Wudi, some classics written in Dazhuan (i.e. "ancient characters") were found inside the walls of Confucius's old house. These texts have become known as "ancient-character classics."

The existence of two different kinds of characters created controversy about the interpretation of Confucius's work. The controversy led to disputes between those who championed the modern-character classics and those who championed the ancient-character classics. These disputes lasted for at least 200 years.

To get a better understanding of the ancient-character and modern-character classics, Xu Shen spent many years writing *Shuowen Jiezi*. Xu Shen championed the ancient-character classics. He lived during the Eastern Han Dynasty. His book was based on his analysis of the structures of ancient characters. In *Shuowen Jiezi*, Xu Shen used the concept of the "six categories" to analyze and summarize existing Chinese Characters. This approach provided an integrated understanding of their forms, pronunciations, and meanings and made a great contribution to China's paleography.

The First Dictionary of Ancient Characters

Shuowen Jiezi consists of 15 volumes. These total together 9,353 characters that are classified into 540 categories.

Using Xiaozhuan as the primary character type, Xu Shen analyzed the forms and structures of written Chinese. He comprehensively explained the forms, pronunciations, and meanings of xiaozhuan, which made the book the first Chinese Dictionary of ancient characters.

Shuowen Jiezi provides an explanation of the meanings of Xiaozhuan characters based on their forms. It, therefore, offers a wonderful opportunity to learn the structures of Chinese characters and to grasp their original meanings. Although Xu Shen did not assess any Jiaguwen characters (which brings into question the reliability of his analysis regarding some characters in the book), his book's basic contents are correct, and it remains a handy reference book on ancient writing, even today.

Xu Shen pioneered the study method of integrating forms, pronunciations and meanings. In *Shuowen Jiezi* he also created an indexing system based on the components of Chinese characters. These two ground-breaking ideas, and the enormous amount of material about ancient characters that *Shuowen Jiezi* contains, make this title one of the most precious treasures for the study of Han philology.

The Formation of the "Six Categories"

In *Shuowen Jiezi*, Xu Shen discussed the formation of Chinese characters. These categories are pictographic characters, indicative characters, associative compounds, phonograms, mutually explanatory characters, and phonetic loan characters. Currently, the first four of these categories are regarded as being linked to the way in which the characters they contain are formed.

Using these six categories, Xu Shen analyzed the formation of 9,353 Chinese Characters. This work made a very significant contribution to the philology of ancient characters in China. Even today, the "six categories" play a role in analyzing the forms and structures of modern Chinese characters.

Components

The system of components was established to make dictionary references easier. It was another of Xu Shen's great inventions. In *Shuowen Jiezi*, Xu Shen classified the 9,353 characters he collected into 540 categories. The characters within each category shared the same component, with the first character in each category being that shared component. Therefore, there were 540 shared components.

The establishment of the component system not only made it easier to look up characters in a dictionary but it also gave prominence to the function of expressing the meanings of Chinese characters and to grasp their original meanings. Although Xu Shen did not assess any Jiaguwen characters, it is also a great help to anyone who wants to learn and use Chinese characters and to grasp their original meanings. Other major Chinese dictionaries later also put the system into use.

1) Answer the following questions.
   (1) During which dynasty was *Shuowen Jiezi* written? What does "the five Confucian classics" refer to?
   (2) What are the two ground-breaking ideas that Xu Shen pioneered in writing *Shuowen jiezi*?
   (3) What does "six categories" refer to? What role does it play?
   (4) What is the significance of the establishment of the component system by Xu Shen?

Passage Two

The Lingering Charm of Chinese Calligraphy

Calligraphy was the visual art form in traditional China. Since the invention of the "Oracle bone script," Chinese calligraphy has experienced several developmental stages, from "Seal script" to "Clerical script," "Cursive script," "Regular script" and "Running script." There are many calligraphers and calligraphic works that were produced and helped constitute a profound tradition of Chinese calligraphy at each stage.

In 2009, Chinese calligraphy was added to the list of UNESCO Masterpieces of the Oral and Intangible Heritage of Humanity.

Oracle Bone Script

The oracle bone script, also known as "Jiaguwen," was used on animal bones or turtles' shells. It is the earliest known form of Chinese writing. Oracle bone inscriptions were discovered in Yinxu in Anyang City, in central Henan Province, as a cultural product of the Shang Dynasty, dating back more than 3,600 years. Moreover, there were bronze items used during the Shang and Zhou dynasties, and some were inscribed with writing, which was later called "Bronze script," also known "Jinwen" or "Zhongdingwen." The structure of the oracle bone script was the base of the bronze script and later Chinese calligraphy.

Seal Script

Seal script, "Zhuanshu" or "simplified picture script," was developed directly from China's most ancient forms of writing. The general term seal script can be used to refer to several types of seal script, including the large seal script and the small seal script. According to the documents, there was no special name for Chinese calligraphy before the Qin Dynasty. The so-called seal script was the official calligraphy and the standard font for official documents in the Qin Dynasty. However, since it's a difficult writing method, the script was replaced by the clerical script after Qin. Also, it was still widely used for decorative engraving and seals, such as name chops, or signets in the Han Dynasty.

Clerical Script

The clerical script, or "Lishu," is an intense font style commonly seen in Chinese characters. As ancient bamboo and wooden slips recorded, the clerical script evolved from the Warring States period to the Qin Dynasty and reached its peak during the Eastern Han or Later Han Dynasty. Clerical script, which was based on the seal script, is the font that is easiest to write. For the convenience of writing on the bamboo and wood slips, ancient people simplified the small seal script. The appearance of the clerical script is an excellent change in ancient writing and calligraphy.

Cursive Script

The cursive script, or "Caoshu," has a simple structure and continuous strokes, which evolved from the clerical script. The cursive script began in the early Han Dynasty. The character "草(cao)" means quick, rough or sloppy, which corresponds to its simple structure and fast writing style. The early cursive script, which broke the strict rules of the clerical script, was a hasty form of writing and called "Zhangcao." Zhangcao was most widespread in the Han and Wei dynasties, and was later revived in the Yuan Dynasty and transformed in the Ming Dynasty. Now, the aesthetic value of the cursive script is far beyond its practical value. The cursive script has a writing method to follow and not random scribbling.

Regular Script

The regular script, also known as "Kaishu," can be compared to Western printing, and is the newest of the Chinese script styles. The script appeared during the Wei Dynasty and matured stylistically around the seventh century, hence it being the most common form in modern writings and publications. The character "Kai" means "the model" in Chinese, which represents the normalized style and standard writing method of this script. The clerical script changed the writing style and aesthetic trend of Chinese characters, thus laying a foundation for the evolution of the regular script and opening a field for the development and prosperity of Chinese calligraphy. In modern times, the regular script is still the standard of writing Chinese characters.

Running Script

The running script, "Xingshu" or "Semi-cursive script," can be compared to Western longhand. There are two types of cursive, including "Xingkai" and "Xingcao," which were developed on the basis of the regular script. Running script is a font between regular script and cursive script, and the appearance of the script is to compensate for the slow writing speed of regular script and the illegibility of cursive script.

Over time, Chinese characters gradually became a system of symbols with strong national ties. For the better promotion of Chinese character culture, China established the National Museum of Chinese Writing (NMCW) in 2009, in Anyang City, Henan Province, where the oracle bone script originated. The NMCW is a state-level museum constructed upon the approval of the State Council for preserving, showcasing and studying the cultural relics.

1) Answer the following questions.
(1) Which script is the earliest known form of Chinese writing? And to which dynasty can it be dated back?
(2) Which script was the official calligraphy and the standard font for official documents in the Qin Dynasty?
(3) When did the clerical script reach its peak?
(4) What are the features of cursive script?
(5) Which script is the most common form in modern writings and publications and the standard of writing Chinese characters?

2) Translate the following terms into English.
(1) 联合国教科文组织
(2)《人类非物质文化遗产代表作名录》
(3) 金文
(4) 竹简与木简
(5) 美学价值
(6) 标准字体

翻译技巧：减词法/省略法（Omission）

所谓减词法，就是把原文中有但译文中不需要的单词、词组等在翻译过程中省略不译。由于汉英两种语言在句法和表达方式上存在很大差异，翻译时可根据目的语的表达习惯酌情省略原文中的一些词，使译文更加简练、清晰。减词法的根本原则是"减词不减意"，也就是说在不改变原文意思的前提下，省略一些在译文中可有可无的词。

Ⅰ. 减词法在英译汉中的运用

一般来说，汉语相较于英语较为简练，英译汉时许多在原文中必不可少的词语，要是原原本本地译成汉语，就会成为不必要的冗词，译文会显得累赘。因此省略法在英译汉中使用非常广泛，其主要作用是删去一些可有可无、不符合汉语表达习惯的词语，如虚词中冠词、介词和连接词的省略，以及实词中代词、动词的省略。

1. 省略冠词

英语中的冠词有 a、an、the，用途极广，用法复杂，而汉语中没有冠词。在英译汉时，应注意区分冠词只是起语法作用还是表达某种实际的意义。对于仅起语法作用而没有实际意义的冠词，在翻译过程中应省略不译。

例 1　原文　*The* earth is larger than *the* moon, but smaller than *the* sun.
　　　　译文　地球比月亮大，但是比太阳小。
例 2　原文　*A* camel is much inferior to *an* elephant in strength.
　　　　译文　骆驼在体力方面远不及大象。

2. 省略介词

大量使用介词是英语的一个显著特点。相较于英语，汉语中介词使用的频率要低得多。因此在英译汉时，很多情况下英语介词要转换为其他词性或省略不译，尤其是表示时间和地点的介词。

例 1　原文　Columbus arrived *in* America *in* the 15th century.
　　　　译文　哥伦布 15 世纪到达美洲。
例 2　原文　There is a temple *at* the top of the mountain.
　　　　译文　山顶上有一座寺庙。
例 3　原文　*On* Sundays we have no school.
　　　　译文　礼拜天我们不上学。

3. 省略连接词

英语句子讲究形式上的严密，句子内部的逻辑关系主要依靠连接词来体现。而汉语句子注重的是意思的连贯而不是形式的严密，所以句子内部的逻辑关系是暗含的，在很多情况下不一定需要连接词。例如汉语句子"他来了，我就走"，这两个分句之间关系是松散的，没有连接词。但是，在英语句子中，这两个分句之间一定要加上连接词，指出他们之间的逻辑关系，比如可以说"*If* he comes, I will go."，也可以说"*When* he comes, I will go."等。因此在英译汉时，英语中的连接词并非都要译出，适当地省略连接词可以使译文更加简洁、自然。

例 1　原文　*If* winter comes, can spring be far behind?
　　　　译文　冬天来了，春天还会远吗？
例 2　原文　The sun is bright, *and* the sky is clear.
　　　　译文　阳光灿烂，晴空万里。
例 3　原文　Modesty helps one to go forward *whereas* conceit makes one lag behind.
　　　　译文　谦虚使人进步，骄傲使人落后。

4. 省略代词

英语中大量使用代词以求得句式的严谨，而汉语中则要避免使用过多的代词，否则表达上会显得啰唆。因此，在英译汉过程中经常需要省略一些代词，包括人称代词、物主代词、充当宾语的反身代词以及用在强调句等特殊句型中的代词 it 等。例如：

例 1　原文　He put *his* hands into *his* pockets and then shrugged *his* shoulders.
　　　　译文　他将双手放进口袋，然后耸了耸肩。

例 2　原文　The brain is the center of *our* nervous system.
　　　译文　大脑是神经系统的中枢。
例 3　原文　I glanced at *my* watch. *It* is already 11 o'clock.
　　　译文　我看了一下手表，已经11点了。
例 4　原文　*It* was in this mountain that this rare kind of plant was found.
　　　译文　正是在这座山上发现了这种珍稀植物。

5. 省略多余的词或短语

英译汉时，出于逻辑或修辞上的考虑，有时要省译多余的、重复出现的、不言而喻的词或短语。

例 1　原文　The treatment did not produce any *harmful* side effect.
　　　译文　这种治病方法没有产生任何副作用。
例 2　原文　*The time-keeping devices of* electronic watches are much more accurate than those of mechanical ones.
　　　译文　电子表比机械表准确得多。
例 3　原文　Copper is a material which has the *property* of elasticity.
　　　译文　铜是一种具有弹性的材料。
例 4　原文　Applicants who have worked at a job will receive preference over *those who have not*.
　　　译文　有工作经验的优先录取。

Ⅱ. 减词法在汉译英中的运用

减词法也同样适用于汉译英的某些情况。汉译英的省略主要是省略冗词赘句，以及一些表示概念范畴的词语和过分详细的描述。

汉语中有些词、词组或成分经常重复使用，以增强句子的气势，如果照原文全部译出，往往不符合英语表达习惯，有时只需译出其中一个，其余可以略而不译。

例 1　原文　我们要培养分析**问题**、解决**问题**的能力。
　　　译文　We should cultivate the ability to analyze and solve problems.

在汉语中有时为了明确信息，往往需要将动词和一些关键性的名词加以重复，翻译时只需出现一次。

例 2　原文　他们为国家**做**的**事**，比我们**做**的多得多。
　　　译文　They have done much more for the country than we have.
例 3　原文　**不**坚持社会主义，**不**改革开放，**不**发展经济，**不**改善人民生活，只能是死路一条。
　　　译文　If we did not adhere to socialism, implement the policies of reform and opening up, develop the economy and raise living standard of the people, we would find ourselves in a blind alley.

英语中有些抽象名词往往已经含有汉语中一些表示状态、品质的范畴概念，如 unemployment 表示"失业现象、失业问题"，housing 表示"住房问题"，emergency 表示"紧急情况"，solution 表示"解决办法"，tension 表示"紧张局势"，stability 表示"稳定局面"。有时为了表达简洁，或是出于主谓搭配的缘故，在汉译英时要省译表示汉语的范畴词。

例 4　原文　我的英语水平提高了。
　　　译文 A　The **level** of my English has improved.

　　　　　译文 B　My English has improved.
例 5　原文　这座大楼的**质量**非常差。
　　　　　译文 A　The **quality** of the building is poor.
　　　　　译文 B　The building is not well built.
例 6　原文　我们可以逐步解决沿海地区和内陆地区的差距**问题**。
　　　　　译文　We can gradually bridge the gap between coastal and inland areas.
例 7　原文　国家要加大对中西部地区的支持**力度**。
　　　　　译文　The state will increase the support for the central and western parts.
例 8　原文　在工作中大家都必须杜绝浪费和低效率的**现象**。
　　　　　译文　It's necessary to put an end to waste and low efficiency in our work.

　　总之，在翻译过程中，可以根据实际的需要适当地运用减词译法，以达到既忠实于原文又符合译文表达习惯的目的，但一定要注意把握最基本的原则，即在不改变原文意思的前提下运用减词法，绝不能随意删减、篡改原文的意思。

段落翻译

1. 汉语概况

现代标准汉语

　　现代标准汉语是中国使用的唯一官方标准语言，也是联合国六种官方工作语言之一。现代汉语的标准语是"普通话"，在新加坡、马来西亚等国被称作"华语"。它以北京语音为标准音，以北方话为基础方言，以典范的现代白话文作为语法规范。普通话为中国不同地区、不同民族人们之间的交际提供了方便。

汉语方言

　　中国地域广阔，人口众多，各地区都有自己的方言。方言俗称地方话，是汉语在不同地域的分支，只通行于一定的地域。汉语方言可分为七大类：北方方言、吴方言、湘方言、赣方言、客家方言、闽方言、粤方言。其中，北方方言是通行地域最广、使用人口最多的方言。

汉字

　　汉字是世界上最古老的文字之一，也是世界上使用人数最多的文字。古往今来，汉字发生了翻天覆地的变化，从最早的图画文字到由笔画构成的符号文字，演变过程历经甲骨文、金文、小篆、隶书、楷书和行书。

难点讲解：

1)"联合国"可译为 the United Nations。
2)"现代白话文"可译为 modern vernacular Chinese。
3)"吴方言、湘方言、赣方言、客家方言、闽方言、粤方言"可译为 the Wu dialect, the Xiang dialect, the Gan dialect, the Hakka, the Min dialect and the Yue or Guangdong dialect。
4)翻译"翻天覆地的变化"时要注意汉语中具体形象的语言在英译时不能机械地逐字翻译，而是要根据英语的表达习惯把原文意思准确地翻译出来。
5)"图画文字"可译为 pictograph。

2. 汉字的造字方法

　　汉字的造字方法主要有四种。象形是指画出事物形状的造字法，如"月"写起来像一个弯弯的月亮。指事是在象形字上加指事符号，或完全用符号组成字的造字法。如"刃"就是在刀锋上加一点，指出这个位置就是刀刃所在。会意是把两个或两个以上的符号组合起来，从而表示一个新的意义。如"明"是由"日"和"月"组成，太阳和月亮在一起，怎么能不"明"呢？形声是用形旁和声旁组成新字。形旁表示字的意义；声旁表示字的读音。如"湖"字，"水"是形旁，说明这是一个与水有关的字，"胡"是声旁，说明这个字的读音和"胡"一致。

难点讲解：

1)本段简要介绍汉字的四种主要造字法，难点是各种造字法以及相关术语的英文表达。"象形"可译为 pictographs 或 pictographic characters。象形字来源于图画文字，是一种最原始的造字方法。中国的甲骨文、埃及的象形文字、古印度文等都是独立地从原始社会最简单的图画发展而来的。

2)"指事"可译为 ideographs、ideographic characters 或 indicative characters。指事字是一种抽象的造字法，也就是说当没有或不方便用具体形象展现某种事物时，就用一种抽象的符号来表示。大多数指事字是在象形字的基础上添加、减少笔画或符号。

3)"会意"可译为 compound ideographs 或 associative compounds。会意字是将两个或两个以上的独体字根据意义之间的关系合成一个字，综合表示这些构字成分合成的意义。

4)"形声"可译为 phono-semantic compounds。形声字由两部分组成：形旁（又称"义符"）和声旁（又称"音符"）。形旁指示字的意思或类属，声旁则表示字的相同或相近发音。

3. 甲骨文

甲骨文是中国的一种古老的文字，是中国商朝用于占卜记事而在龟甲或兽骨上刻的文字。商朝王室贵族上自国家大事，下至私人生活，无不求神问卜，以得知吉凶祸福，并以此来决定行止。于是，占卜成了国家政治生活中的一件大事，朝廷设置了专门的机构和卜官。有刻辞的甲骨都作为国家档案保存起来，堆存在窖穴之中。因此，甲骨上的卜辞成为研究商代历史的第一手材料，它反映了公元前1000多年社会生活的各个方面。

难点讲解：

1)"占卜"可译为 divination。

2)"王室贵族"可译为 royal family and nobility。

3)"国家大事"可译为 affairs of state 或 state affairs。

4)"求神问卜"可译为 to seek divine guidance through divination。

5)"吉凶祸福"可译为 good or bad fortune 或 auspiciousness and misfortune。

6)"窖穴"意指地下室或者地下洞穴，通常指在地下的封闭空间，可能用于存储物品或躲避危险，可翻译为 underground chamber、pit 或 cellar。

4. 汉语热

"汉语热"是指近年来越来越多的外国人开始学习汉语的现象。在很多国家，学汉语的人数在迅速增长。一项调查显示，外国人学习汉语的主要目的是去中国旅游、从事贸易活动、了解中国和中国文化。汉语热背后的原因是中国经济的飞速发展，它使中国的国际地位和影响力得到了提升。全球"汉语热"传达了世界各国人民渴望了解中国文化的信息。随着"一带一路"的推进，中国与世界各国的交流会越来越多、越来越深入，"汉语热"也必将迎来一个新的时期。我们不妨抓住这个机会，主动对接全球学汉语的需求，向学汉语的人提供更多来中国学习交流的机会，使"汉语热"成为中国联系世界、世界了解中国的切入点。

难点讲解：

1)"一带一路"是"丝绸之路经济带"和"21世纪海上丝绸之路"(the Silk Road Economic Belt and the 21st-Century Maritime Silk Road)的简称。2013年9月和10月，中国国家主席习近平分别提出建设"新丝绸之路经济带"和"21世纪海上丝绸之路"的合作倡议。"'一带一路'倡议"应译为 Belt and Road Initiative。

2)"汉语热"可译为 Chinese language craze/fever。

3)"越来越多"可译为 a growing number of 或 more and more。

4)"显示"可译为 to indicate 或 to show。

5)"从事"可译为 to engage in 或 deal with。

6)"贸易活动"可译为 trade activity。

7)"背后的原因"可译为 underlying reason 或 reason behind。

8)"国际地位"可译为 international status。

9)"传达"可译为 to convey 或 to deliver。

5. 中国书法

中国书法是中国汉字特有的一种传统艺术。传统书法字体有篆书、隶书、楷书、草书和行书。每种都有不同的书写技法。书法的书写工具，是被人们称为"文房四宝"的笔、墨、纸、砚。在中国艺术史上，书法和绘画具有同等重要的地位。自古以来，汉字书法都因其美学价值而获得欣赏。中国书法因其艺术美和复杂性而被誉为无言之诗、无形之舞、无图之画、无声之乐。中国历史上有许多著名的书法家，如王羲之、欧阳询、颜真卿、柳公权、赵孟頫等。他们经过多年的勤学苦练，开创了不同的风格和流派，使中国的书法艺术达到了很高的水平。

难点讲解：

1)"美学价值"可译为 aesthetic value。

2)"被誉为"可译为 be acclaimed as、be praised as 或 be crowned as。

3)"无言之诗、无形之舞、无图之画、无声之乐"可译为 poetry without words, dance without movement, painting without pictures, and music without sound。

6. 谚语

谚语是广泛流传于民间的短小精悍的格言，通常经口头流传下来，大都反映了劳动人民的生活实践经验。谚语类似成语，但口语性强、通俗易懂，因而很有感染力。谚语往往能反映一个民族的地理、历史、社会制度、社会观点和态度。比如，有些民族住在沿海一带，靠海为生，他们的谚语往往涉及海上航行、经受风雨、捕鱼捉蟹等。游牧民族的谚语则多涉及沙漠、草原、羊、马、骆驼、豺狼等。人们的经历和对世界的认识在不少方面是相似的。因此，汉语和英语中有很多相同或相似的谚语。

难点讲解：

1)"经口头流传"可译为 to be passed down orally 或 by word of mouth。

2)"口语性强、通俗易懂"可译为 highly colloquial, easily understood。

3)"经受风雨、捕鱼捉虾"是汉语中典型的具体形象的表达，英译时可将其转换为抽象表达，译为 weathering the storm and fisheries。汉语中有大量运用具象来表达抽象的例子，如画饼充饥(feed on illusions/fancies)、弱不禁风(be in delicate health)等。相对而言，英语中的抽象表达方式更加普遍，如 work with meticulous care（精雕细刻）、accept sth uncritically（生吞活剥）、be full of fears and misgivings（前怕狼后怕虎）等。因此，在汉英互译中不能死抠原文词语和语言结构。

4)"游牧民族"即 nomads。

拓展阅读

Reading A

Some Distinctive Features of the Chinese Language

In the Chinese language, the messages borne by the sentence are not expressed by way of grammatical pattern, but by way of the words according to the inherent interrelations and the circumstances. The semantic element and the usage element in the sentence are more important than the syntax element in a sentence in western languages. Sentences formed by this method can carry the maximum amount of message and express multiple meanings, giving the Chinese language a very high manifestation power. Take a lyric composed by Ma Zhiyuan for example:

秋思

枯藤老树昏鸦，

小桥流水人家，

古道西风瘦马，

夕阳西下，

断肠人在天涯。

Longing in Autumn

Withered rattans, old trees, ravens in the evening,

A small bridge, a running brook, a house,

Age-old road, west wind, thin horse,

Sunset in the twilight,

The broken-hearted man in the corner of the world.

The first three lines are all simply collocated nouns without the grammatical elements as in western languages. The readers are left to see the inherent grammatical relations by themselves. But the things expressed by these nouns are connected with each other, giving a beautiful picture of a mountain village and an autumn scene. The lyric involves colors, sounds, the near perspective, the far perspective, the static things and moving things, as well as the sorrowful sentiment of the writer. The lyric is imbued with deep sentiments and a lasting appeal. The Chinese language is fully capable of conveying ideas and emotions, even though the Chinese sentences do not adhere to the grammatical structure as in western languages.

A sentence in western languages must have the important structural elements such as subject, predicate, object, etc., or the sentence will be untenable. In the Chinese language, sentences with no subject, no predicate or no object are often found. Sentences without subjects are widely used in the Chinese language. For example, 下雨了, 上课了 or 爱护花草, 随手关门 are all sentences without subjects. Sentences without a verb in the predicate are frequently used in daily conversations in China. For example, 这张画漂亮 (This painting magnificent) or 今天星期五 (Today Friday).

A western language tends to be reconstructive and the Chinese language tends to be accumulative in the use of words. Western languages are phonographical and tend to be more variable. This greater variability is manifested in two respects. First, it is common not to use the same words and phrases to express something that has changed somewhat. Second, western languages are characterized by reconstruction, the frequent changes in word orders and sentence patterns.

In contrast, the Chinese language has a greater degree of stability and invariableness, which is closely related to its use of ideographs and pictographs. The Chinese language has multiple dimensions and relative stability, manifested first of all in the accumulativeness of words or phrases. In this way, a Chinese word can have a set of multiple meanings. For instance, 闻 used in 耳闻 (listen by ear), 听闻 (hear of), and 新闻 (news) can mean "hear"; 闻 used in 闻到气味 (smell an odor) can mean "smell."

With the accumulative semantic development, the Chinese word can have a greater generality and flexibility. A child, for example, if he is aware of the concept 车 (chariot) can speak out a pile of terms, such as 火车 (train), 汽车 (car), 马车 (horse-drawn cart) and 三轮车 (tricycle), etc. Therefore, the Chinese primary and middle school students can write letters and compositions if they get a mystery of 2,000 to 3,000 characters.

The Chinese words are isolated words. The relations among the words are constituted mainly through the use of functional words and the word order. For example, 太阳红 (The sun gets red) and 红太阳 (the red sun) have different meanings. Through the different word orders, a different grammatical relationship is expressed. On the other hand, functional words are used to express word relationships. As quoted below, the same words in the phrase 写字 (write words) will express quite different meanings when functional words are inserted. For example, 写了字 (has written words), 写过字 (wrote words) and 写着字 (is writing words) express different tenses.

The phonetic characteristic of the Chinese language results in its obvious musicality—pleasant in sound, gentle in tone, clear in tempo and harmonious in rhythm. The classical Chinese poems exploit this characteristic to arrange the regular yet varied rhythmic units.

The repetition of syllables is another important characteristic, showing the high aesthetic expressive power of the syllables of the Chinese language. The Chinese language has an outstanding aesthetic characteristic phonically. For instance, the lyric entitled "Slow, Slow Song" composed by Li Qingzhao exemplifies the unique skills of the writer in using repeated syllables. With respect both to its artistic form and its aesthetic effect, the lyric has become a great poetic masterpiece of all times.

The starting point of the traditional Chinese thinking is the entirety and the unification of the subjective and objective. This thinking mode stands out for its pictographic and its experiential characteristics. The Chinese language is dominated by this dialectical thinking mode, which emphasizes the interrelations within and governing of the forms by the essence.

Exercises

1 **Answer the following questions according to the text.**

1) Do you agree that "The western language is characterized by reconstruction"?

2) What's the difference between Chinese and English?

2 **Tell whether the following statements are true or false. Write T if the statement is true and F if it is false.**

1) In the Chinese language the messages borne by the sentence are expressed by way of grammatical pattern.

2) A sentence in the Chinese language must have the important structural elements such as subject, predicate, object, etc., or the sentence will be untenable.

Reading B

Chinese Couplets

Couplets refer to two lines of verse, usually in the same meter and joined by rhyme. Couplets appeared frequently in Early Modern English poetries, especially in Shakespeare's sonnets. For example, in Sonnet 18, "So long as men can breathe or eyes can see, so long lives this, and this gives life to thee," it just showed the rhyming couplet in the last word of two sentences. Chinese couplets are also composed of pairs of balanced lines with the same meter in the poetry. But there are two principles that need to follow when people write Chinese couplets. Firstly, characters in two lines must be equal in number. Secondly, characters at the opposite position must be equal in the lexical category. Take 喜滋滋迎新年，笑盈盈辞旧岁 as an example, the number of characters in two sentences are identical with each other. Additionally, the lexical category of words is also in common. Both 喜滋滋 and 笑盈盈 are adjectives; 迎 and 辞 are verbs; 新年 and 旧岁 are nouns.

Chinese couplets represent a significant part of Chinese traditional culture. It has been continued for thousands of years. In ancient times, people would carve couplets on the surface of bamboo, woods or pillars. But nowadays, people merely write couplets on papers or fabrics.

The origin of Chinese couplets can be traced back to Zhou Dynasty (1046 – 256 BCE), called *taofu*(桃符) at first to guard against evil. But the earliest written Chinese couplet was from Tang Dynasty (618 – 907) that archaeologist found at the Mogao Grottoes in Gansu province. It was recorded in Dunhuang Manuscripts (敦煌遗书), which meant everything comes back to life at the springtime, and people will usher in the new year of a brand-new life.（三阳始布，四序初开。福庆初新，寿禄延长。）

Couplets did not become popular and secular until to the Song Dynasty (960 – 1279). During the Song Dynasty, people began to paste couplets on their doors. The famous poet Wang Anshi (1021 – 1086) in Northern Song Dynasty even created a poem to depict the spectacular scene of pasting Spring Festival couplets, called "New Year's Day" (《元日》). To the Ming Dynasty, couplets got officially appreciated and spread widely by the Hongwu Emperor (1328 – 1398). It was also him who invented the word **春联** and stipulated for writing Spring Festival couplets on red paper.

After hundreds of years, couplet came to its heyday during the Kangxi and Qianlong reign periods of the Qing Dynasty (1636 – 1912). Before the Qing Dynasty, couplets were only written for the Spring Festival. Out of the economic and cultural development, couplets turned into many different kinds other than Spring Festival couplets. Furthermore, the content of couplets was related to politics, economy, and social events like weddings and funerals.

Couplets can be divided into various categories according to its character numbers and usages.

Based on the number of characters, couplets can be fallen into short couplets, moderate couplets, and long couplets. Short couplets generally consist of ten characters, while moderate couplets contain no more than a hundred characters. And as for long couplets, they are composed of more than a hundred characters with no upper limit.

From the usages, there are Spring Festival couplets, congratulatory couplets, and elegiac couplets. Spring Festival couplets, just as its name implies, are only pasted in the Spring Festival. Congratulatory couplets are always written by people to express their sincere blessing for somebody's birthday, wedding or pregnancy. If there is a funeral, people will also write elegiac couplets to mourn the deceased.

Exercises

1. Talk about the history and categories of Chinese couplets.
2. List some of the classic Chinese couplets with English translation.

翻译佳作赏析

乡愁

余光中

小时候，乡愁是一枚小小的邮票，我在这头，母亲在那头。

长大后，乡愁是一张窄窄的船票，我在这头，新娘在那头。

后来啊！乡愁是一方矮矮的坟墓，我在外头，母亲在里头。

而现在，乡愁是一湾浅浅的海峡，我在这头，大陆在那头。

译文：

Homesick

By Yu Guangzhong

When I was a child, my homesickness was a small stamp linking Mum at the other end and me this.

When I grew up, I remained homesick, but it became a ticket by which I sailed to and from my bride at the other end.

Then homesickness took the shape of a grave, Mum inside of it and me outside.

Now I am still homesick, but it is a narrow strait separating me on this side and the mainland on the other.

(陈文伯 译)

解析：

本文作者是诗人、散文家余光中。作者谈及本文时曾说："小时候上寄宿学校，要与妈妈通信；婚后赴美读书，坐轮船返乡；后来母亲去世，永失母爱。前三句思念的都是女性，到最后一句我想到了大陆这个'大母亲'，于是意境和思路便豁然开朗。"全文四句都很对称，每句都有一个比喻，都用了一个叠词作为修饰语。

本文是一篇散文诗。"乡愁"一词重复四次，翻译时两次译成名词 homesickness，两次译成形容词 homesick，使译文有所变化。"在这头……在那头"重复了三次，译文有的省略了一部分，有的改译成其他词语。原诗使用了四个叠词，分别是"小小""窄窄""矮矮""浅浅"。翻译者将"小小"和"浅浅"分别翻译成单词 small 和 narrow，而非叠词；另两个叠词"窄窄"和"矮矮"因考虑到句子结构而未译。

翻译练习

1. 从字音来看，汉字是音节字。汉语是声调语言，属于汉藏语系（而英语是语调语言，属于印欧语系）。作为音节字的汉字，其音节结构简单，一字只有一个音节。词的信息靠音节的声音结构和声调来承担，这就说明了为什么汉语中同音字特别多。不同的音调能传达不同的意思，一个典型的例子就是"ma"，赋予其不同的音调就有不同的意思，它可以是"妈"，或"麻"，或"马"，或"骂"。汉语是由大量同音不同义的字组成的语言，区别这些同音词的标志是声调，也就是某些音节上音高的升降。普通话有四个基本声调，阴平、阳平、上声、去声，还有第五种轻声。汉语声调变化不仅具有语义功能，还具有语法形态上的功能。

2. 草书比其他字体写起来更快，但对于那些不熟悉草书的人来说难以辨认。汉语中的"草"也有"粗野、简单、粗略"之意思，"草书"这个词中的"草"便是这个意思。术语"草书"具有广义和狭义之分。从广义上讲，它是非时间性的，可以指任何匆匆书写的汉字。从狭义上讲，它指的是汉代的特定笔迹风格。草书又分章草和今草两种风格。用章草书写的汉字，虽然写得很快、很流畅，但是每个字都是分开独立的，点画也没有附着在其他笔画上。今草于东汉时期兴起，在晋朝和唐朝兴盛，至今广受欢迎。今草的精髓是笔画行云流水，汉字很快就写成了，字与字通常连在一起写，上一个字的最后一笔和下一个字的第一笔连在一起。同一幅作品中的汉字大小不一，看起来就像是创作者即兴发挥出来的。唐代草书书法家张旭就以不按章法随性发挥而著名。据说，他不喝得酩酊大醉不会执笔写字，这就是他的风格。笔刷在纸上驰骋，一个个连续的笔画弯曲伸展，蜿蜒回环。现在我们还能看到刻有他字迹的碑石，该碑石保存于西安碑林博物馆。

3. 汉语成语和寓言故事是中国语言文化和智慧宝库中耀眼夺目的璀璨明珠。事实上，每则成语皆有一段历史典故，寓意深刻、哲理经典。寓言故事是人类最通俗的语言，是历史最形象的表达。每则寓言都是一个包含了某种道理的故事，有时这个道理是显而易见的常识，有时则需要我们去体会和感悟。寓言故事所具有的道德教育功能远胜于其文学价值。寓言故事短小简洁，经过千百年来的锤炼，有些已精炼为成语，被人们普遍接受并广泛使用。成语能使谈吐焕彩、文章生辉，意味隽永。成语和寓言故事反映了中国人的传统价值观，例如正义战胜邪恶、智慧胜过力量等。这些价值观通过语言的代代相传而深入人心。

4. 碑林是我国收藏古代碑石墓志时间最早、名碑最多的艺术宝库，它不仅是中国古代文化典籍刻石的集中地点之一，也是历代著名书法艺术珍品的荟萃之地，有着巨大的历史和艺术价值。"碑林"一名始于清朝，有"碑石丛立如林"之意。今日的西安碑林博物馆收藏了历代大量碑石、墓志。作为我国收藏古代碑石最多的一座宏伟艺术殿堂，它经历了九百余年的历史。大家非常熟悉的《九成宫》《圣教序》的碑刻实物都在西安碑林博物馆，所以西安碑林博物馆是书法家非常向往的一个书法圣地。

5. 流行语是指新的或已经存在的、在特定的时期或者背景下变得流行的词或短语。中文热词或流行语通常反映社会变化和社会文化。例如，"打工人"和"逆行者"这两个词是2020年下半年的网络热词。"打工人"的字面意思是"劳动人民"，以前指从农村迁移到城市从事蓝领工作的劳动力。该词经过演变并用来称呼整个工薪阶层或受雇员工。"逆行者"的字面意思是"逆流而上的人"。从广义上讲，这个短语与英文对应词的含义相似，描述了敢于与主流不同、超越职责和在危险面前不顾自己人身安全拯救他人生命和财产的人。

6. 歇后语是中国人民在生活实践中创造的一种特殊的语言形式。它由前后两部分组成：前一部分提供描述或情境，而后一部分则以机智或幽默的方式给出一个与前一部分有关联的回答，两部分往往通过双关语或其他文字游戏的方式联系在一起。歇后语根据语义的表达方式可分为两大类：喻义型歇后语和谐音型歇后语。喻义型歇后语的前一部分描写一个事实，后一部分从意义上对这个事实加以解释、说明，后一部分才是表义的真实目的。例如：黄鼠狼给鸡拜年——不怀好意。谐音型歇后语的前一部分提出一个事由，后一部分借助音同或音近关系，故意"言在此而意在彼"，是一种妙语双关。例如：腊月里的萝卜——（冻）动了心。歇后语俏皮幽默、通俗形象，在交际中它以特有的表达方式和表达效果增加了语言的表现力。

7. 战国时期，楚襄王统治楚国时，国势不振。楚王和重要的大臣都荒淫无能，他们一直沉溺于奢侈享乐之中，大臣庄辛预见楚国会发生危险。一天他劝谏楚王说："陛下，无论您走到哪儿，身旁总是那些奉承您的人，他们想尽办法让您高兴，您就忘了处理国事。长此以往，国家迟早会灭亡的。"

楚王大怒："大胆！你居然用这种恶毒的话来诅咒我的国家，蓄意挑起人民的不满！"庄辛解释说："我不敢诅咒楚国，但我可以预言楚国正面临着巨大的危险。"庄辛见楚王如此宠信那些腐败的大臣，相信楚国必定要亡国。于是他向楚王请求离开楚国，到赵国居住一段时间。

楚王同意了，庄辛便到赵国去了。五个月之后秦军果然入侵楚国并占领了大片土地。楚王被迫流亡。这时，他想起了庄辛的劝谏，于是派人接庄辛回来。楚王见了庄辛，便问："现在我该怎么办呢？"

庄辛回答说："丢了羊，就把羊圈修好，不算迟。"然后他提出许多如何重振国家、收复失地的谋略。楚王非常高兴。

成语"亡羊补牢"便由此故事而来。

Unit 5

哲学思想

> **Unit Goals**
>
> In this unit, you are going to
> - grasp words and expressions concerning Chinese philosophy;
> - acquire knowledge about Chinese philosophies which are the gems of Chinese culture and civilization;
> - know how to translate compound sentences from Chinese into English by applying combination;
> - grasp translation skills of paragraphs on Chinese philosophy.

Related Words and Expressions

甲骨文 inscriptions on oracle bones; oracle bone script; oracle bone inscriptions
青铜器 bronze ware
三皇五帝 Three Sovereigns and Five Emperors
禅让制 Abdication System; crown abdication
大禹治水 King Yu tamed the flood
奴隶制 slavery
诸子百家 Hundred Schools of Thought
百家争鸣 the Contention of a Hundred Schools of Thought
儒家 Confucianism
孔子 Confucius
孟子 Mencius
荀子 Xuncius; Xunzi
道家 Taoism; Daoism
老子 Laozi; Lao Tzu
庄子 Zhuangzi; Chuang Tzu
孙子 Sunzi; Sun Tzu
无为 Wu-wei; non-action
墨家 Mohism
法家 Legalism; Legalist School
名家 School of Names
阴阳家 School of Naturalists; School of Yin and Yang

纵横家 School of Diplomacy
杂家 the Eclectics
农家 Agriculturalism
医家 School of Medicine
兵家 School of the Military
《孙子兵法》*The Art of War*; *Art of Wars*
四书五经 *Four Books and Five Classics*
《大学》*The Great Learning*
《论语》*The Analects*（*of Confucius*）
《中庸》*The Doctrine of the Mean*
《孟子》*The Book of Mencius*
《诗经》*The Book of Songs*; *The Book of Poetry*; *The Book of Odes*; *The Classic of Poetry*
《书经》*The Book of History*
《礼记》*The Book of Rites*
《易经》*The Book of Changes*; *I-Ching*
《春秋》*The Spring and Autumn Annals*
《韩非子》*The Book of Master Han Feizi*
《左传》*Zuo's Commentary on the Spring and Autumn Annals*
《国语》*The Discourses of the States*
《战国策》*Strategies of the Warring States*
六韬 *Six Secret Teachings*
《商君书》*The Book of Lord Shang*
管子 Guanzi
韩非子 Han Feizi
法经 Canon of Laws
《竹书纪年》*Bamboo Annals*
食客 retainer
商鞅变法 Reform of Shang Yang in State Qin
商纣王 King Zhou of Shang
周武王 King Wu of Zhou
齐桓公 Duke Huan of Qi

Lead-in Activities

 Answer the following questions.

　　1）In the pre-Qin period, a hundred schools of thought contended. What are the main schools of thought?

　　2）What are the core ideas of different schools in the pre-Qin period?

　　3）Which school do you think has the most far-reaching influence on our social development? Why?

Listen to a brief introduction to Confucius and fill in the blanks with the words you hear.

　　Confucius was a Chinese ＿＿＿＿＿＿＿＿, whose teachings and philosophy have deeply influenced the thoughts and lives of Chinese, Korean, Japanese, and Vietnamese peoples, among others.

His philosophy emphasized personal and governmental morality, correctness of social relationships, _____. During the Han Dynasty, these values _____ over other doctrines in China, such as _____. Confucius's thoughts have been developed into a system of philosophy known as _____. It was introduced to Europe by Matteo Ricci, who was the first to Latinize the name as "Confucius."

His teachings may be found in _____, a collection of "brief aphoristic fragments," which _____ many years after his death. Modern historians do not believe that any _____ can be said to have been written by Confucius himself, but for nearly 2,000 years he was thought to be the editor or author of all of _____, a collection of works including *The Book of Rites* (of which he was the editor), and *The Spring and Autumn Annals*.

3 Read the following passage and then do the exercises.

The Contention of a Hundred Schools of Thought

As an era of great cultural and intellectual expansion in China, the Hundred Schools of Thought lasted from 770 to 222 BCE. Known as the Golden Age of Chinese Thought and the Contention of a Hundred Schools of Thought, the period saw the rise of many different schools of thought. Many of the great Chinese classic texts that originated during this period have had profound influences on Chinese lifestyle and social consciousness lasting to the present day.

The intellectual society of this era was characterized by itinerant intellectuals, who were usually employed by various state rulers as advisers on the methods of government, war, and diplomacy.

Confucianism is the body of thought that has arguably had the most enduring effect on Chinese life. Also known as the School of the Scholars, its written legacy lies in the Confucian Classics, which later became the foundation of the traditional society.

The representative of this thought is Confucius. He believed that the only effective system of government necessitated prescribed relationships for each individual: "Let the ruler be a ruler and the subject a subject." Furthermore, he contended that a king must be virtuous in order to rule properly.

Mencius was a Confucian disciple who made major contributions to the spread of humanism in Confucian thought, declaring that man, by nature, was inherently good. He argued that a ruler could not govern without the people's tacit consent, and that the penalty for unpopular, despotic rule was the loss of the "mandate of heaven."

Another Confucian follower was Xunzi who preached that man is innately selfish and evil. He asserted that goodness is attainable only through education and conduct befitting one's status. He also argued that the best form of government is one based on authoritarian control, and that ethics is irrelevant in the context of effective rule.

Legalism greatly influenced the philosophical basis for the imperial form of government. During the Han Dynasty, the most practical elements of Confucianism and Legalism were taken to form a sort of synthesis, marking the creation of a new form of government that would remain largely intact until the late 19th century.

As the second most significant stream of Chinese thought, the Zhou period also saw the development of Taoism. Its formulation is often attributed to the legendary sage Laozi and Zhuangzi. The focus of Taoism is on the individual within the natural realm rather than the individual within society. According to Taoism, the goal of life for each individual is to seek to adjust oneself and adapt to the rhythm of the natural world, to follow the way of the universe, to live in harmony.

The school of Mohism was founded upon the doctrine of Mozi. Though the school did not survive through the Qin Dynasty, Mohism was seen as a major rival of Confucianism in the period of the Hundred Schools of Thought. Its philosophy rested on the idea of universal love: Mozi believed that "all men are equal before heaven," and that mankind should seek to imitate heaven by engaging in the practice of collective love. His epistemology can be regarded as primitive materialist empiricism; he believed that our cognition ought to be based on our perceptions—our sensory experiences, such as sight and hearing—instead of imagination or internal logic, elements founded on our capacity for abstraction.

In a word, the scene of "contention of a hundred schools of thought" and the emergence of various schools of thought and their exponents such as Laozi and Confucius all occupy a very important position in the world history of philosophy.

1) Answer the following questions.
   (1) When did the Hundred Schools of Thought happen?
   (2) Which thought has the most influential effect on Chinese life? Who are the representatives of this thought?
   (3) What is the goal of life according to Taoism?
2) Translate the following words or phrases into English.
   百家争鸣
   诸子百家
   儒家典籍
   和谐生活
   兼爱
3) Translate the following paragraph into English based on what you have learned from the above article.

孔子生于公元前551年，是历史上对中国文化影响非常大的人。他出身贫寒，为了求学访遍名师。他创立的儒家思想注重人的自身修养，强调要与人建立一种和谐关系，对待长辈尊敬有礼，与朋友交往真诚守信，统治者应致力于让人民生活幸福。孔子还是一位伟大的老师，他倡导每个人都有受教育的权利。孔子是华夏文明精神上的引导者。两千多年来，孔子的思想影响着中国乃至世界。

翻译技巧：合译法（Combination）

所谓合译法，是指把原文中两个或两个以上的句子合并起来，翻译成一个句子。英汉两种语言在结构上存在很多差异。汉语重"意合"，句子与句子之间缺乏必要的连接词，积词成句，积句成章，流水句较多，呈线性排列，一句接一句，短句较多，句子结构呈竹竿型分布。英语重"形合"，连接词使用频率较高，句子结构层层包孕，句子在空间上呈大树型结构，长句较多。此外，汉语的修饰语一般前置且不是很长，而英语的修饰语可后置，修饰语可以很长。因此，在汉译英时，为了更清楚地表达原文意思且使译文符合目的语表达习惯，往往需要对原文的句子结构进行调整。采用合译法进行翻译时可以从以下几个角度去考虑：

- 在关联处合译；
- 为保持内容连贯而合译；
- 从主语变换处合译，常出现主从句。

例1 原文　史密斯先生拿起电报，他的手指在微微颤抖着。

　　　译文　Mr. Smith picked up the telegram, his hands slightly trembling.

　　　评析　原文由两个分句构成，翻译时从主语变换处将两个分句合并为一个整句，第一个分句为主句，第二个分句用独立主格结构作伴随状语，这样处理使译文读起来生动且富有画面感。

例2 原文　这家小工厂经过技术改造，发展很快，使人感到惊讶不已。

　　　译文　This small factory underwent technological innovation, thus developing with surprising speed.

　　　评析　原句由三个分句构成，根据内容，第一个分句与后面两个分句形成因果关系，因此可将第二个分句与第三个分句合译，作第一个分句的伴随状语。

例3 原文　他的眼睛疲惫地闭着，但是有时又忽然睁开看看岸上的路，看看水面。没有什么动静。他含糊地哼了一声，又静下去了。

　　　译文　His eyes were closed wearily, but once in a while he would open them suddenly and stare at the path along the shore, or look at the water. When he saw that nothing was stirring, he would mutter something to himself and again doze off.

　　　评析　原文由三个句子构成。根据内容，第一个句子由三个分句构成，第一分句与第二、第三分句之间构成转折关系，第二和第三分句之间又构成并列关系。第二个句子与第三个句子可合译为主从复合句，第二个句子是时间状语从句，第三个句子为主句。第三个句子包含两个分句，两个分句间为并列关系，可合译为一个句子，中间用 and 连接。

例4 原文　我们必须抓住新的机遇，迎接新的挑战，采取更加有力的措施，以更为积极的姿态扩大对外开放，力争对外贸易和吸收外资有新的增长。

　　　译文　We must seize new opportunities and meet new challenges. We must open ourselves wider to the outside world more actively and take more effective measures to expand foreign trade and absorb more foreign funds.

　　　评析　原文包含五个小分句。根据内容上的逻辑关系，可以发现第一分句和第二分句是并列关系，可以通过 and 合译成一句；第三分句和第四分句是并列关系，第五分句是第三、第四分句的目的，这三个分句可以合译成一个句子。第三、第四分句在译文中调整了顺序，先表明态度，再说做法，更加符合目的语的表达习惯。当然，这两个部分之间还存在着总分关系，前两句说得比较笼统，后三句说明了具体的措施和做法，英语句子体现具体信息的部分往往可以利用分词结构表达，所以本句还有一种译法：

We must seize new opportunities and meet new challenges, opening ourselves wider to the outside world more actively, and taking more effective measures to expand foreign trade and absorb more foreign funds.

例5 **原文** 党领导人民自信自强、守正创新，创造了新时代中国特色社会主义的伟大成就。

译文 The Party has led the people in bolstering self-confidence and self-reliance and in innovating on the basis of what has worked in the past, thereby bringing about great success for socialism with Chinese characteristics in the new era.

评析 原文包含两个分句。根据内容上的逻辑关系，可以判断两个分句构成因果关系，翻译第二个分句时可用现在分词作结果状语。

总之，在汉译英时，要先找出句子的主谓框架，构建句子的主干，然后将各种关系词、短语（介词短语、名词短语）、附加成分（同位语、插入语）、分词结构、从句（定语从句、状语从句、同位语从句）等添加到主干，使树木枝繁叶茂。翻译汉语的多个分句时，注意分析各个分句之间的逻辑，确定好主从关系，采用恰当的方式进行连接。

段落翻译

1. 周文化

周文化融合了居住在渭水流域的各个民族的文化。在向外拓展领土的同时，周人还接受了臣服的商文化，用龟骨占卜、铸造祭祀用的铜器及丧葬仪式等都与商时相同。在吸收借鉴他人的同时，周人也创造了自己的辉煌文化。西周、春秋、战国是我国古代文化大发展时期，主要文化成就体现在三个方面：一是五经，包括《诗》《书》《易》《礼》《春秋》；二是思想领域里出现的"百家争鸣"的局面；三是卓越的文学成就。西周至战国时期文学的代表作有《诗经》和《楚辞》。

难点讲解：

1)"臣服的"可译为 subdued。

2)翻译第二句时可使用分译法。翻译"用龟骨占卜、铸造祭祀用的铜器"时可将动词转化为名词，译为 oracle bone divination 和 bronze casting for sacrificial purposes。

3)第四句中的"春秋"可译为 the Spring and Autumn Period，"战国"可译为 the Warring States Period。翻译该句时，主句谓语动词使用 witnessed（见证、经历）可使译文更加生动。

4)"五经"可译为 Five Classics，《诗》《书》《易》《礼》《春秋》可分别译为 *The Book of Songs*, *The Book of History*, *The Book of Changes*, *The Book of Rites* and *The Spring and Autumn Annals*。

5)"百家争鸣"可译为 the Contention of a Hundred Schools of Thought。

6)"《楚辞》"可译为 *Elegies of Chu*。

2. 诸子百家

诸子百家指的是中国古代先秦至汉初大量涌现并繁荣发展的各个学术派别的总称。春秋战国时代是从奴隶社会向封建社会转变的时代，涌现出了众多思想家和思想流派，思想家们纷纷著书立说，相互论战，形成"百家争鸣"的局面。这一时期也被称为中国哲学思想的黄金时代。在众多思想流派中，最著名的是儒家、墨家、道家和法家。后来，秦王朝的崛起和随后的"焚书坑儒"宣告了这一时代的结束。汉武帝时推行"罢黜百家，独尊儒术"的政策，于是以孔子和孟子为代表的儒家思想成为正统，统治中国思想与文化两千余年。

难点讲解：

1）"诸子百家"译为 Hundred Schools of Thought，是专有名词，故实词的第一个字母大写；"涌现并繁荣发展"可译为 emerged and flourished。

2）第二句内容多，句子长，可采用分译法译为三句。"春秋战国时代是……的时代"译为一句，可用动词 witnessed 使译文地道生动。"涌现出了……"可译作"There emerged …"，后面可接一个带非限定性定语从句的名词性短语。"形成'百家争鸣'的局面"的翻译也比较灵活，在译文中可自成一句，增加主语 This phenomenon 承前启后，衔接自然；"百家争鸣"译为 the Contention of a Hundred Schools of Thought。

3）第三句中"被称为"可译为 be known as。

4）第四句中"儒家、墨家、道家和法家"可译为 Confucianism, Mohism, Taoism, and Legalism。

5）第五句中"焚书坑儒"可译为 burning of books and burying of scholars。

6）第六句是一个长句，可采用分译法，原因和结果分译为两句。"罢黜百家，独尊儒术"的"百"是虚数，指其他众多思想派别，不宜直译为 one hundred。"罢黜百家，独尊儒术"可译为 rejecting the other schools of thought and respecting only Confucianism。"于是以……成为正统"可用 As a result 开头，不仅起到衔接作用，也指明了与上一句之间的因果关系。

3. 中国传统思想流派

中华民族的传统文化博大精深，源远流长。早在两千多年前就出现了以孔孟为代表的儒家学说和以老庄为代表的道家学说，以及其他许多也在中国思想史上有一定地位的学说流派，这就是有名的"诸子百家"。中华民族传统文化有许多珍贵品质，其本质体现在它的人民性和民主性。比如强调仁爱，强调群体，强调和而不同，强调天下为公。"天下兴亡，匹夫有责"的爱国情怀，"民为邦本""民贵君轻"的民本思想，"己所不欲，勿施于人"的待人之道，以及吃苦耐劳、勤俭持家、尊师重教的传统美德，都对家庭、国家和社会起到了巨大的维系与调节作用。

难点讲解：

1）第一句可采用合译法，将两个分句合二为一，"源远流长"可译为 starts far back and runs a long course。

2）第二句中，"以……为代表的"可用 represented by 作后置定语。

3）第三句中，在翻译"其本质体现在它的人民性和民主性"时可使用词性转换技巧，原句中的名词"本质"可译为副词 essentially，"人民性和民主性"可译为形容词 populist and democratic。

4）第四句中，"和而不同"可译为 seeking harmony without uniformity；"天下为公"可译为 the world is for all。

5）"天下兴亡，匹夫有责"可译为 everybody is responsible for the rise or fall of the country；"民为邦本"可译为 people are the foundation of the country；"民贵君轻"可译为 people are more important than the monarch；"己所不欲，勿施于人"可译为 treat others as you want to be treated。

4. 儒家思想

儒家思想是在中国影响最大的思想流派。自汉代以来，儒家思想就是封建统治阶级（feudal ruling class）的主导思想之一。儒家思想的核心实际上是一种人道主义。它提倡自我修养，认为人是可教化的、可完善的。儒家思想的一个宏大的目标就是实现"大同社会"，在这样的一个社会中，每个人都能扮演好自己的角色，并与他人维持良好的关系。《论语》是儒家思想的代表作，它是对孔子及其弟子(disciple)言行的记录。数个世纪以来，《论语》一直极大地影响着中国人的哲学观和道德观，也影响着其他亚洲国家人民的哲学观和道德观。

难点讲解：

1)"思想流派"可译为 school of thought。

2)"主导思想"可译为 ruling doctrine。

3)"自我修养"可译为 self-cultivation。cultivate 除了有"耕种；照料"之意，还可以表示"修养；改善"。

4)"可教化的、可完善的"都可以使用动词加上"-able"这一形容词后缀的构词法，分别译为 teachable 和 improvable

5)"大同"即为"和谐"之意，"大同社会"可译为 harmonious society 或 perfect society。

6)"每个人"除可译为 everybody、everyone 以外，还可译为 each individual，更加强调个体。"扮演好某人的角色"即 play one's part/role well。

7)"代表作"可译为 representative work。representative 为形容词，意为"典型的，有代表性的"。

8)"道德观"中的"观"即"观点、看法"，可译为 moral outlook。

9)最后一句中"也影响着……的哲学观和道德观"重复出现，只翻译一次即可，最后一个分句可直接译为 that of the people of other Asian countries as well。

5. 四书五经

四书五经是中国儒家的经典书籍，也是儒家思想的核心载体，体现了儒家思想的核心价值和思想体系。四书包括《大学》《中庸》《论语》《孟子》。明清时期，四书成为科举考试的核心科目。五经是儒家作为研究基础的五本古代经典书籍的合称，包括《诗》《书》《礼》《易》和《春秋》。西汉时期，儒家思想被推为正统，五经也因此变得更加重要，到明清时期被用作科举考试的教科书。四书五经是中国传统文化的重要组成部分，更是中国历史文化古籍中的宝典。它在世界文化史、思想史上也具有极高的地位。

难点讲解：

1) 原文第一句是并列句，可译为简单句，使用分词短语作状语，使结构主次分明，表达更加自然。

2)第二句中，"《大学》《中庸》《论语》《孟子》"可译为 *The Great Learning*，*The Doctrine of the Mean*，*The Analects of Confucius* and *Mencius*。

3)第三句中，"科举考试"可译为 imperial civil examinations。

4)第五句可采用分译法，以时间为节点，将原句分译为两句话。

5)第六句可用"not only… but also…"连接两个分句。"重要组成部分"可译为 an integral part；"宝典"可译为 treasured books。

6)最后一句中"具有极高的地位"可译为 rank very high，表达自然。注意 rank 在这里是半系动词，后面用形容词 high，而不是副词 highly。

6. 孟子

孟子本名为孟轲，是战国时期伟大的思想家、教育家、政治家。孟子继承并发扬了孔子的思想，被认为是继孔子之后儒家学派最重要的代表。孟子继承了孔子的德治思想，主张仁政，即对人民"省刑罚，薄税敛"。当权者若无视人民需求或统治残暴，人民可将其推翻或诛灭。孟子还继承了孔子的性善学说，主张性善论。他认为人天生具有道德意识，可通过内省和道德教育去保持和扩充，以免腐化堕落。孟子对孔子学说的诠释、发展与推广和孔子学说一样对中国传统思想影响深远，二者的思想被称为"孔孟之道"。孟子的思想收录在《孟子》中，由孟子及其弟子收集记录。《孟子》是四书之一，和《论语》一样，也是儒家学说的经典之一。

难点讲解：

1）第三句中有一些具有中国文化特色的词，如"德治""仁政"，可分别意译为 idea of governing by virtue 和 a benevolent government。此外，"省刑罚，薄税敛"出自《孟子·梁惠王章句上》，意为"减免刑罚，减轻赋税"，"省"和"薄"都是"减少"的意思，所以译文中可仅出现一个动词 reduce。

2）第五句涉及儒家的核心学说"性善"，是指人天生是善良的或人的本性是好的，所以可译为 innate goodness of human nature。

3）第六句后半句是对前半句"道德意识"的说明，可采用 which 引导的非限定性定语从句使句法紧凑。

4）"孔孟之道"可译为 Doctrine of Confucius and Mencius。

5）最后一句可分译为两句，《孟子》是四书之一"单独译为一句，也可译为"Just like *The Analects of Confucius*，*Mencius*，one of the Four Books，is the classic of Confucianism."。

7.《孙子兵法》

《孙子兵法》是中国古代最重要的军事著作之一，是我国优秀传统文化的重要组成部分。孙子，即该书作者，在书中揭示的一系列具有普遍意义的军事规律，不仅受到军事家们的推崇，还在领导艺术、人生追求甚至家庭关系等方面发挥着重要的指导作用。《孙子兵法》中的许多名言警句富有哲理、意义深远，在国内外广为流传。

难点讲解：

1）第二句可使用合译法进行翻译。句子的主干为"孙子揭示了军事规律"，后半部分通过定语从句说明其重要意义。"普遍意义的"可译为 universal，"人生追求"可译为 the pursuit of life。

2）最后一句包含两个分句，可使用合译法进行翻译。

3）"名言警句"有很多表达方法，如 famous quotes、wise words、famous aphorism、famous epigrams 等，但根据此处语境可知，这些名言警句必然是从《孙子兵法》中选出的，因此用 quote（引语）一词更为恰当，此处可译为 famous quotes。

4）"意义深远"可翻译为 profound meanings。

5）"广为流传"可翻译为 widely circulated，其中 circulate 一词在这里有"流传，传播"之意。

8. 天下大同

"大道之行也，天下为公"源于两千多年前的儒家经典《礼记》。书中孔子将理想社会描述为"天下大同"（Universal Harmony）。在这个理想社会中，把有贤德、有才能的人选拔出来，人人讲求诚信，崇尚和睦。此外，老年人能终其天年，中年人能为社会效力，幼童能顺利地成长，寡妇、孤儿等弱者都能得到供养。自然资源要为大家的利益而充分利用，而不是为私利而挪用。人们为社会贡献自己的力量，是为了公益，而不是为了私利。"天下大同"这一概念常用来解释中国的外交政策，表达中国人民对美好世界的展望。"大道"是指公平、正义等人类共同价值观，"天下大同"是构建人类命运共同体这一理念的体现。

难点讲解：

1）"大道之行也，天下为公"可翻译为"When the Great Way prevails, the world is for everyone."。

2）"源于"可译为 originate from。

3）第三句和第四句可采用合译法，用 in which 将两句连接起来。"讲求诚信，崇尚和睦"可译为 fidelity and friendliness are valued。

4)"为……的利益"可用 for the benefit of 来翻译。

5)"人类共同价值观"可译为 the shared values of humanity;"构建人类命运共同体"可译为 building a community with a shared future for humanity。

拓展阅读

Reading A

Introduction to *I Ching* (*The Book of Changes*)

I Ching, also *Yi Jing* or *The Book of Changes*, is thought to be the oldest and most abstruse classic in Chinese history. Reputedly, it originated with Fu Xi, who is a mythical sovereign being the first of the three primogenitors (始祖) of Chinese civilization. It is also called *Zhou Yi* reputedly because it is not until the Western Zhou Dynasty that the whole context of *I Ching* was understood. The first king of Zhou, King Wen, concentrated on the study of the mystery of changes when he was put in prison for seven years. It has been an aid to foretell the future and make decisions for thousands of years. However, it means more than a book of divination (占卜).

In Chinese, Yi means change, an eternal truth to describe the world's motion. Jing means the way or classic. So, *I Ching* is a classic text to expatriate inexhaustible changes. Rich philosophic viewpoints lurked in the thoughts have provided a case of guiding significance. It is a well-built philosophic ideology, which is for most of the people obscure and difficult to follow. Hence there are a lot of eisegesis (肆意诠释). After King Wen's composition and commentary, *I Ching* was expanded from the range of divination to science. It is said that the earliest extant *I Ching* was written on bamboo slips during the Warring States Period. In the Han Dynasty, *I Ching* inspired the Taoism to create many theories of regimen which were derived from Yin-Yang, Five Elements, and Bagua. It was first introduced to the western world by missionaries in late Ming Dynasty and explained by German mathematicians with binary code (二进制代码). *I Ching* affected Confucianism very much and it was the foundation of Taoism. It survived the "Burning of the books and Burying of the Scholars" Qinshihuang committed. Then, it could continue functioning to have impact on taijiquan (Shadowboxing), feng shui in architecture, Chinese Go game and many aspects in Chinese culture.

Yin-Yang

Yin-Yang is a materialistic concept of Taoism which dialectically describes that everything in the world has contrary sides, and these contrary forces are interconnected and interdependent in the natural world. For example, the south of a mountain refers to Yang, similarly the north of a river, upper side of a leaf, man and the sun, and conversely Yin refers to the north of a mountain, south of a river, reverse side of a leaf, women and the moon. Seen from the taiji symbol, when the Yang energy is at the peak time, the Yin energy has gradually shown up. This is a profound philosophy saying that things at the worse will mend. Many branches of traditional Chinese medicine and philosophy adopted the Yin-Yang theory as their primary guidelines.

Here is the description in *I-Ching* about how world began:

The infinite produces limitations and this is the supreme ultimate (taiji or the absolute);

The taiji produces two forms, Yin and Yang;

The two forms produce the four phenomena, shao yin, tai yin (the Moon), shao yang, tai yang (the Sun);

The four phenomena act on the eight trigrams (Bagua): sky, earth, mountain, water, wind, fire, thunder and lake/marsh.

There is another description: when the world began, there are heaven (sky) and earth. They mated to give birth to everything in the world. Heaven is called the Qian trigram (Qian Gua) and the earth is Kun trigram (Kun Gua). The remain trigrams are Dui, Li, Zhen, Xun, Kan, Gen respectively representing lake, fire, thunder, wind, water and mountain.

Yin-Yang and Chinese Medicine

Body visceral organs (内脏器官), channels and collaterals all have yin and yang sides. The upper part of the body is assigned to Yang, while the lower part to Yin. Health is based on the balance of yin and yang. Yin vacuity will represent heat sensations, dry mouth, night sweats, dark urine, etc, while the yang vacuity will represent cold limbs, slow pulse, bright white complexion, etc.

Bagua (Eight Trigrams)

Bagua is a set of symbolic signs. Each of the eight trigrams consists of three signs, having the special meaning. The combination of the eight trigrams produces 64 trigrams which symbolize all the things and phenomena in the nature and life. In Chinese traditional medicine, Bagua refers to the eight acupuncture points around the hollow of hands. It also refers to the gossip in the world of entertainment.

Chinese character "卦" (Gua) is comprised of two parts, left part meaning a mud pillar used to observe the shadow of the sun, and right part meaning measurement. Bagua means to observe the sun shadow from every quarter in order to know the seasons and guide the agricultural production. In *I Ching*, the meaning of Gua was extended to be the phenomenon in the universe. There are two arrangements of Bagua Hexagram, Early Heaven or Fuxi Bagua, and Later Heaven or King Wen Bagua.

Each trigram corresponds to an aspect of life and cardinal direction. Therefore, the Bagua Hexagram is also a tool in Feng Shui used to map a room or location. The explanation on each trigram is complicated. It is undoubtedly the classic of ancient cosmic principles.

Exercises

1 Match the English expressions in Column A with the Chinese translations in Column B.

Column A   Column B

1   *The Book of Changes*   a   竹简
2   abstruse classic   b   焚书坑儒
3   an eternal truth   c   八卦
4   bamboo slips   d   《易经》
5   Five Elements   e   深奥的经典著作
6   Burning of the books and Burying of the Scholars f   经络
7   Yin vacuity   g   永恒的真理
8   the eight trigrams   h   五行
9   channels and collaterals   i   穴位
10 acupuncture points   j   阴虚

Answer the following questions.

1) Why is *The Book of Changes* also called *Zhou Yi*?

2) What do Yin vacuity and Yang vacuity represent in traditional Chinese medicine?

Reading B

The Art of War

The Art of War is the greatest military theoretical work in ancient China. It is also one of the most respected Chinese books and has a tremendous amount of influence worldwide. The book deals with both strategic thought and philosophical ideas, which have since been widely applied in the areas of the military, politics, and economics.

Completed more than 2,500 years ago, the book is the earliest military theoretical work in the world, written around 2,300 years earlier than *On War* by Karl von Clausewitz.

The book's author, Sun Wu, was a great Chinese strategist during the Spring and Autumn Periods and is honored as Military Sage. He came to Wu State to escape the war and was nominated as a general by the king of Wu State. He defeated 200,000 Chu State soldiers with an infantry(步兵)of only 30,000 soldiers. This established his fame and prestige in the military field. After reflecting on his experiences, he wrote *The Art of War*, which discusses a series of universal military rules and proposes a complete military theoretical system.

With more than 6,000 Chinese characters, *The Art of War* has 13 subjects in 13 chapters. For example, the strategy chapter talks about the merits of waging a particular war. It reminds the reader of the strong relationship between war, politics and the economy. It speaks of the five basic elements decisive for war—politics, timeliness, favorable geographical location, commanders and law—among which the politics is the most important. The fight chapter discusses the best way to carry out the war. The chapter on attack strategies is about how to attack the enemy. Sun Wu believes battles should be won with the least cost, such as capturing an enemy's castle without a direct fight or conquering an enemy state without an enduring war. He thinks the best way to win a war is through political strategy. Failing that, he advises diplomatic measures followed by force, and finally attacking the enemy's castle. In terms of attack strategies, it is important to have a clear idea not only about one's own strengths but also that of the enemy. In the chapter regarding the use of spies, he says various spies must be used to obtain a wide range of information before a war.

The Art of War consists of a great deal of valuable philosophical thoughts. The verse "if you know others and know yourself, you will not be imperiled in a hundred battles" has become popular among the Chinese people. There are many dialectic thoughts in the book as well, which discusses such contradictions as the guest and the host, the majority and the minority, the strong and the weak, attack and defense, triumph and failure, interest and trouble, and others. *The Art of War* encourages one to study these contradictions and use it to form the basis of war strategies. The dialectic thought contained in the book holds a significant position in the history of Chinese dialectic development.

The Art of War has been widely applied by countless militarists since it was completed, and the stories and strategies in the book are well known to the Chinese public. The meticulous military and philosophical thought system, the profound philosophy, and the lessons on strategy and tactics have made it an influential work around the world. It has been translated into many languages including English, Russian, German and Japanese, and several thousand editions have been printed worldwide. Many countries even use it as a textbook in military schools.

The Art of War is also widely applied in social and commercial areas. Many entrepreneurs, both at home and abroad, use thoughts from the book to enhance their management and marketing abilities.

Exercises

1 *Answer the following questions.*

1) What do you know about Sun Wu? What established his fame and prestige in the military field?

2) What is the implied meaning of the verse "If you know others and know yourself, you will not be imperiled in a hundred battles"? Please give an example or your personal experience to illustrate it.

2 *Translate the following sentences into English.*

1)《孙子兵法》是中国古代最伟大的军事理论著作,也是最受推崇的中国古典著作之一,在世界范围内影响巨大。

2) 他写了决定战争的五个基本要素:道、天、地、将、法,其中"道"是最重要的。

3) "知己知彼,百战不殆"这句话在中国家喻户晓。

4)《孙子兵法》中缜密的军事哲学思想体系、深邃的哲学思想,以及对战略战术的借鉴,使其成为全世界颇有影响力的一部著作。

5)《孙子兵法》还广泛应用于社会和商业领域。国内外许多企业家都借鉴这本书的思想来提高自己的管理和营销能力。

翻译佳作赏析

月下独酌

李白

花间一壶酒,独酌无相亲。
举杯邀明月,对影成三人。
月既不解饮,影徒随我身。
暂伴月将影,行乐须及春。
我歌月徘徊,我舞影零乱。
醒时同交欢,醉后各分散。
永结无情游,相期邈云汉。

译文：

Last Words

By Li Bai

An arbor of flowers
    and a kettle of wine：
Alas! In the bowers
    no companion is mine.
Then the moon sheds her rays
    on my goblet and me，
And my shadow betrays
    we're a party of three!
Though the moon cannot swallow
    her share of the grog,
And my shadow must follow
    wherever I jog，
Yet their friendship I'll borrow
    and gaily carouse，
And laugh away sorrow
    while spring-time allows.
See the moon—how she glances
    response to my song；
See my shadow—it dances
    so lightly along!
While sober I feel，
    you are both my good friends；
While drunken I reel，
    our companionship ends，
But we'll soon have a greeting
    without a goodbye，
At our next merry meeting
    away in the sky.

（Herbert A. Giles 译）

赏析：

  好的译诗，应是形象与音韵俱佳。此首李白的五言古诗，节奏明快，醉意酣畅，意象叠生，意境高远，而英国著名汉学大师翟理斯（Herbert A. Giles）的译诗也基本上做到了这些，且能发挥英诗长处，自创格局，一行五字分作两节译，使得语气从容而意境豁然，读之别有一番风味。翻译诗的标题也可灵活，甚至可以别具一格，只要不离要旨，起到提醒和点睛的作用即可。翟理斯把李白的《月下独酌》译为 Last Words，而多数译者会采取直译的策略，如 Drinking Alone with the Moon、Drinking Alone in the Moonlight、Drink Alone under the Moon、On Drinking Alone by the Moonlight，也有其他灵活处理的方式，如 We Three，似嫌太略，不如 Three with the Moon and His Shadow。标题以简洁达意为要，以上诸例，得失自见。

首句译诗拆"花间"与"一壶酒"：An arbor of flowers 和 and a kettle of wine 相缀成句，相映成趣，省却动词，以名词结构传递出句意，清新自然。接着译下句"独酌无相亲"，突然间一叹词"Alas!"成独词句，将感慨呼出，再重复"花间"义，又与上句略有不同。前者为 arbor（花枝结成之凉棚），此处用 bower（花枝所生之阴凉），略去"独酌"字面，突出"无相亲"，即"In the bowers no companion is mine."。

第二句将明月引出，使其光照"我"与杯中酒，又以"我"的影呈现，与"我"共为三人："Then the moon sheds her rays on my goblet and me，/And my shadow betrays we're a party of three!"。其中 sheds her rays on（光照……）、betrays（显露）和 a party of three（三个人的聚会）都有英诗的味道。这里虽省略了汉语的"举""邀""对""成"等字，但无损诗境。若照字面直译为"I raise my cup to invite the moon who blends. Her light with my shadow and were three friends."则有平铺直叙的过程而无心理感受的隐义，句子连贯有余而诗情跳跃不足，并有拼韵脚之嫌。

接下来用比较从容的步调，把"月既不解饮，影徒随我身。暂伴月将影，行乐须及春"一气译出："Though the moon cannot swallow her share of the grog（酒会），/And my shadow must follow wherever I joy，/ Yet their friendship I'll borrow and gaily carouse（痛饮），/And laugh away sorrow while spring-time allows"。其中除了连接词的使用（如 though、and、yet、and）使语义连贯，如英诗常见的表达风格，还能于语气连贯之中，把心中不悦一吐为快。而 her share of the grog、their friendship I'll borrow、while spring-time allows 等表达也具有英诗风格，使译文更容易为目的语读者所接受，而又与原意甚为吻合。只有一处加词 And laugh away sorrow（满腹忧愁一笑而去），即便有填节奏之嫌和夸张之意，但若联想到前文已用"欢宴"（grog）、"痛饮"（carouse）进行铺垫，此处的豪情正好推向极致而别生佳意。

"我歌月徘徊，我舞影零乱"对仗工整，节奏明快，语气坚定，又首次连用两个"我"开句，使主体意识得到高扬。英译则依原诗节奏，行之犹嫌不足，连用两个 see（瞧），使角色分离，妙趣骤生。其后的描述，又用 how（如何）和 so（如此）以状其貌，其诗境、诗意达到高潮，且有过之而无不及："See the moon—how she glances response to my song；/ See my shadow—it dances so lightly along!"此种诗句，如原诗风格，看似用字平易，反以句法取胜。

最后，诗人似以较为超脱的态度，从诗境梦幻中苏醒，又以评论式的语气，抒发感慨，寄托理想。诗曰："醒时同交欢，醉后各分散。永结无情游，相期邈云汉。"译者借助对仗和转折，挥洒自如地译完全诗："While sober I feel，you are both my good friends；/ While drunken I reel，our companionship ends，/ But we'll soon have a greeting without a goodbye，/At our next merry meeting away in the sky."。"无情游"和"邈云汉"虽没有按字面译出，但因发挥了英文人称代词和物主代词的用法，使"醒时同交欢，醉后各分散"的直叙转换为你我对话的倾诉衷肠，又因 greeting 和 merry meeting 的仪式化处理，诗的结尾更富于戏剧性。总体而言，翟理斯的英译已能将原诗的神韵较好地传达出来。

翻译练习

1. 百家争鸣时期始于公元前770年，终于公元前222年，被誉为中国思想的黄金时代，它见证了不同思想学派的兴起。这个时期的不少中国古典著作直到今日对中国人的生活方式和社会意识还有着深远的影响。在这一时期，许多知识分子游走于各国，作为不同诸侯王的策士，针对治国之道、治军之道和外交手段提出建议。

2. 孔子是我国古代私人办学的先驱。相传他有弟子三千。儒家的代表人物还有孟子和荀子。孟子继承并发展了孔子的学说,其学说的核心是"仁""义"。他主张人性本善,行"仁政""保民",反对诸侯混战,反对残酷的剥削和压迫,对当时各国的政治和战争进行抨击,其主要学说多收录在《孟子》一书中。荀子名况,时人尊称他为荀卿,是赵国人。荀子虽为儒家学者,但有较浓厚的法家思想。与孟子不同,他认为人性本恶,其主要学说多收录在《荀子》一书中。

3. 山东曲阜是中国历史上伟大的思想家、政治家、教育家和儒家学派的创始人孔子的故里。中国悠久灿烂的汉文化,其思想根源都可追溯到先秦时期孔子的儒家思想。曲阜作为历代帝王、文人名士仰慕的地方,有大量的文物古迹,其中最著名的是孔庙、孔林、孔府。孔府紧靠孔庙,府内收藏大量的历史档案、文件和文物。

4. 法家是反映新兴地主阶级利益的思想流派。前期法家的代表人物有李悝、商鞅和申不害,后期法家的代表人物是韩非。韩非(约公元前280—公元前232年)出身于韩国贵族,和李斯同是荀子的学生,其文章由后人收集整理为《韩非子》一书。他崇尚法治,反对儒家说教,也反对民间的游侠群体。他主张"明主之国,无书简之文,以法为教;无先王之语,以吏为师。"韩非的主张很为秦王所重视。后韩非自韩至秦,李斯嫉妒他的才能,将其谋害。

5. 《道德经》又称《老子》。虽然简短,但它在中国文化发展中的作用很大。《道德经》是道家哲学思想的重要来源。道家主张"重人贵生",崇尚清静无为,修身养性。"道可道,非常道;名可名,非常名。无名,天地之始,有名,万物之母。故常无欲,以观其妙,常有欲,以观其徼。"这便是老子的至理名言。《道德经》的思想也对中国人的民族特性、思维倾向和审美趣味产生了重要影响。

6. 《易》也称作《易经》或《周易》,是我国最早的占卜用书。它对自然或社会变化的论述,富有朴素的辩证法观点。相传该书为周公所编。《礼》是春秋战国时期的部分礼仪制度的汇编,共有十七篇,一说周公制作,一说孔子修订。《春秋》是我国最早的一部编年体历史著作,以鲁国的历史为主。

7. 礼仪文化的发展有其历史渊源,可以追溯到久远的过去。可以说,中华民族的历史掀开第一页的时候,礼仪就伴随着人的活动、伴随着原始宗教而产生了。中国人对于礼的认知,首先来自对大自然的敬畏。随着人类社会生活的发展,人们表达敬畏、祭祀的活动日益纷繁,逐步形成种种固定的模式,最终形成礼仪规范。在中国古代,礼体现了皇权天授的威严,也体现了等级。礼在民间意为人民和谐交流,长幼有序。发自内心的礼,是中国人对天、地、人的敬重。

8. 中华文明历来崇尚天人合一、道法自然,追求人与自然和谐共生。中国将生态文明理念和生态文明建设写入《中华人民共和国宪法》,纳入中国特色社会主义总体布局。中国以习近平生态文明思想为指导,贯彻新发展理念,以经济社会发展全面绿色转型为引领,以能源绿色低碳发展为关键,坚持走生态优先、绿色低碳的发展道路。

Unit 6

古今教育

Unit Goals

In this unit, you are going to
- grasp words and expressions concerning ancient and contemporary Chinese education;
- acquire knowledge about ancient and contemporary Chinese education;
- know how to translate sentences with serial verbs from Chinese into English;
- grasp translation skills of paragraphs concerning ancient and contemporary Chinese education.

Related Words and Expressions

官学教育 official education system

私学；私塾 private school; old-style private school; home school with a private tutor

国子监/翰林院 the Imperial College

书院 academies of classical learning

科举制度 the imperial examination system

八股文 eight-part essay form

殿试 palace examination; final imperial examination (presided over by the emperor)

会试 general examination (for the successful candidates of all the provincial civil examinations)

乡试 triennial provincial civil service examination for the degree of juren (held in provincial capital during the Ming and Qing dynasties)

春闱；春试 imperial examination held in spring

秋闱；秋试 imperial examination held in autumn at the provincial level

状元 zhuangyuan; the first-place winner at palace examination; Number One Scholar (title conferred on the one who came out first in the highest imperial examination)

榜眼 bangyan; the second-place winner at palace examination

探花 tanhua; the third-place winner at palace examination

进士 jinshi; advanced scholar (successful candidate in the highest imperial examination held in the palace under the emperor's supervision)

举人 juren (successful candidate in the imperial examinations at the provincial level)

秀才 xiucai (a scholar in the Ming and Qing dynasties who passed the imperial examination at the county level); scholar

士大夫 literati and officialdom in feudal China; scholar-officials in feudal China

九年义务教育 nine-year compulsory education
寄宿制学校 boarding school
学前教育 preschool education
普通/通识教育 general education
职业教育 vocational education
全日制教育 full-time education
应试教育 exam-oriented education
素质教育 well-rounded education; quality-oriented education
高考 college entrance examination
高校扩招计划 the college expansion plan
大学城 university town
初等教育 elementary education
高等教育 higher education
重点高校 key colleges and universities
世界一流大学和一流学科 world-class universities and disciplines
教育事业 educational cause
高等学府 institution of higher education/learning
综合性大学 comprehensive university
文科院校 college of (liberal) arts
理工科大学 college/university of science and engineering
师范学院 normal college
中等职业学校 secondary vocational school
民办学校 privately-run/non-governmental school
继续教育 continuing education; further education
考研 take the Postgraduate Entrance Examination; take part in the entrance exams for graduate schools
课外活动 extracurricular activity
核心课程 core curriculum course
必修课 required/compulsory course
选修课 selective/elective/optional course
基础课 basic course
专业课 specialized course
课程表 school timetable
教学大纲 teaching program; syllabus
学分 credit
转换学分 transfer credit
启发式教学 heuristic method of teaching; heuristic education
录取 admit/admission
标准化测试 standardized test
成绩单 school record/report
绩点 GPA (Grade Point Average)

填鸭式教学 cramming method of teaching

补考 make-up examination

交换生 exchange student

走读生 non-resident student

住宿生 boarder

本科生 undergraduate student

研究生 graduate student；postgraduate

大专生 junior college student；associate-degree student

自费留学 self-funded study abroad

应届毕业生 graduating student；current year's student

学龄前儿童 preschool children

学前教育 pre-school education

校园数字化 campus digitalization

学士学位 Bachelor's degree

硕士学位 Master's degree

博士学位 Doctor's degree

访问学者 visiting scholar

客座教授 guest professor

创新思维 innovative thinking

实践能力 practical ability

文凭 diploma

证书 certificate

德智体美劳 morality, intelligence, physique, aesthetics and labor

德智体美劳全面发展 all-round development of morality, intelligence, physical fitness, aesthetics, and labor skills

希望工程 Project Hope

教育界 educational circles/world

教育投入 input in education；educational investment fund

远程教育 distance learning

网上课程 online course

Lead-in Activities

 Answer the following questions.

1) Exemplify some famous educators or celebrities in the educational field that you have known. Who do you admire most and why?

2) How much do you know about the imperial examination system? And what's your opinion on it?

3) How much do you know about contemporary Chinese education system? And what do you think is the most excellent part of it compared with the ancient one?

2 **Listen to a brief introduction to the Chinese imperial examinations and fill in the blanks with the words you hear.**

The Chinese imperial examination, or keju, was a _____ in imperial China used for _____ for the state bureaucracy. The concept of choosing bureaucrats by merit rather than birth started early in Chinese history but using written examinations as _____ _____ started in the mid-Tang period. The system became _____ during the Song Dynasty and lasted until it was _____ in the late Qing Dynasty.

The exams served to ensure a common knowledge of writing, the classics, and _____ _____ among state officials. This common culture helped to _____ and ___ _____ gave legitimacy to imperial rule. The examination system played a significant role in _____ of hereditary aristocracy and military authority, and in the rise of a gentry class of scholar-bureaucrats.

3 **Read the following passage and then do the exercises.**

The Birth of the Imperial Examination System and Its Transition to Scholar-Bureaucracy

Keju, or the Chinese imperial examination, was a civil service examination system, which helps with selecting candidates for the state bureaucracy during imperial China. The idea of choosing talents for state officials arose very early in Chinese history, but the practice of using written exams as a selection tool became popular in the mid-Tang Dynasty. The examination system dominated the Song Dynasty until it was abolished in 1905 during the reform of the late Qing Dynasty. The test aims to ensure that state officials have a common understanding of writing, classics and literary styles. This shared culture helped unify the empire, and the ideal of merit gave it legitimacy. The imperial examination system played an important role in moderating the power and military authority of hereditary aristocrats and in the rise of the scholar-bureaucrat and gentry class.

The examination-based civil service promoted stability and social mobility. The Confucianism-based examinations meant that the local elites and ambitious would-be members of those elites all over China were taught with similar values. Even though only a small fraction (about 5 percent) of those who attempted the examinations actually passed them and even fewer received titles, the hope of eventual success sustained their commitment. Those who failed to pass did not lose wealth or local social standing; as dedicated believers in Confucian orthodoxy, they served, without the benefit of state appointments, as civilian teachers, patrons of the arts, and managers of local projects, such as irrigation works, schools, or charitable foundations.

The original purpose of the imperial examinations as they were implemented during the Sui Dynasty was to strike a blow against the hereditary aristocracy and to centralize power around the emperor. The era preceding the Sui Dynasty, the period of Northern and Southern Dynasties, was a golden age for the Chinese aristocracy. The power they wielded seriously constrained the emperor's ability to exercise his power in court, especially when it came to appointing officials. The Sui emperor created the imperial examinations to bypass and mitigate aristocratic interests.

This was the origin of the Chinese examination system. The imperial examination system played an important role in moderating the power and military authority of hereditary aristocrats and in the rise of the scholar-bureaucrat and gentry class.

The short-lived Sui Dynasty was soon replaced by the Tang, who built on the examination system. The emperor placed the palace exam graduates, the *jinshi*, in important government posts, where they came into conflict with hereditary elites. During the reign of Emperor Xuanzong of Tang, about a third of the Grand Chancellors appointed were jinshi, but by the time of Emperor Xianzong of Tang, about three fifths of the Grand Chancellors appointed were jinshi.

This change in the way government was organized dealt a real blow to the aristocrats, but they did not sit idly by and wait to become obsolete. Instead, they themselves entered the examinations to gain the privileges associated with it. By the end of the dynasty, the aristocratic class had produced 116 jinshi, so that they remained a significant influence in the government. Hereditary privileges were also not completely done away with. The sons of high ministers and great generals had the right to hold minor offices without taking the examinations. In addition, the number of graduates were not only small, but also formed their own clique in the government based around the examiners and the men they passed.

1) Answer the following questions.
   (1) Why was it very important for state officials to have a common understanding of writing, classics and literary styles in feudal China?
   (2) What might be the future of those who failed the examinations?
   (3) What was the initial intention of the Sui emperor to carry out the imperial examinations?
   (4) What was the conflict among the emperor and hereditary elites in the Tang Dynasty?
   (5) What was the focus of emperors in the Song Dynasty?
2) Translate the following words or phrases into English.
   世袭贵族
   士大夫与乡绅阶级
   中央集权
   宰相
   派系，私党

翻译技巧：连动句(Sentences with Serial Verbs)

我国著名语言学家王力曾经说过："就句子的结构而论，西洋语言是法治的，中国语言是人治的。"这句话是说，英语注重的是结构，而汉语注重的是语义。英汉两种语言的差异主要存在于语法层面。英语简单句呈以主谓句为主轴、动词谓语为核心的中心辐射样态；汉语简单句呈无主谓语主轴、无动词谓语为核心的平铺直叙样态。所以，英文中的句子都是以动词作谓语为核心去展开，动词独立性弱，须根据主语、时态、语态作出相应的变化。而汉语语法意义不强，动词丰富灵活，有很强的独立性，可将多个动词连用构成句子，表现形式各式各样，与英文构句差异很大。这种差异使得英语偏向一种静态语言，而汉语呈现出动态的特点，包含大量兼语句、连动句这样的特殊句式。语言中的特殊句式一直是翻译中的难点，下文将以汉语中的连动句为例，对其英译方法进行具体讲解。

Ⅰ. 连动句的定义和特点

"连动句"也叫"连谓句""连动式"，是指谓语由两个或两个以上存在逻辑关联的动词或动词词组组成的句子。连动句的句型通常可总结为"主语＋动词(短语)＋动词(短语)"。

例1 他走进来拿了一本书。

例2 我正在学习用钢笔写字。

例1是由"走进来"和"拿了一本书"这两个动词短语组成的连动句，两个动词短语共用一个主语，都作"他"的谓语。例2则是由一个动词"学习"和两个动词短语"用钢笔""写字"组成的连动句，都是主语"我"的谓语。从这两个例子可以看出，汉语中连动句的多个谓语动词共用同一个主语，是同一个主语的多个动作，彼此之间没有联合、偏正、动宾、主谓和补充等关系，他们紧密结合在一起表示整体意义。

周志培在其《英汉对比与翻译中的转换》中提出连动句有以下特点：

- 连动短语中的各个动词项都要与一个主语联系，都是由主语表示的同一个人或事物进行的行为和做的动作；
- 这些行为动作可以是连续性的，可以是并发性的，也可以从不同方面合述某一行为和事件；
- 连动项之间没有停顿，书面上不能有逗号，动词项之间也不能带连词。

Ⅱ. 连动句的分类

由定义可知，连动句的谓语由两个或两个以上的动词或动词词组组成。按照连续动作的数量，连动句可以分为双项和多项连动句两大类。

1. 双项连动句

双项连动句可根据两个动作短语间的逻辑关系进一步分为以下几类。

接续关系：前后动词表示连续发生的动作，例如"小明拿出钥匙骑车"。

目的关系：后面的动作表示前面动作的目的，例如"他去图书馆读书"。

方式关系：前面的动作表示后面动作的方式或工具，例如"他用毛笔写字"。

时间/原因关系：前面的动作表示后面动作的时间或原因，例如"女儿看见蛇尖叫了起来"。

重复关系：重复使用一个动词，后面的动词往往由前面的动词演变而来，例如"小红写字写错了"。

正反关系：一个动作用肯定式，另一个动作用否定式，表示否定的动作往往是前一个动作的持续，或是对前一动作的描述，两个动作相互补充，因此也可以称为互补关系，例如"爸爸出门没回来"。

"有"作为谓语动词："有"作为谓语动词的连动句在汉语中也很常见，例如"我们有办法找到目的地"。

2. 多项连动句

多项连动句包括连贯式多项连动句和并行式多项连动句。

连贯式多项连动句：前后动词表示连续发生的动作。例如"她站起来披上衣服赶紧开门拿外卖"。

并行式多项连动句：动词之间具有逻辑语义上的状语意义，如方式、目的、条件、时间、正反、重复等。例如"小明看书看累了就坐在沙发上睡了"。

Ⅲ. 英语中连动意义的表达方法

英语是重视语法规范的语言，一个句子的核心一般只有一个谓语动词，其他成分围绕动词被置于相应的语法位置。若一个句子包含两个或两个以上的动作，则必须将动词用逗号隔开，或者用连词 and 连接。从形式上看，英语当中没有连动句这一句式，但并不意味着英语无法表达连动含义。英语中句子的连动含义也可通过适当的语法变形来实现。

1. 非谓语动词形式表达连动意义

英语中可用非谓语动词作状语来表示汉语中的连动意义，具体包括不定式作状语、非谓语动词 v-ing 和非谓语动词 v-ed 作状语三种情况。

▶ 不定式作状语

用不定式作状语来表目的，可体现连动句中表示目的关系的连动意义。

例 1　He went to the library to read some books.
　　　他去图书馆读书。

例 2　She went to France to study architecture.
　　　她去法国学建筑。

▶ 非谓语动词 v-ing 作状语

非谓语动词 v-ing 作状语同样可以表示连动句中含有时间关系、因果关系、方式关系等的连动意义。除此之外，v-ing 作主语补语时表示目的或状态的意义，比如 go shopping、like doing 等。

例 3　Seeing a snake, my daughter gave a scream.
　　　我女儿看到蛇尖叫了起来。

例 4　Holding a book, our teacher came into the classroom.
　　　老师带着一本书走进了教室。

例 5　Leaving home, he forgot to take the key with him.
　　　他出门忘带钥匙了。

例 6　She likes playing football.
　　　她喜欢踢足球。

▶ 非谓语动词 v-ed 作状语

非谓语动词 v-ed 作状语具有完成含义，也能够表达汉语中的连动意义。

例 7　Faced by failure, she wasn't afraid at all.
　　　她面对失败毫不恐惧。

2. 英语中某些介词的连动意义

如前文所述，相较于汉语，英语少用动词，呈现出静态的特点。英语在表达连动意义时，除使用状语从句和非谓语动词之外，还可使用介词来表达动作意义，例如 with、for、over 等。用介词短语表达连动含义更体现出英文静态、简洁的语言特点。

例 1　He found his mother over the crowds.
　　　他穿过人群找到了他的母亲。

例 2　Tom came into our classroom with a smile.
　　　汤姆微笑着走进教室。

Ⅳ. 汉语连动句的翻译

连动句是汉语的特殊句式之一，种类多样且较为复杂，但在实际的翻译操作中，由于英文表达连动的形式丰富，英译连动句并不复杂。下面将根据连动句句式的分类，举例分析连动句的翻译策略和技巧。

1. 双项连动句

▶ 表示接续关系的连动句

处理接续关系的连动词时，可以采用两种翻译策略。第一种是将两个谓语动词用连词 and 并列起来；第二种则是将一个动词作为核心谓语，另一个动词处理为状语从句、非谓语动词或介词短语的形式构成完整的句子。

例 1　小英关上门悄悄打开了电视。

译文 1　Xiaoying closed the door and opened the television quietly.

译文 2　After she closed the door, Xiaoying opened the television quietly.

译文 3　Closing the door, Xiaoying opened the television quietly.

译文 4　Xiaoying opened the television quietly with the door closed.

▶ 表示目的关系的连动句

翻译这类句子时可以采用三种翻译策略。第一种同样是将两个谓语动词用连词 and 并列起来；第二种是将非表目的的动词作为谓语，表目的的动作处理成状语从句、非谓语动词或介词短语的形式构成完整的句子；第三种是将表目的的动词作为谓语，非表目的的动作处理成状语从句、非谓语动词或介词短语的形式构成完整的句子。

例 2　我骑自行车到奶奶家去。

译文 1　I rode my bike and went to my grandma's home.

译文 2　I rode my bike to my grandma's home.

译文 3　I went to my grandma's home by riding my bike.

译文 4　Riding my bike, I went to my grandma's home.

▶ 表示方式关系的连动句

翻译这类句子时可以采用三种翻译策略。第一种同样是将两个谓语动词用连词 and 并列起来；第二种是将表方式的动词作为谓语，非表方式的动作处理成状语从句、非谓语动词或介词短语的形式构成完整的句子；第三种则是将非表方式的动词作为谓语，表方式的动词处理成状语从句、非谓语动词或介词短语的形式构成完整的句子。

例 3　老师带着本英语书走进教室。

译文 1　Our teacher brought an English book and came into the classroom.

译文 2　Our teacher brought an English book when coming into the classroom.

译文 3　Our teacher came into the classroom with an English book.

▶ 表示时间/原因关系的连动句

这类句子的译法有两种。第一种同样是将两个谓语动词用连词 and 并列起来；第二种可以根据时间先后，用主从句、非谓语动词等方式进行表达。

例 4　请站起来回答问题。

译文 1　Stand up and answer my question.

译文 2　Stand up before you answer my question.

译文 3　Stand up if you want to answer my question.

译文 4　Before answering my question, you'd better stand up.

▶ **表示重复关系的连动句**

翻译这类句子时可以采用三种策略。第一种同样是将两个谓语动词用连词 and 并列起来；第二种是将第一个动词翻译成谓语，将重复的动词用非谓语动词、形容词、副词、介词短语以及从句的形式作状语，表示第一个动作的状态等。第三种是将重复的动词作谓语，第一个动词用非谓语动词、形容词、副词、介词短语以及从句的形式补充。

例 5　他打球打累了。

译文 1　He played basketball and got tired.

译文 2　He played basketball tiredly.

译文 3　He got tired after playing basketball.

▶ **表示正反关系的连动句**

翻译这类句子时可以采用四种翻译策略。第一种同样是将两个谓语动词用连词 and 并列起来；第二种是将肯定式的动词作谓语，否定式的动词用非谓语动词、介词短语、从句的形式将意义补充完整；第三种是将否定式的动作译为谓语，肯定式的动词译为非谓语动词、介词短语或从句的形式；第四种是将肯定式和否定式合并处理为句子的谓语部分。

例 6　同学们站在操场上不说话。

译文 1　Students were on the playground and they didn't talk.

译文 2　Students stood on the playground without talking.

译文 3　Standing on the playground, students didn't talk.

译文 4　Students kept silent on the playground.

▶ **"有"作为谓语动词的连动句**

翻译这类连动句时可以采用两种翻译策略。第一种是将"有"作为谓语，第二个动词处理为非谓语动词、介词短语、从句等形式充当句子的状语或其他成分；第二种是将"有"处理为 there be 句型，第二个动词译为非谓语动词、介词短语、从句等形式充当句子的状语或句子的其他成分。

例 7　我有办法解决问题。

译文 1　I have a way to solve the problem.

译文 2　There are ways to solve the problem.

此外，当"有"后面的名词表示某种资格或能力时，可以将其合并为系表结构，将第二个动词译为非谓语动词、介词短语、从句等形式充当句子的状语或其他成分。

例 8　玛丽有能力胜任这项工作。

译文　Mary is capable of this job.

2. 多项连动句

▶ **连贯式多项连动句**

翻译这类连动句时可以采用两种策略。由于连贯式多项连动句表示几个连续发生的动作，因此第一种译法同样是将两个谓语动词用逗号和连词 and 并列起来；第二种是将核心动词作为谓语，其余动词通过非谓语动词、介词短语、从句等形式译为句子的状语或其他成分。

例 1　她站起来披上衣服赶紧开门拿外卖。

译文 1　She stood up, put on clothes, quickly opened the door and got the delivery.

译文 2　She stood up and put on clothes, quickly opening the door to get the delivery.

译文 3　Standing up with the clothes put on, she quickly opened the door and got the delivery.

▶ 并行式多项连动句

该类连动句的动词之间具有一定的逻辑关系，如方式、目的、条件、时间等，因此翻译的时候可以根据其逻辑关系来确定句子结构。翻译方法可以是选择多项动词中的一个为核心词作谓语，其余动词用非谓语动词、介词短语、副词、从句等译成形式状语或句子的其他成分。

例2 小明看书看累了就坐在沙发上睡了。

译文1 Tired after reading books, Xiaoming slept on the sofa.

译文2 After reading books, Xiaoming got tired so that he slept on the sofa.

综上所述，翻译汉语连动句时，可以根据连动句动词之间的逻辑关系用非谓语动词、介词短语、从句等结构进行灵活处理，使译句更符合英语的句法规则和语言表达习惯。

段落翻译

1. 国子监

国子监是中国古代最高学府和教育管理机构，成立于晋武帝时期，旨在教育贵族。古代在国子监读书的学生被称为"监生"。国子监不仅接纳全国各族学生，还接待外国留学生，曾为培养国内各民族人才、促进中外文化交流起到积极的作用。

难点讲解：

1) "国子监"可直接音译为 Guozijian，或释译为 the Imperial College；"监生"可直接音译为 Jiansheng。

2) "中国古代最高学府"可译为 the national central institution of higher learning。

2. 书院

书院是中国帝制时期的教育机构，出现于唐朝时期，是宋代以后民间教育的重要形式。书院是学者们讲授和研究经典的地方，也是存放来自全国各地的书卷之所。与官办学校不同，书院通常由私人建立，远离城市或城镇，提供安静舒适的环境，使学者得以安心潜修，不受世俗纷扰。在宋代，私人书院在全国各地兴起，较为著名的是被誉为四大书院的白鹿洞书院、岳麓书院、嵩阳书院和应天书院。

难点讲解：

1) 书院可直接音译为 Shuyuan，或释译为 academies of classical learning。

2) "民间教育"指与官学相对的私学，可译为 private education。

3) "安心潜修，不受世俗纷扰"可译为 pursue their studies, unencumbered by restrictions and distractions。"安心"二字不必刻意译出，后面紧跟着的非谓语结构 unencumbered by 已能传达该词的意义。

4) 四大书院的名字采用音译法即可。

3. 科举考试

在科举考试中，大多数考生无法通过考试，而且通常是数次落榜，这是无可避免的现象。在唐代，殿试的通过率只有百分之一或百分之二；在宋代，会试的通过率约为百分之二；在明清时期，乡试的通过率约为百分之一。虽然大多数考生都是有一定收入的男性，但也不乏家境贫寒的人倾尽所有参加考试，以求一个光明的前程。

难点讲解：

1)"这是无可避免的现象"可译为"it was inevitable that…"。

2)比率可用直观的数字符号来表达，如"1∶100""2∶100"或"1%""2%"。

3)"倾尽所有"地做某事，有孤注一掷、赌上一切之意，可译为"risk everything on…"。

4. 应试教育与素质教育

受应试教育思想影响，许多学校片面追求升学率，只重视智育而忽视其他方面的教育，导致学生学业负担过重，影响学生的全面发展。为此，加强对素质教育思想的认识，是一项艰巨而紧迫的战略任务。素质教育是指一种以提高学生诸方面素质为目标的教育模式。它重视学生的思想道德素质、能力培养、个性发展、身体健康和心理健康。

难点讲解：

1)"应试教育"与"素质教育"可分别译作 exam-oriented education 和 quality-oriented education。

2)"片面追求"可理解为过度追求，译作"excessively pursue…"。

3)"全面发展"可译为 all-round cultivation/development。

4)"战略任务"可译为 strategic task。

5)"重视……"可译为 attach importance to doing sth 或 emphasize on doing sth。

5. 教育和教育事业的发展

教育是人类文明进步与繁荣的重要标志，是经济社会发展的重要动力。在人类的历史进程中，教育承担了不可替代的使命，发挥了至关重要的作用。早在两千多年前，中国古代的一部经典著作《大学》(*The Great Learning*)就曾提出，大学的宗旨在于彰显人类自身的美德，重塑他人，追求至善至美。这一教育思想几千年来薪火相传，至今仍具有蓬勃的生命力。1949年中华人民共和国成立以来，中国政府一直十分重视教育，并且颁布了一系列法规，保护不同群体的公民受教育的权利，尤其是保护少数民族、妇女、儿童和残疾人受教育的权利。几十年来，通过持续不断的努力，中国的教育事业取得了长足的进步，九年义务教育(compulsory education)已在全国有计划分阶段地普及。高等教育、职业教育、各种形式的成人教育和少数民族教育迅速发展。一个多层次、多元化、多学科的教育体系已经在中国形成。

难点讲解：

1)第一句如果用英语中主系表结构的简单句对应翻译出来，则显得句子不够简洁。由于两个分句主语都为 education，故可译为"As an important driving force for economic and social development, the education signifies the progress and prosperity of human civilization."。

2)第二句中的两个分句在翻译时可处理成由 and 连接的两个并列的动词短语。

3)第三句中的"重塑他人"即用教育改造人，可译作 the remolding of people。"追求至善至美"是"以完美为目标"的意思，用 the pursuit of perfection 表达较为恰当。

4)翻译第四句时需要注意汉语中四字成语的特点。"薪火相传"可以译为 has been handed down over generations。

5)第五句中的"十分重视……"可以翻译成"pay great attention to…"或者"attach great importance to…"，而使用"place…on one's higher agenda"会让人眼前一亮。"一系列"可以译为 a series of；"不同群体的公民"可以译为 citizens of different groups。

6)第六句中的"持续不断的努力"可以译为 uninterrupted efforts，也可译为 continuous efforts。"在全国……普及"就是指"在全国范围内实施"，可以译为 be implemented nationwide。

拓展阅读

Reading A

Stories behind Rejected Candidates and Their Papers in the Late Imperial China

In contrast to modern examinations, the official recruitment examination system of late imperial China did not translate the achievements of the candidates into comparable units, such as grades or ranks expressed in figures. Numerical assessments were not introduced in China until the late nineteenth century and were never adopted in the imperial examinations. In every examination until the system's abolition in 1905, only a few of the candidates entered official records after being ranked and awarded official degrees. Not being granted any rank, title, or grades, those who had not passed were deprived of any clear indicator of their situation vis-à-vis（与……相比）the rest of the candidates and the examination system in general. How then did they make sense of what they had been able to achieve?

Rejected candidates expected to see their graded papers and were routinely able to identify and interact with the examiners who had graded them. And indeed, since at least the mid-fifteenth century, the fact that failed papers should be returned to candidates was recognized in official discourse. This practice was eventually codified in the late seventeenth century: in the Qing examination code failed papers were to be returned to the candidates, so that they might understand how their papers had been graded. The relative openness of this made failed papers a medium of communication between examiners and candidates, a means by which—in theory at least—the examiners became personally responsible to the candidates. Of course, the information that candidates could extract from their failed papers was often limited and uncertain, as the examiners' markings varied in both format and quantity. But the failed candidate's access to his paper did create a sense of accountability, as he could at least identify the examiners involved in the marking process.

Controversies over examination grading tended to be negotiated and settled personally between examiners and candidates. If this was the usual case, then it might have been difficult for rejected candidates to mobilize other rejected candidates in some kind of collective action. The personalization of the examinee-examiner relationship could also make it hard for individual candidates to raise protests in the literary field. Equipped with the information from a failed paper, candidates should have been able to articulate challenges against particular examiners in their writings. Yet as we shall see, open criticism of examiners was quite rare throughout the late imperial period.

Furthermore, the access candidates had such information as the comments on their papers and the identity of examiners does not seem to have encouraged petitions for official review of examination results. Although the candidate might take legal action against the examiner, this might not be the option eventually chosen by the candidate. But certainly, the state is bound to take measures to limit any personal networking between examiners and rejected candidates that might undermine its authority.

Exercises

1 Match the English expressions in Column A with the Chinese translations in Column B.

Column A	Column B
1 numerical assessment	a 公务员考试
2 vis-à-vis	b 请愿
3 civil service examinations	c 打分制
4 petition	d 损害……的权威
5 undermine one's authority	e 与……相比

2 Answer the following questions.

1) What's the difference between rejected candidates and the takers of university entrance examinations in contemporary China in terms of their papers?

2) Why was it difficult for rejected candidates to settle controversies over examination grading?

Reading B

Higher Education in China, 2050: Moving to High-Quality Popularized Higher Education

In 1973, American sociologist Martin Trow presented his report titled "Problems in the Transition from Elite to Mass Higher Education" at the Conference on Future Structures of Post-secondary Education held by the World Economic Cooperation and Development Organization (OECD). His report proposed a three-phase model of higher education development for the first time and used the gross enrollment rate of higher education as an indicator to measure the expansion scale of a certain country's higher education system as well as divide its development stages.

According to his argument, the elite stage of higher education development means that the gross enrollment rate is less than 15%, while the massification stage means that the gross enrollment rate is greater than 15% and less than 50%. When the gross enrollment rate is greater than 50%, a higher education system can be regarded as entering the stage of popularization.

Since China's mainland implemented the reform and open policy in the late 1970s, after more than 40 years of rapid development, China's higher education has not only achieved the goals of massification and popularization in 2002 and 2019, respectively, but also achieved a transformation from scale expansion to quality improvement.

According to China's present socioeconomic development trends and long-term plan China Education Modernization 2035, it seems appropriate to anticipate that China's higher education will enter a new stage of high-quality popularization in 2050, which means a further improvement of higher education penetration rate, quality and equity. A more open higher education system with further optimized structure will be established.

Increase in the penetration rate of higher education

The high-quality higher education popularization first means a higher gross enrollment rate. Along with the continuous development and transformation of China's economy and society, especially the arrival of the wave of college-age youth in the "post one-child policy era," higher education will continue to be popularized in China. According to data released by UNESCO in 2018, the gross enrollment rate of higher education in developed countries has reached an average of over 80%.

According to the current gross enrollment rate of higher education in developed countries around the world, it seems that the scale of China's higher education still has a lot of room for development in the next 30 years. By 2050, China's higher education gross enrollment rate will reach a higher level, and perhaps will approach or even exceed some developed countries. Factors including population ageing and declining birthrate may contribute to this trend to a certain extent. As the birthplace of standardized examinations, ancient China has a long history of imperial civil service examinations. No matter how the penetration rate of higher education increases, the college entrance examination will still be the most important way for Chinese higher education institutions to recruit students in the foreseeable future. Taking test scores as an important criterion in the process of admissions has become a major feature of higher education in East Asian countries that is different from Western countries.

Improvement in China's higher education quality

Quality is the lifeline of higher education, and high-quality development is an important dimension of the popularization of higher education. According to Outline of China's National Plan for Medium and Long-term Educational Reform and Development Plan (2010-2020) issued by the State Council in 2010, the policy of China Education Modernization 2035 issued in 2018, as well as other series of national-level policies for guiding the development of higher education, further improving the quality is an important goal of China's higher education reform and development in the future.

Based on the historical experience of developed countries, it seems obvious that after a certain higher education system enters the phase of popularization, it will perhaps undergo significant changes in terms of admission opportunities, institutional scales, intuitional diversity and teaching reform. One of the greatest changes might be that receiving higher education is no longer the privilege of a few people but has become a choice for most people.

The major goal of providing higher education services will be to prepare the entire population for future life. Therefore, in the next 30 years, China will inevitably improve the overall quality of higher education via optimizing its structure and diversification in order to meet most Chinese people's demands. Moreover, students' choices will be more rational. Fulfilling the needs of individual development will become the major motivation for entering universities. In the coming era of artificial intelligence, higher education in China will also be more diverse and flexible.

Enhancement of higher education equity

From a global perspective, improving education equity is always a major approach to promoting social equity. Promoting higher education equity is therefore a common task faced by all countries around the world. For a long time, due to various historical, geographical, economic, and cultural factors, higher education in China has always had problems of regional imbalance and inequality between urban and rural areas. For instance, in terms of the distribution of high-quality higher education resources, the prestigious "Double First-Class" universities in China's eastern region are far more than that in the central and western regions. In 2017, the population proportions of the central and western regions were 26.5% and 27.1%, respectively.

The Chinese government has already attached great importance to these issues and has implemented various policy interventions, such as attempting to get provinces and the Ministry of Education to jointly provide support for the development of universities in less-developed regions, and giving priority to admit ethnic minority students and students from the middle and western regions as well as rural areas. Along with the equalization of the allocation of higher education resources and the entrance opportunities, it seems appropriate to anticipate that the higher education equity will be further improved in China.

Promote a more developed higher education system

A more developed or mature higher education system means that it can cultivate different kinds of talent to meet the needs of a country's socioeconomic development. As the world's largest developing country under the continuous promotion of "Reform and Opening Up" development strategies, China's economy and society will face comprehensive and profound transformations in the next 30 years, which include the transformations in the fields of agriculture, manufacturing, commerce, service industry, technology, culture, and education. Such transformations will bring new challenges to universities in the dimensions of talent training, conducting research, providing social services, as well as disseminating traditional culture.

In order to deal with such challenges, higher education in China needs to undergo serious transformations in terms of the major educational goals, the methods of major program settings, as well as the models and methods of talent training. High-level research universities (e.g., China's "Double First-Class" universities), local-level institutions which specifically serve local economic and social development, as well as higher education level vocational colleges which serve the modernization of manufacturing all need to optimize their respective development models for achieving functional complementarity.

Therefore, it seems appropriate to anticipate that China's higher education system will become more diversified in types (and levels), more appropriate in its overall structure, and more comprehensive in its functions while entering the relatively mature stage of higher education popularization in 2050. And some universities in China will grow up as the top-level or high-level universities in the world.

Construct a more open higher education pattern

Opening to the outside world is not only an important symbol of higher education internationalization but also a crucial part of China's "Opening Up" national strategy. Since the 1980s (when "Opening Up" became a fundamental national strategy), international higher education exchanges and cooperation, as well as higher education level student mobility have become important pathways for China to achieve "Opening Up." According to statistics published by China's Ministry of Education, in 2017, a total of 489,200 foreign students, including 75,800 master and doctoral students, from 204 countries and regions studied in 935 Chinese universities in 31 provincial level regions. This number has increased by 18.62% compared to 2016, making China the largest destination country for studying abroad in Asia. The internationalization of higher education will be further developed via online communication.

By 2050, it seems also appropriate to anticipate that China's higher education system will be more open and inclusive. In addition to the expansion of the scale of higher education internationalization, China will also focus on improving the quality of internationalization process to further promote cultural exchanges and talent mobility between countries and regions around the world, in order to enhance international understanding and friendship, and contribute to constructing a better community of shared future for mankind.

Exercises

 Translate the following words or expressions into English.

毛入学率

实现从规模扩张到质量提升的转变

"双一流"大学

高等教育资源分配均等化

建设更美好的人类命运共同体

 Answer the following questions.

1) What are the reasons for the increase of China's higher education?

2) According to the passage, why is receiving higher education no longer the privilege of a few people but has become a choice for most people?

3) How can China construct a more open higher quality education pattern?

翻译佳作赏析

我们要积极发展教育事业，通过普及教育，启迪心智，传承知识，陶冶情操，使人们在持续的格物致知中更好认识各种文明的价值，让教育为文明传承和创造服务。我们要大力发展科技事业，通过科技进步和创新，认识自我，认识世界，改造社会，使人们在持续的天工开物中更好掌握科技知识和技能，让科技为人类造福。我们要大力推动文化事业发展，通过文化交流，沟通心灵，开阔眼界，增进共识，让人们在持续的以文化人中提升素养，让文化为人类进步助力。

译文：

We should develop education more actively. Education can open people's minds, impart knowledge, and cultivate temperament. The continued process of learning will enable our people to better appreciate the value of different civilizations. In this sense, education is an effective vehicle for the continuation and creation of civilizations. We should develop science and technology more vigorously. Scientific advancement and innovation can help people understand themselves and the world and be in a stronger position to change their society for the better. The continued process of exploiting nature will enable our people to master still more knowledge and skills. In this sense, science and technology are a powerful tool to make the world a better place for mankind. We should promote cultural undertakings more energetically. Cultural exchanges can help open our hearts to each other, broaden our horizon and build greater consensus among us. The continued process of cultivating people morally and intellectually will result in a higher standard of humanity. In this sense, culture is a big booster for human progress.

赏析：

原文选自习近平2014年3月27日在巴黎联合国教科文组织总部发表的演讲，选段强调了教育之于个人、社会乃至国家发展的重要意义。原文属于政治类文体，简洁的四字表达居多，排比句式整齐，语言气势较强，以第一人称叙述，反复通过"我们要……通过……"来表达强烈的号召。因此，译文也应在文体和语言风格上与原文相符，避免复杂的词汇和表达，使句式简洁而有气势。

从用词上看，译文并未使用任何晦涩难懂的词语，"发展"即develop，"推动"即promote，"陶冶""提升"即cultivate，清晰达意，一目了然。而在用词精简的同时，译文亦未因此遗漏原文的韵味，如将"让文化为人类进步助力"改译为"In this sense, culture is a big booster for human progress."（从这一意义上看，文化是人类文明进步的强大助力），流畅地承接了前文对大力推动文化事业发展的益处的解释说明。

从句式上看，译文保持了与原文一样的排比句型。三处"我们要……通过……"均以"we should… can…"的句式译出，排列整齐而有气势。受英语单词长度和表达习惯影响，相同内容的英语句子通常会比汉语句子更长。为使句子更简洁有力、向原文靠近，译文灵活地对原文进行了断句重组。例如将"使人们在持续的天工开物中更好掌握科技知识和技能"这一句子成分与前文的四字格脱离，断句重组为"The continued process of … will …"，使句子变得相对简短，也未割裂与上下文的关系。此外，译文对中式四字格的处理也值得学习，如将"传承知识"译作impart knowledge，将"陶冶情操"译作cultivate temperament，保持了"动词＋名词"的规整形式，使译文表达同样铿锵有力。

总而言之，译文在内容上准确传达了原文的思想内容，同时又做到了与原文文体风格保持一致。

翻译练习

1. 中国封建帝制晚期，科举制度是中央政府选拔地方人才的主要机制。科举制度根据省和县的名额分配官职，这意味着，朝廷官员是从全国范围内选拔，人数与每个省的人口成一定比例。因此，偏远落后地区的人才和精英也有机会在科举考试中获得成功，为自己谋得一官半职。

2. 元、明、清时期的科举考试，僵化死板的"八股文"风占据了主导地位。这一时期的士人因当时的政治环境相对无法自由发言和创作。一些人指责"八股文"的固定格式扼杀了创新思维，限制考试规定的题目，导致当时的中国知识分子缺乏学习理科或进行实验的动力，这可能是导致该时期中国科学和经济发展落后于欧洲的原因。1905年，清政府废除科举制度，士大夫逐渐消失。

3. 理论上讲，科举制度将培养出精英统治阶级，让最优秀的学者管理国家。科举考试为社会阶层向上流动提供了途径，赋予许多人追求政治权力和名誉的机会，鼓励人们寻求正规的教育。然而，尽管官僚制度以科举考试为基础，高度重视儒家思想，确保学识渊博之人得以就任高阶官职，但这一体制缺乏预防政治腐败的措施。

4. 近年来，职业教育的发展以及对社会的贡献改变了不少人对它的消极看法。职业教育对社发展意义重大。职业教育培养了大量的技术工人和专家满足国家建设的需要；中国政府投入了大量精力，发展不同层次的职业教育，以满足不断发展的国家经济的需要。数据显示，近年来中等职业学校的入学率有了明显增长。

5. 中国拥有世界上规模最大的教育体系。2021年6月，中国有1,078万考生参加高考，教育投资约占中国国内生产总值的4%。1986年，中国政府通过了义务教育法，规定所有中国儿童必须接受九年义务教育。2020年，教育部启动了"强基计划"，将允许包括北京大学、清华大学和复旦大学在内的部分中国顶尖高校选拔有志于服务国家重大战略需求的优秀高中毕业生。根据"强基计划"，这些大学将重点招收近年来较为冷门的数学、物理、化学和生物等专业的学生。

6. 改革开放以来，中国的教育事业得到了快速发展，取得了引人瞩目的成就。中国政府把教育摆在优先发展的地位，坚持科教兴国，全面提倡素质教育；同时，积极推进教育公平，保障人人有受教育的机会。中国的教育成就反映在两个不同的层面：一个是全面普及了九年义务教育；另一个是实现了高等教育大众化。教育的发展为中国的经济发展和社会进步作出了重大贡献。近年来为适应社会、经济发展的需要，中国政府不断加快培养各领域急需的人才。

7. 我们处在一个几乎所有信息都可以从网络上获得的新时代，这也使人们不再那么依赖实体学校。网络课程，作为一种远程教育的形式，为人们的学习提供了极大的便利，人们可以在最方便的时间和地点学习，也可以按照自己的节奏进行学习。然而，与线下学习相比，网络课程并不能够很好地实现师生互动和同学间交流。此外，若无法连接网络，网络课程就无法进行。网络课程并不适合所有人，只有适当利用网络资源，才能得到最好的学习效果。

Unit 7

科技成就

Unit Goals

In this unit, you are going to
- grasp words and expressions concerning scientific and technological achievements;
- acquire knowledge about scientific and technological achievements which can be traced back to thousand years ago;
- know how to translate passive sentences from Chinese into English;
- grasp translation skills of paragraphs on Chinese scientific and technological achievements.

Related Words and Expressions

四大发明 four great inventions in ancient China
造纸术 papermaking
指南针 compass
火药 gunpowder
印刷术 printing
中医 traditional Chinese medicine (TCM)
针灸 acupuncture
共享单车 shared bicycle; bike sharing
网购 online shopping
人工智能 artificial intelligence (AI)
虚拟现实 virtual reality (VR)
区块链 block chain
珠算 abacus
《神农本草经》 Shennong's Herbal Classic
《黄帝内经》 Yellow Emperor's Inner Canon
《伤寒杂病论》 Treatise on Febrile and Miscellaneous Diseases
《太初历》 Taichu Calendar
《梦溪笔谈》 Dream Pool Essays
《本草纲目》 Compendium of Materia Medica
地动仪 seismograph
高铁 high-speed train

移动支付 mobile payment

移动服务 mobile services

数字货币 digital currency

中国天眼 FAST（Five-hundred-meter Aperture Spherical Radio Telescope）

探月工程 lunar exploration

嫦娥五号 Chang'e-5

科技创新 sci-tech innovation

科教兴国 invigorate China through science and education

高新技术 new and high/high and new technology

前沿科学 frontier science

前沿技术 cutting-edge technologies

达到或接近国际先进水平 reach or approach advanced international standards

赶上或超过国际先进水平 catch up with or even surpass advanced world levels

信息技术 IT（information technology）

信息化 informationize/informize；IT application

互联网＋ the Internet Plus

产学研深度融合 integration of enterprises，universities and research institutes

研发投入 research and development（R&D）spending

创新 make innovations

创新驱动的发展 innovation-driven development

知识产权 intellectual property/intellectual property rights

科技人员 scientists and engineers

研究人员 researcher

研究所 research institute

科研项目 research projects

科技成果转化 application of scientific and technological achievements

国家科技重大项目 major national science and technology project

激励政策 incentive mechanism

坚决打击侵权行为 crack down on infringements

网络 networking

数字化 digitalization

智能科技 smart technology

互联网企业 Internet-based company

移动互联网 the mobile Internet

物联网 IoT（Internet of Things）

云计算 cloud computing

信息消费 spending on information goods and services

宽带用户 broadband Internet users

科创板 Sci-Tech innovation board

社交网站 social network site
社交网络 social networking
社交媒体 social media
注册 register
粉丝 followers
网民 netizen; net citizen; cyber citizen
上网/网上冲浪 surf the Internet
网上交易平台 online trading platform
网友 net friend; key pal
电脑黑客 hacker
短信 text message; text
笔记本电脑 laptop
掌上电脑 palmtop
平板电脑 tablet
个人数字助理 PDA (Personal Digital Assistant)
潜水 lurk
帖子 thread
论坛版主 moderator
秒杀 seckill
漂浮广告 floating ad
人肉搜索 human-powered search
垃圾邮件 junk mail/spam
U盘 USB disk; USB flash disk; memory stick
应用程序 application; app
智能卡 smart card
刷卡 swipe the card
数字化时代 digital age
3D打印机 3D printers
智能手机 smartphone
多媒体 multimedia
智能处理 intelligent processing
智能家居 smart home
5G时代 the 5G era
低头族 smartphone addicts; phubber
保护发明创造 protect inventions and creative work
硬件/软件 hardware/software
数字制造业 digital manufacturing
工业互联网 industrial Internet
二维码 QR code (quick response code); two-dimensional code
扫码 scan a QR code
人脸识别支付 face scan payment

电讯，通信 telecommunication

通信卫星 communications satellite；telecommunication satellite

全球定位系统 global positioning system（GPS）

北斗导航系统 Beidou navigation system

量子通信 quantum communication

量子卫星 quantum satellite

发射运载火箭 launch a carrier rocket

载人航天飞行 manned space flight

发射无/载人宇宙飞船 launch an unmanned/a manned spaceship（space vehicle）

神舟十一号 Shenzhou-11

运载火箭 carrier rocket

可回收卫星 retrievable satellite

探月工程 the lunar exploration program

生物技术 biotechnology，biotech

基因 gene

转基因食品 genetically modified/altered food；GM food

杂交水稻 hybrid rice

试管婴儿 test-tube baby

无人探索 unmanned probe

载人宇宙飞船 manned spacecraft

长征五号 B 运载火箭 Long March 5B

载人空间站 manned space station

空间实验室 space lab

返回舱 the re-entry capsule

推进舱 propelling module

轨道舱 orbital module

既定轨道 definitive orbit

卫星地球同步 Geosynchronous orbit

国际空间站 International Space Station

发射台 launch pad

无人机 UAV（unmanned aerial vehicle）；unmanned drone

氢能源汽车 hydrogen fuel cell vehicle

燃料电池电动汽车 FCEV（Fuel Cell Electric Vehicle）

Lead-in Activities

 Answer the following questions.

1）Do you know the four great inventions of ancient China? And what are they?

2）Do you know the new four great inventions of modern China?

3）How many scientific innovations have appeared in recent years? Can you give some examples?

2 **Listen to a brief introduction to the Four Great Inventions of ancient China and fill in the blanks with the words you hear.**

_____: these four inventions have been recognized as _____ for great civilizations. The focus on these four _____ as the most important was not made by the Chinese but by foreign scholars. For example, in the seventeenth century, Francis Bacon wrote how printing, gunpowder and the _____ had changed the world with literature. In the twentieth century, Dr. Joseph Needham _____ the four great inventions and pointed out that China had achieved many of the world's firsts. Before paper was made, Chinese characters were _____ animal bones and cast onto bronze objects. Then, from the _____, in the fifth century BCE, _____ were used. Though lighter than bones or bronze, these were still quite heavy. Silk, too, was used—but it was too expensive for most people.

3 **Read the following passage and then do the exercises.**

A Fruitful Year for China's Manned Space Program

It has been a busy year for China's manned space program. In 2023, the country welcomed the return of its Shenzhou-15 crew, sent two manned spaceships and one cargo spacecraft to its space station and harvested fruitful scientific research results in the space. Let's look back at the memorable moments of China's manned space program during 2023.

The launch of the Tianzhou-6 cargo spacecraft

China launched the Tianzhou-6 cargo spacecraft on May 10, which later docked with its space station.

The primary purpose of the Tianzhou-6 was to deliver essential supplies and spacesuits to the Shenzhou-15 crew, which arrived at the space station in November 2022. The cargo craft also transported maintenance components, application facilities and propellant to support the operation of the space station.

Its successor, the Tianzhou-7 cargo craft, is scheduled to be launched in early 2024 to deliver supplies for the astronauts.

The return of the Shenzhou-15 crew

On November 29, 2022, China launched the Shenzhou-15 manned mission, which wrapped up the last stage of the construction of its space station. Since then, the China Space Station (CSS) entered a new phase of application and development, which will span more than 10 years.

After an over 180-day stay in the CSS, the re-entry capsule with the Shenzhou-15 crew members Fei Junlong, Deng Qingming and Zhang Lu aboard touched down at the Dongfeng landing site in north China's Inner Mongolia Autonomous Region on June 4.

During their stay, the three Chinese astronauts, or taikonauts, accomplished four extravehicular activities, setting a new record for Chinese astronaut crews in spacewalks. They also conducted a series of scientific experiments and tests, including installing an extravehicular extension pump set and a cross-cabin cable installation and connection.

The Shenzhou-15 crew not only achieved a milestone in extravehicular activities but also witnessed the historic moment when the CSS was fully completed in 2022.

The CSS welcomes the Shenzhou-16 crew

The Shenzhou-16 manned spacecraft embarked on its journey to the CSS on May 30. It is the first manned mission since the space station entered its application and development phase.

The Shenzhou-16 crew consisted of mission commander Jing Haipeng, spaceflight engineer Zhu Yangzhu and payload expert Gui Haichao. Gui became the first Chinese civilian in space, the first payload specialist to go to the CSS and the first taikonaut wearing glasses.

The crew returned to Earth after a five-month stay at the space station. The three taikonauts completed a series of tasks during their trip, including an extravehicular activity, a science lecture titled "Tiangong Class" and multiple extravehicular installation tasks. Closely cooperating with the ground crew, the Shenzhou-16 crew also carried out a slew of space science tests and experiments concerning human factors engineering, space medicine, life ecology, biotechnology, materials science, fluid physics and astronautical technology.

On their way back, the crew captured the first images of the complete configuration of the CSS with Earth in the backdrop.

The Shenzhou-17 taikonauts join their colleagues in space

The Shenzhou-17 taikonauts arrived at the space station on October 26, just a few days before the return of the Shenzhou-16 crew on October 31.

The Shenzhou-17 crew, the country's youngest lineup by average age since the CSS's construction began, comprises commander Tang Hongbo, 48, and operators Tang Shengjie and Jiang Xinlin, aged 34 and 35, respectively.

The Shenzhou-17 crew will undertake a series of tasks, including in-orbit tests of space science and application payloads, extravehicular activities, installation of extravehicular payloads, and space station maintenance.

1) Answer the following questions.
   (1) What scientific experiments and tests did the Shenzhou-15 crew members do during their stay?
   (2) What subject areas are involved in the space science tests and experiments that the Shenzhou-16 crew carried out?
2) Translate the following words or phrases into English.
   中国载人航天计划
   航天员
   着陆场
   返回舱
   舱外活动

翻译技巧：被动句(Sentences with Passive Voice)

语态是动词的一种形式，用以说明主语与谓语动词之间的关系，语态包括主动语态和被动语态两种。主动语态即主语是动作的执行者，被动语态则表示主语是动作的承受者。汉英两种语言中都存在主动语态和被动语态，而被动语态在英语中的广泛应用，是英语区别于汉语的一大特点。英语重客体思维，侧重句子的语法与结构；汉语重主体思维，侧重主观意识和人的能动性，因此汉语使用被动句的频率更低。这样的语言思维差异让汉译英中的被动句成为难点。下面将从英汉被动句特点、英语被动意义的表达形式、汉语被动意义的表达形式这三个方面，分析英语中被动句的汉译技巧。

Ⅰ. 英汉被动句特点

被动语态往往以物为主语，表达上较为客观。英语是注重形合并强调客体思维的语言，被动句的特点恰恰符合英语语言的表达习惯，因此在英语中广泛使用。大多情况下英语中的被动句能够起到强调动作承受者、在语法结构上保持完整性、使上下文连贯等作用。

汉语与英语恰恰相反，汉语注重意合，强调主题而非主语。严格来说，汉语中不存在被动语法结构，只有一些含有被动意义的字、词、句式。在现代汉语中，"被"字句常用来表达负面意义或对动作承受者产生不利影响的意义，比如"我被你害惨了""房子被大水冲垮了"等，有时也可以表达积极、客观的含义。汉语经常用主动句来表被动含义，形成形式上是主动语态而逻辑意义上是被动语态的句子特点。汉语中大多数被动句都以这种形式出现。

Ⅱ. 英语被动意义的表达形式

英语被动意义的表达形式有两种：结构被动语态和自然被动语态。

结构被动语态即用动词的被动语态从结构上来表示被动意义，即"be＋v-ed"形式，有时在口语中 be 常常由 get 代替。

例1 Environment should be protected by everyone on the earth.

自然被动语态指句子不用动词的被动形式也具有被动意义，即用主动形式表示被动意义。这类句子占比相对较少，常见于含有感官动词的句子。

例2 The food tastes well.

Ⅲ. 汉语被动意义的表达形式

汉语的被动句也可分为两种：有标识被动句和无标识被动句。有标识被动句除了由"被"标识外，还常用"受""让""遭""给""叫""由""靠""加以""予以""得到""由……所""为……所""被……所"等来表示。汉语中最常见的是无标识被动句，即用主动形式表示被动意义，省略标志被动意义的"被"等标志词。除此之外，汉语也常用主动句来表示被动意义。例如：小明因为见义勇为得到了大家的尊重。

Ⅳ. 英语被动句的汉译技巧

了解英汉两种语言的差异及各自被动句的表达形式，有利于译者在翻译被动句时选择恰当的策略。汉译英语被动句时，译者需要依据汉语的表达习惯灵活处理被动语态，同时准确表达原文意思。下文介绍了汉译英语被动句的几个常见翻译技巧。

1. 英语结构被动句翻译为汉语有标识被动句

英语中结构被动句的被动形式为"be＋v-ed"，汉语中虽然没有特定某种语法结构的被动句，但有很多表示被动意义的词，译者可根据具体语境选择恰当的表达。

1) 在英语结构被动句中，若强调谓语动词本身，且动词带有负面、消极的含义时，可以将其翻译为带"被""受""遭"等字的有标识被动句。

例 1　He was punished by his English teacher because he didn't finish his homework.
　　　他没有完成家庭作业，所以受到英语老师的惩罚。

例 2　Mary was shocked by the sudden loud sound.
　　　玛丽被这突如其来的巨响吓了一跳。

例 3　The new policy of the government was criticized by the public.
　　　政府的新政策遭到了民众的批评。

2) 英语中的结构被动句若是强调正面、积极的含义，翻译时可用"加以""予以""得到"来表达被动含义。

例 4　He was praised by his classmates for providing help to the elders.
　　　他帮助老人，得到了同学们的赞扬。

例 5　Later，the details of the work will be discussed.
　　　稍后将对工作细节问题加以讨论。

3) 英语结构被动句中的动词若表达中性意义，可以将其翻译为带有"叫""由""让""靠""以"等字的被动句。

例 6　Not all things in the world are consisted by molecules.
　　　世界上不是所有的物质都是由分子构成的。

例 7　The way to the exit of the maze has been found by you.
　　　让（叫）你找到迷宫出口了。

4) 当英语结构被动句强调动作执行者（即由 by 引出动作执行者）时，可以用"由……所"等结构来翻译。

例 8　The work will be finished by the team that performs well.
　　　这项工作将由表现好的队伍来完成。

例 9　The room was cleaned by the couple.
　　　这个房间是由这对夫妻打扫的。

5) 将英语结构被动句翻译成汉语的无标识被动句。在汉语中，无标识被动句很普遍。这类句子与主动语态没有区别，但主语却是动作的承受者。在翻译英语被动句时，若去掉标识词也能够清楚表达被动含义，则可以省略标识词，将其翻译为无标识被动句。

例 10　The 2008 Olympics was successfully held in Beijing.
　　　 2008 年奥运会在北京成功举办。

例 11　The living room was decorated to look like a garden.
　　　 客厅装扮得像个花园。

6) 当英语中的被动语态表示事物的状态、性质、过程时，即与系表结构相似时，可以用汉语的判断句"是……的"句型来翻译。

例 12　The watch is made in Switzerland.
　　　 这款手表是瑞士生产的。

例 13　The building was established by a great architect.
　　　 这个建筑是一位伟大的建筑师建造的。

例 14　The gift to the boy was conditioned on his good behavior.
给孩子的礼物是以他的表现好坏为条件的。

2. 英语结构被动句翻译为汉语无主句

汉语是一门注重主题的语言，很多句子没有主语但同样可以将意思表述清楚，因此英语结构被动句也可翻译为汉语无主句。通常情况下，表示命令、建议、请求、要求或在汉语中不需要提出执行者的句子，都可以翻译成汉语的无主句，即将行为承受者放在动词之后作宾语。

例 1　Attention should be paid to control the temperature of plants.
应该注意控制植物的温度。

例 2　Children must be taught to be polite.
必须教孩子们变得礼貌。

例 3　Efforts must be made to prevent the spread of the pandemic.
必须努力防止疫情扩散。

3. 英语结构被动句译为汉语主动句

在汉语的长期发展中，形成了用主动句来表达被动含义的语言习惯。因此在翻译英语结构被动句时，大多数情况下都可以采取符合汉语表达习惯的主动句。英语中常为了衔接上下文、避免重复或追求客观表达，用无生命的事或物来充当主语，而汉语多用人来作主语。

1) 当英语中用无生命的事或物作主语时，可将原文的执行者译为主语，承受者译为宾语，从而翻译为汉语的主动句。

例 1　The thief was caught by the police.
警察抓住了小偷。

例 2　Efforts weren't made by the little boy to improve his study.
小男孩没有努力提升学业。

例 3　The book was introduced by my brother last year.
去年我的哥哥向我推荐了这本书。

2) 当英语结构被动句中未提及执行者，但根据句意可以推断出执行者是人的时候，译成汉语时可以补充执行者，比如增译"人们""有人""大家"等具有泛指意义的名词或代词作主语。

例 4　Red is known as the lucky color for the Chinese.
人们都知道红色是中国人的吉祥颜色。

例 5　Smoking is regarded as a killer to people's health.
人们认为，吸烟是威胁人体健康的杀手。

3) 对于英语中 it 作形式主语，后接被动语态以及主语从句的句型，翻译时可以用"据了解""据说""众所周知"等表达转译为主动句，将主语从句译为宾语。

例 6　It's reported that there were 10 people hurt in the accident last night.
据报道，昨晚的意外中有10人受伤。

例 7　The Great Wall is known as the one of the most famous places in China.
众所周知，长城是中国最著名的景点之一。

例 8　It's said that artificial intelligence will replace many people to do various jobs.
据说，人工智能将代替人们进行各种工作。

4. 英语自然被动句译为汉语无标识被动句或主动句

英语中自然被动句出现比例较少，这类句子通常含有 feel、taste、sound、appear、look、

smell、sell、wash、write、cook、wear、open、drive、begin、adjourn、require、need、want 等动词。还有一些介词短语在形式上主动但在逻辑上被动。这类句子可以译为汉语无标识被动句或主动句。

例 1　His voice sounded strange on the phone.
　　　他的声音在电话里听着怪怪的。

例 2　The pencil writes well.
　　　这个铅笔很好写。

例 3　The house needs painting.
　　　这房子需要粉刷了。

例 4　Everything is under the control.
　　　一切都在控制当中。

段落翻译

1. 网购

网购是电子商务的一种形式，顾客轻点鼠标，足不出户就可以通过网络购买商品或服务。物美价廉的网络商品吸引了越来越多的消费者。网购随时随地都可以进行，极为便利，在年轻一代中很受欢迎。据预测，中国网购人数将以更快的速度持续增长。但网购的迅猛增长也给快递业带来不小压力。为了按时送达大量的网购商品，很多快递员（courier）不得不夜以继日地工作。

难点讲解：

1) 第一句可以与第二句合译为一句。在译文中，可使第一句作主句，第二句处理成定语从句，对主句内容进行补充说明。

2) "物美价廉的网络高品"可译为 high quality online goods at fair prices。

3) 第三句包含三个分句，第一个分句与后两个分句之间存在因果关系，因此译文可用 so 连接第一个分句和后两个分句。后两个分句可用 and 连接，译为 it's very convenient and quite caters for the young generation。

4) 第四句中"据……"一般处理成"It ＋ be ＋ v-ed ＋ that 从句"的结构。例如："据报道"可译为"It is reported that…"；"据谣传"可译为"It is rumored that…"。

2. 数字货币

数字货币是指主要在互联网上管理、存储或交换的任何货币或类似货币的资产。数字货币具有与传统货币相似的属性，但它们通常不具有实体形式（如印刷的纸币或铸造的硬币）。因为数字货币不具有实体形式，所以网上的交易几乎能在瞬间达成，并去除了分发纸币和硬币相关的成本。数字货币可以用于购买实体商品和服务，但也可能仅用于某些场合，如在线上游戏中使用。

难点讲解：

1) 本段不涉及生词难词，难点在于将长句间的逻辑关系表达准确。

2) "实体形式"可译作 physical form。

3) 翻译"网上的交易……瞬间达成"时可将动词短语转化为名词短语，以求译文更简洁，可译作 instantaneous online transactions。

3. 基因测序

基因测序是确定基因中核苷酸精确顺序的过程。基因序列相关知识已经成为基础生物学研究中不可或缺的部分,应用于许多领域。比较健康和突变的基因序列有助于诊断不同的疾病,包括各种癌症。掌握快速的基因测序方法,可以使医疗护理更高效、更个性化。此外,这一技术还能锁定个人病变基因,有助于疾病的预防和治疗。近年来,对该技术的研究在实验室与实际应用均取得了进展。基因测序逐渐成为医学界热门的话题。可见,基因测序有望成为下一个改变世界的技术。

难点讲解:

1)本段翻译涉及少许医学专有名词,难点在于正确译出长句的逻辑关系。"基因测序"译作 DNA sequencing 或 gene sequencing,"核苷酸"译为 nucleotides。

2)"成为……不可或缺的部分"可直译为"become indispensable part for…"。

3)"突变的基因序列"可译为 mutated DNA sequences。

4)"有助于疾病的预防和治疗"可译为 be conducive to prevention and treatment of diseases。

4. 移动支付

过去几年里,移动支付市场在中国蓬勃发展。随着移动互联网的出现,手机购物逐渐成为一种趋势。一项研究表明18到30岁的年轻人构成了移动支付市场的最大群体。由于现在移动支付很便捷,许多消费者在购物时更喜欢用手机付款,而不是用现金或信用卡。移动支付开创了新的支付方式,使电子货币开始普及。专家预测,中国移动支付市场未来仍有很大发展潜力。

难点讲解:

1)第一句要用现在完成时进行翻译。此句比较简单,"过去几年里"可译为 during the past few years,句中的"蓬勃发展"可以用 thrive 来表达。

2)翻译第二句时,"随着……的出现"可用固定表达方式"with the advent of…",这一表达方式常用来描述重要事件或发明的出现。"成为一种趋势"可简单地翻译为 become a trend。

3)翻译第三句时,"18到30岁的年轻人"可以翻译为 young people aged between 18 and 30。"构成了"可以翻译为 account for,也可以翻译为 constitute 或 make up。

4)翻译第四句时,句中的"更喜欢……而不是……"可译为"would rather … than …",注意 would rather 和 than 后面的动词都要用原形。

5)翻译第六句时,可用分词结构形式。"未来仍有很大发展潜力"可翻译为 still has great potential for development in the future。

5. 北斗卫星导航系统

北斗卫星导航系统是中国着眼于国家安全和经济社会发展需要,自主建设的卫星导航系统。北斗卫星导航系统由两个独立的卫星星座组成,可在全球范围内为各类用户提供高精准度的定位导航服务。总体而言,北斗卫星导航系统的建成促进了我国卫星导航事业的发展,体现了我国综合国力的提升。此外,北斗卫星导航系统的建成使我国在卫星应用方面摆脱了对国外卫星导航系统的依赖,打破美国 GPS 的垄断,同时还带动了一大批高科技产业的发展,形成了新的经济增长点。

难点讲解:

1)这一段涉及的复合词较多,难点在于中式复合词和长句的翻译。第一句中"北斗卫星导航系统"译为 The Beidou navigation satellite system,后文用简称 BDS 代替即可,无须多次重复。"经济社会发展"可译为 socio-economic development。

2)第二句中"卫星星座"译为 satellite constellations。"高精准度"可译为简洁的复合词 high-precision。

3)最后一句"经济增长点"可译为 economic growth point。

6. 科教兴国

我们要实施科教兴国的战略。科技进步是经济发展的决定性因素,发展教育是科技进步的基础。世界范围内日趋激烈的经济竞争和综合国力的较量，归根结底是科技和人才的竞争。我国只有大力发展教育和科技事业，把经济发展切实转到依靠科技进步和提高劳动者素质的轨道上来，才能加快现代化进程，缩小与发达国家的差距。科教工作的根本任务，是提高全民族的思想道德素质、科学文化素质和创新能力。这是我国现代化事业进一步发展的需要，也是适应世界科技革命和经济竞争新形势的需要。

难点讲解：

1）该段属于典型的国情翻译，需要译者掌握相关的专业术语表达。例如，"科教兴国"一般翻译成 invigorating China through science and education。

2）翻译中有时汉语的一个词语在英语中的不同语境下需用不同词来表达，属于一对多的关系。本段中"素质"一词反复出现，如"劳动者素质""思想道德素质""科学文化素质"，在这些表述中素质应分别翻译成 quality、standards、level。

3）在翻译该段的动词时需注意题材特点，应使用正式的书面表达语。例如，"实施"一词可以译为 implement，"缩小……差距"可译为 narrow the gap，"加快"可译为 accelerate。

拓展阅读

Abacus and Calculation with an Abacus

In 2007, the British newspaper *The Independent* listed 101 small inventions that changed the world, among which, the Chinese abacus which has enjoyed a history of 2,000 years or so, ranked the first.

The abacus was a great invention in ancient China. The abacus was invented on the basis that Chinese used the counting-rod for a long period. In ancient times, people used small rods to count. Later, with the development of productivity, the amount requiring calculation was greater, and calculation with counting-rods limited the calculation. Thus, people invented a more advanced counter—the abacus.

The earliest known painting of the Chinese abacus can be found in the famous long scroll *Riverside Scene at Qingming Festival* painted by Zhang Zeduan (1085 – 1145) during the Song Dynasty. There, an abacus is clearly seen lying beside an account book on the counter of an apothecary's.

The abacus is rectangular with wooden frame on the four sides and small rods fixed inside strung with wooden beads; a girder across the middle separates the abacus into two parts: each rod has two beads on its upper part, each representing five, and five beads on the lower part, each representing one.

With the application of the abacus, people summarized many abacus rhymes, increasing the calculating speed. By the time of the Ming Dynasty, people could use the abacus in addition, subtraction, multiplication and division, which were widely used in calculating weight, amount, space and volume.

Since it is simple to make an abacus and cheap to buy one, and it is easy to remember abacus rhymes, simple and convenient to calculate with an abacus, it is widely used in China. There are many experts in the use of the abacus in all trades and professions, and some people can use an abacus with two hands at the same time.

Later the abacus was gradually spread into Japan, Korea, and countries and regions in Southeast Asia. People found that using an abacus can improve thinking and practical abilities in addition to providing convenient calculation. Since it requires cooperation of the mind, eyes and hand, it is a good way to improve the comprehensive reaction ability.

Exercises

1 Match the English expressions in Column A with the Chinese translations in Column B.

Column A	Column B
1 comprehensive reaction ability	a 珠算口诀
2 addition, subtraction, multiplication and division	b 算盘
3 abacus	c 各行各业
4 weight, amount, space and volume	d 综合反应能力
5 in all trades and professions	e 加减乘除
6 *Riverside Scene at Qingming Festival*	f 珠算
7 calculation with an abacus	g 重量、数量、面积、体积
8 abacus rhymes	h 《清明上河图》

2 Answer the following questions.

1) Why is the abacus widely used in China?

2) How does the abacus improve people's comprehension and reaction abilities?

翻译佳作赏析

原文：

1. 算数求积尺之法，如刍萌、刍童、方池、冥谷、堑堵、鳖臑、圆锥、阳马之类，物形备矣，独未有隙积一术。

2. 若止印三二本，未为简易；若印数十百千本，则极为神速。

3. 其法并上下广折半以为之广，以直高乘之，又以直高为股，以上广减下广，余者半之为勾。勾股求弦，以为斜高。

译文：

1. In mathematics, there are many methods to calculate the volumes of various polyhedrons such as "chumeng," "chutong," "fangchi," "minggu," "qiandu," "bienao," "yuanzhui" and "yangma," however, only the "xiji" method is missing.

2. If only two or three copies are printed, the advantage of this method is not conspicuous. But when tens or hundreds of copies are printed in this way, the speed will be greatly quickened and its convenience and efficiency will be fully revealed.

3. If we take the height of the object as the longer leg of a right triangular while half of the difference between the widths of the top base and the bottom base as the shorter leg of a right triangular, the hypotenuse of the triangular can be calculated out by using the Pythagorean theorem, which is length of the inclined side "qiandu."

赏析： 这三个例子均来自《梦溪笔谈》，此书以其科学技术价值闻名于世，自然科学条目约占全书的三分之一，书中所记述的许多科学成就均达到了当时世界的最高水平。科技条目主要介绍当时中国的科学技术发展，侧重于解释某一技术、表述某一发明的事实，属于信息型文本，所以其英译本也应该呈现出信息型文本特征。换言之，译者可以将文本类型理论作为指导，采取相应的翻译策略。

科技专业术语的音译就是用相同或相近的语言把源语言中的词语表达出来。在汉译英时是用汉语拼音来翻译。《梦溪笔谈》科技条目中的科技术语很特殊，多是古汉语表述的专有名词。如果将其直译为英文，会使外国读者不知所云。所以，一些古语形式的科技术语可以用音译的方式保留其原意。

在第一个例子中，有很多算术中求体积的方法，这些方法就是典型的科技术语，这些科技术语具有中国文化特色，既是专有名词，又是古汉语名词。如果译者把"圆锥"直译为 cone，会让外国读者产生疑惑，cone 是一种圆锥体，怎么会成为一种求体积的方法？所以，这里就采用音译的策略，让读者知道这是中国古代求体积的一种方法。

在《梦溪笔谈》科技条目文本中，有许多非人称主语句。这些非人称主语句能够清晰简明地表达科技条目文本中的相关信息。译者在将这类句子翻译成英文时，多用被动句转换。如第二个例子的译文中连用四个被动语态，体现了科技条目的客观真实性。

英语复合句可以清晰地表达句子中不同成分之间存在的逻辑关系，还可以使句子中的信息呈现出紧凑、严谨的特征。《梦溪笔谈》科技条目文本侧重描述科学事实，讲述科学发明和技术使用的过程，常出现长句。一个长句中会出现多个从句。将这样的句子翻译成英文时，译者应将长句中的句子结构和关系梳理清楚，采用不同的复合句来表达。第三个例子中，原文意思是以直高为股，用其上底面宽与下底面宽的差的一半为勾，用勾股定理求出弦，这就是"堑堵"的斜边长。译文是一个复合句，包含一个条件状语从句、主句和定语从句，条件状语从句中包含前后并列的两个小句，讲述股和勾的定义。虽然译文很长，但是复句的句子结构明了、清晰。

这些翻译策略的使用使得译文文本类型清明，表述得体，突显了文本功能，有助于外国读者了解古代中国的科学技术发明，更好地传播中国优秀传统文化。

翻译练习

1. 目前中国的网民中有 80% 的人经常浏览或偶尔浏览电子商务网站。价格相对较低的图书、音像制品、礼品以及票务服务是如今网上消费的主要热点。网民最常使用的网络服务是电子邮件，平均每位用户拥有 2 至 3 个账号。除了发送电子邮件、浏览网上新闻和搜索信息之外，上网听音乐和看电影也变得更加流行。而网民最反感的问题是网络病毒、弹出式（pop-up）广告和网络攻击。

2. 所谓 5G 网络，是指第五代移动通信网络。5G 技术是全球新一轮科技和产业革命的关键技术，具备高速率、低延时和大容量等特征。在 2019 年的全国两会上，新闻中心首次实现了 5G 信号全覆盖，"部长通道"首次进行了 5G＋VR 直播，全新的技术加持，进一步丰富了媒体的报道方式和手段，也为传递两会盛况注入了新的活力与元素。

3. 港珠澳大桥全长 55 千米，是我国一项不同寻常的工程壮举。大桥将 3 个城市连接起来，是世界上最长的跨海桥梁和隧道系统。大桥将 3 个城市之间的旅行时间从 3 小时缩短到 30 分钟。这座跨度巨大的钢筋混凝土大桥充分证明中国有能力建造创纪录的巨型建筑。它将助推区域一体化，促进经济增长。大桥是中国发展自己的大湾区总体规划的关键。

4. 中国的创新正以前所未有的速度蓬勃发展。中国的大学和研究所正在积极开展创新研究，这些研究覆盖了从大数据到生物化学、从新能源到机器人等各类高科技领域。中国的大学和研究所还与各地的科技园合作，使创新成果商业化。从"嫦娥"探月到"长五"飞天，从"蛟龙"入海到航母入列，中国以一系列创新成就实现了历史性飞跃，创新高原之上耸立起尖端科技高峰。

5. 中国目前拥有世界上最大、最快的高速铁路网，高铁列车的运行速度还将继续提升，更多的城市将修建高铁站。高铁大大缩短了人们出行的时间，准时且基本不受天气或交通管制的影响。高铁还极大地改变了中国人的生活方式。如今，它已经成为很多人商务旅行的首选交通工具。越来越多的人也在假日乘高铁外出旅游。不少年轻人也选择在一个城市工作而在邻近城市居住，每天乘高铁上下班。

6. 随着中国创新的重心从消费互联网转向工业互联网，中国科技生态系统的活力将越来越多地体现在信息技术的工业应用上。中国已成功部署功能强大的"新基础设施"——云计算、5G网络、智慧城市和监控网络等——以促进向工业互联网过渡。在未来五年，中国的技术生态系统将日臻成熟，很有可能实现从消费互联网到工业互联网的转型。具体而言，中国政府将尝试利用人工智能和5G等强大的新兴技术来改造和升级中国城市及制造业、农业、能源和交通等传统产业。

7. 新能源汽车共享项目已在北京、上海等多个城市展开。这种新型的服务有望在未来几年为中国共享经济注入新的活力。要享受共享汽车服务，人们需要先下载客户端，然后注册会员，上传本人身份证和驾照实物照片，经审核通过并交纳押金（deposit）后，即可通过扫描二维码使用租车服务。押金主要用于车辆损坏、违章以及发生行政处罚所产生的费用。租车费用依据实际里程（mileage）和实际用车时间计算。

8. 科技是第一生产力，教育是百年大计。社会的进步、国家的富强、人民生活水平的提高离不开科技和教育。半个多世纪以来，全世界的科技和教育取得长足发展。人类已经被送上太空，探索浩瀚的宇宙；计算机和互联网成为人们获取和处理信息、完成工作及休闲娱乐的重要手段；新的通信和社交渠道改变了人们的交流方式，渗透到日常生活的方方面面。

Unit 8

文学艺术

Unit Goals

In this unit, you are going to
- grasp words and expressions concerning Chinese literature and art;
- acquire knowledge about Chinese literature and art which are the gems of Chinese culture and civilization;
- know how to translate compound sentences from Chinese into English by applying division;
- grasp translation skills of paragraphs on Chinese literature and art.

Related Words and Expressions

《楚辞》 *Chuci*; *Songs of Chu*; *Elegies of Chu*; *Elegies of the South*

《离骚》 *Lisao*; *Sorrow after Departure*; *An Elegy on Encountering Sorrow*

《九歌》 *The Nine Songs*

《九章》 *The Nine Elegies*

《天问》 *Asking Heaven*

《史记》 *Records of the Grand Historian*

《过秦论》 *On the Faults of Qin*

《陌上桑》 *The Mulberry by the Road*

《孔雀东南飞》 *Southeast the Peacock Flies*

《红楼梦》 *A Dream of Red Mansions*; *Dream of the Red Chamber*; *Story of the Stone*

《三国演义》 *Romance of the Three Kingdoms*

《西游记》 *Journey to the West*; *Pilgrimage to the West*

《水浒传》 *The Water Margin*; *Outlaws of the Marsh*; *All Men Are Brothers*; *The Marshes of Mount Liang*

《西厢记》 *Story of the West Chamber*; *The Romance of the West Chamber*

《聊斋志异》 *Strange Stories from a Chinese Studio*; *Strange Tales from a Scholar's Studio*; *Stories of Ghosts and Foxes*

《牡丹亭》 *Peony Pavilion*

《桃花扇》 *Peach Blossom Fan*

诸子散文 proses of the masters

骈文，骈体文 parallel prose

乐府民歌 yuefu folk songs
散曲 the individual aria
杂剧 zaju; variety plays
旧体诗 classical verse
白话诗 verse written in vernacular
唐诗 Tang Poetry
宋词 Song ci; Song ci Poetry; Song Verse
打油诗 doggerel/satirical poetry; ragged verse
民谣 ballad
元杂剧 Yuan dramas
诗仙 Poet Immortal; Immortal of Poems
诗圣 Poet Sage; Sage of Poems
唐宋八大家 the Eight Masters of the Tang and Song
京剧 Beijing Opera; Peking Opera
昆曲 Kunqu; Kunqu Opera
评剧 Pingju Opera
豫剧 Yuju Opera; Henan Opera
黄梅戏 Huangmei Opera
秦腔 Qinqiang Opera; Shaanxi Opera
唱念做打 Singing, Speaking, Acting and Acrobatic Fighting
板眼 musical beat
台步 stage walk
亮相 make a stage pose
翻筋斗 turn a somersault
国画技巧 technique in the traditional Chinese painting
山水画 landscape painting; mountains-and-waters painting
人物画 figure painting
花鸟画 flower-and-bird painting
工笔画 painting done with delicate strokes; detailed brushwork painting; fine brushwork painting; traditional Chinese realistic painting characterized by fine brushwork and close attention to detail
写意画 painting of freehand brushwork
水墨画 ink and wash painting; ink painting
水彩画 watercolor painting
宫廷画 imperial painting
题跋 annotations or remarks on a painting
篆刻 carve in seal script
刻印章 to engrave a seal; to carve a seal

Lead-in Activities

1 **Answer the following questions.**

1) How many famous Tang poems or Song ci poems have you ever memorized? What are your favorite poems?

2) Have you ever read any classical works of Chinese literature? What are they?

3) Have you finished reading four great classical novels of Chinese literature? Which character do you like best? Why?

2 **Listen to a brief introduction to Chinese literature and fill in the blanks with the words you hear.**

Chinese literature has a long and rich tradition. Spanning an uninterrupted history of more than 3,000 years, a considerable number of _____ have created a rich variety of genres as well as a wealth of _____ of high aesthetic value. As an important part of _____, Chinese literature contributes its own _____. In general, _____ can be roughly outlined by the following words by Guo Shaoyu (1893 – 1984), a very famous historian of Chinese literary criticism:

"As far as classical literature is concerned, the Zhou and Qin dynasties were famous for _____; the State of Chu for songs of the south; the Han Dynasty for fu; the Wei, Jin and Six Dynasties for _____; the Tang Dynasty for poetry; the Song Dynasty for ci; the Yuan Dynasty for dramas; and finally the Ming Dynasty for novels and dramas. During the Qing Dynasty, no particular genre _____ other forms. Generally speaking, its literature was all-embracing, with all genres developing _____."

3 **Read the following passage and then do the exercises.**

Traditional Chinese Painting

As an important part of the country's cultural heritage, the traditional Chinese painting is distinguished from Western art in that it is executed on xuan paper (or silk) with the Chinese brush, Chinese ink and mineral and vegetable pigments.

To attain proficiency in this branch of art, it calls for assiduous exercise, a good control of the brush, the knowledge of the qualities of xuan paper and Chinese ink.

Before setting a brush to paper, the painter must conceive a well-composed draft in his mind. He must draw on his imagination and wealth of experience. Once he starts to paint, he will normally have to complete the work in one go. It denies the possibility of any alteration of wrong strokes.

Xuan paper is most suitable for Chinese painting. It is just the right texture to allow the writing brush, wet with Chinese ink and held in a trained hand, to move freely on it, making strokes vary from dark to light, and from opaque to nearly transparent. These strokes soon turn into life-like human figures, plants and flowers, birds, fish and insects.

Many a Chinese painter is at the same time a poet and calligrapher. He will often add a poem on the painting, which invariably carries an impression of his seal. The resulting piece of work is usually an integrated whole of four branches of Chinese art—poetry, calligraphy, painting and seal-engraving.

Chinese paintings can be divided into two major categories: freehand brushwork and fine brushwork. The former is characterized by simple and bold strokes intended to represent the exaggerated likenesses of the objects, while the latter features close attention to details. Employing different techniques, the two schools try to achieve the same end, the creation of beauty.

It is difficult to tell how long the art of painting has existed in China. Five or six thousand years ago, pots were painted in colour with patterns of plants, fabrics, and animals, reflecting various aspects of the life of primitive clan communities. These may be considered the beginnings of Chinese painting.

China entered the slave society about 2000 BCE. Though no paintings of that period have ever come to light, that society witnessed the emergence of a magnificent bronze culture, and bronzes can only be taken as a composite art of painting and sculpture.

In 1949, from a tomb of the Warring States Period (475 – 221 BCE) was unearthed a painting on silk of human figures, dragons and phoenixes. As the earliest work on silk which had been discovered in China, it measures about 30 cm long by 20 cm wide.

From this and other early paintings on silk, it may be easily seen that the ancients were already familiar with the art of the writing or painting brush, for the strokes show vigour or elegance whichever was desired. Paintings of this period are strongly religious or mythological in themes. Paintings on paper appeared much later than those on silk for the simple reason that the invention of silk preceded that of paper.

In 1964, when a tomb in Jin Dynasty (265 – 420) was excavated at Astana in Turpan, Xinjiang, a coloured painting on paper was discovered. It shows, on top, the sun, the moon and the Big Dipper and, below, the owner of the tomb sitting cross-legged on a couch and leisurely holding a fan in his hand. A portrayal in vivid lines of the life of a feudal landowner, measuring 106.5 cm long 47 cm high, it is a world-famous painting on paper of such antiquity in China.

1) Answer the following questions.
   (1) What's the major difference between traditional Chinese painting and western painting?
   (2) Why is xuan paper suitable for Chinese painting?
   (3) What are the characteristics of free hand brushwork and detailed brushwork paintings?
2) Translate the following words or phrases into English.
   植物颜料
   画笔
   写意
   工笔
   人像
3) Translate the following paragraph into English based on what you have learned from the above article:
   中国画可以追溯到六千多年以前的新石器时期(the Neolithic Age)。早期的国画很少用颜色。画家主要依靠线条和着墨来达到想要的效果。例如，郑板桥的竹画就完全依靠墨的浓淡来体现中国画所说的力、神、韵。中国画的另一个特点是集诗、书、画、印为一体。杰出的画家都擅长诗歌和书法。对他们来说，诗是"无形的画"，而画是"有形的诗"。"诗中有画，画中有诗"一直是优秀国画的标准之一。

翻译技巧：分译法（Division）

分译法也叫拆句法或断句法，是指把汉语原文中的一句话译成两句或两句以上的英语句子。汉语的长句之所以要分译，是因为汉语句子结构比较松散，句内逻辑关系往往不是很明显。采用分译法会使译文句子结构清晰、层次分明、易于理解，更符合英语语言的表达习惯。断句时可以从以下几个角度去考虑：

- 按内容层次断句；
- 在主语变化处断句；
- 在总说-分述处或分述-总说处断句；
- 在反问句、感叹句处断句；
- 为了强调某个句子而断句。

例1 原文 这是民国六年的冬天，大风刮得正猛，我因为生计关系，不得不一早在路上走。

译文 It happened during the winter of 1917. A bitter north wind was blowing, but to make a living, I had to be up and out early.

评析 原文全部由逗号连接，但实际上可以分为两层意思。第一层意思交代了故事发生的时间；第二层意思描写当时的天气和人物的活动。两层意思之间有隐含的转折关系：尽管大风很猛，但"我"为了生计不得不一早在路上走。所以英译时可在第一个分句和第二个分句之间断句，而且在翻译第二层意思时需添加转折词 but，将隐含的转折关系体现出来。

例2 原文 现在中年以上的人差不多都有过儿时骑"竹马"的历史，所谓"竹马"其实就是骑在胯下的一根竹竿，儿童的想象力在这根竹竿上得到了充分的张扬。

译文 Almost all middle-aged people have the experience of riding bamboo horses. The toy was actually a bamboo stick, which fed the children's imagination.

评析 原文由三个分句组成，每个分句都有不同的主语。第一个分句的主语是"中年以上的人"，第二个分句的主语是"竹马"，第三个分句的主语是"儿童的想象力"。译者进行英译时在第一个分句和第二个分句之间断句，将第一个分句译为独立的一句话，保留了原来的主语"中年以上的人"，第二个分句和第三个分句合译成主从复合句，将第二个分句的主语"竹马"译为 the toy，把第三个分句处理成了定语从句，实现了句式的紧凑和行文的流畅。

例3 原文 王冕天性聪明，年纪不满二十岁，就把那天文、地理、经史上的大学问，无一不贯通。

译文 Wang Mian had genius. While still in his teens, he mastered the whole field of astronomy, geography, the classics and history.

评析 原文的第一个分句和后面的分句构成总分关系。翻译时，将总说的句子单独成句，可使译文的逻辑关系更清晰。

例4 原文 灾难深重的中华民族，一百年来，其优秀人物奋斗牺牲，摸索救国救民的真理，是可歌可泣的。

	译文	For a hundred years, the finest sons and daughters of the disaster-ridden Chinese nation fought and sacrificed their lives, in quest of the truth that would save the country and the people. This is really moving.
	评析	原文的前四个分句和最后一个分句构成分总关系。因此，译者将最后一个分句与前面的各分句断开，独立成句，使得译文的逻辑关系清晰明了。
例 5	原文	应当承认，每个民族都有它的长处，不然它为什么能存在？为什么能发展？
	译文	It must be admitted that every nation has its strong points. If not, how can it survive? How can it progress?
	评析	原文最后是两个反问句，在一般情况下，反问句需要单独成句，因此原文在翻译时断为三句。
例 6	原文	我们的民族将再也不是一个被人欺辱的民族了，我们已经站起来了。
	译文	Ours will no longer be a nation subject to insult and humiliation. We have stood up.
	评析	为了强调"我们已经站起来了"，译者进行了断句处理，在翻译时拆分为两句。

段落翻译

1.《诗经》

《诗经》是中国第一部诗歌总集，收录了自西周初年至春秋中叶的诗歌作品，共 305 篇。根据音乐性质的不同，这些诗歌被划分为《风》《雅》《颂》三大类。《诗经》中的诗歌多以四言为主，写作手法主要是赋、比、兴。《诗经》中的很多诗歌描述了平民的生活，包括日常活动、欢乐与悲伤、艰苦的劳作和兵役。《诗经》是中国现实主义文学的开端。它的思想和艺术成就对后世文学的发展有着深远的影响。

难点讲解：

1)《诗经》可以采用意译法或直译法译为 The Book of Songs，The Book of Poetry，The Book of Odes 或者 The Classic of Poetry。

2)第一句话为一个长句，第一个分句和后面的分句构成总分关系。翻译时，可将总说的句子单独成句，使译文的逻辑关系更清晰。"自西周初年至春秋中叶"可译为 from the early Western Zhou Dynasty to the middle of the Spring and Autumn Period。

3)"被划分为"可译为 be classified into、be divided into、be categorized into 或 fall into。

4)《风》《雅》《颂》和"赋、比、兴"可以直接采用音译法进行翻译，也可采用音译加注解的方法进行处理，例如：feng (folk songs), ya (odes or court hymns) and song (hymns)。

5)"思想和艺术成就"可译为 ideological and artistic achievements。

6)"对……有着深远的影响"可译为"have profound and lasting influence on/upon …"或"exert far-reaching impact on/upon …"。

2. 屈原

屈原是中国古代伟大的诗人，非常有学问。楚国都城被秦军攻破后，他悲愤绝望，跳进汨罗江自杀。传说屈原投江的日子是中国的农历五月初五，人们为了纪念他，会在这一天赛龙舟、吃粽子（rice dumpling）。赛龙舟是为了把鱼吓走；包粽子喂鱼是为了让鱼不要去吃屈原的尸体。屈原采用楚国方言，利用民间歌谣的形式，创造出一种新的诗歌形式，即楚辞体。他写了许多优秀的诗篇，以《离骚》最为著名。他的作品语言优美,想象奇特。

难点讲解:

1)"非常有学问"可译为 extremely knowledgeable。

2)"被……攻破"可以理解为"被……夺取",即"was seized by…"。

3)"跳进汨罗江自杀"可译为 drowned himself in Miluo River。其中 drown oneself 意为"自溺身亡",即投江自杀。

4)"把鱼吓走"可译为 scare fish away。

5)"以《离骚》最为著名"可译为非限制性定语从句:among which "Li Sao" is the most famous。

6)"他的作品语言优美,想象奇特"可译为"His works are characterized by beautiful language and fancy imagination."其中"be characterized by…"表示"以……为特点,具有……的特征"。

3. 唐诗

唐朝是中国古代诗歌发展的黄金时期。唐代诗歌的发展可以分为四个阶段,即初唐、盛唐、中唐和晚唐。四位杰出诗人王勃、杨炯、骆宾王和卢照邻被称作"初唐四杰"。盛唐时期涌现出了整整一代文学巨匠,代表人物有"诗仙"李白和"诗圣"杜甫。盛唐时期有两大诗派,一派是以王维、孟浩然为代表的"田园诗派",他们描写秀丽恬淡的自然美景和淳朴的乡村生活。另一派是以高适、岑参为代表的"边塞诗派",他们在诗中描写的主题是戍卫边疆士兵的雄心壮志、艰辛的生活和乡愁。中唐和晚唐是王朝衰落时期,中央政权发展为分裂的地方统治者。这一时期的代表人物是白居易。他的许多诗作深刻地反映了下层阶级的苦难,并揭露了贵族的腐败。

难点讲解:

1)"初唐""盛唐""中唐"和"晚唐"可译为 Early Tang、High Tang、Middle Tang 和 Late Tang,属于专有名词,书写时注意英文字母的大小写。

2)"初唐四杰"可译为 Four Literary Eminence of the Early Tang。

3)"盛唐时期涌现出了整整一代文学巨匠,代表人物有'诗仙'李白和'诗圣'杜甫。"此句由两个分句组成,分别有不同的主语,因此可采用分译法将其翻译为两个独立的句子。"诗仙"可译为 Poet Immortal,"诗圣"可译为 Poet Sage。

4)"盛唐时期有两大诗派,一派是以王维、孟浩然为代表的'田园诗派',他们描写秀丽恬淡的自然美景和淳朴的乡村生活。"此句由三个分句构成,有三个不同的内容层次,因此可以采用分译法翻译为三个独立的句子。"田园诗派"可译为 the Landscape and Pastoral Poets Group。

5)"另一派是以高适、岑参为代表的'边塞诗派',他们在诗中描写的主题是戍卫边疆士兵的雄心壮志、艰辛的生活和乡愁。"此句由两个分句构成,有两个不同的内容层次,因此可以采用分译法翻译为两个独立的句子。"边塞诗派"可译为 the Borders and Frontier Fortress Poets Group。

4. 宋词

两宋时期,中国文学的主要形式是词。词在宋朝达到全盛时期。它起源于唐朝,是和着音乐演唱的歌词,经由民间歌女和坊间乐师表演而普及。与五言律诗和七言律诗不同,宋词每一行的字数并不相等。按照长短,宋词可分为三类:58字以内为小令,59至90字为中调,超过90字为长调。根据内容和风格的不同,宋词可分为婉约派和豪放派两大流派。婉约派词作浪漫、悦耳,结构简洁,风格清新。豪放派词作以题材广泛、音韵自由、文笔奔放为特点。婉约派词人以柳永、李清照为代表,豪放派词人则以苏轼、辛弃疾为代表。

难点讲解:

1)第一句和第二句根据内容逻辑关系可以合译为一句。"达到全盛时期"可译为 reach its heyday

或 reach the peak。

2）原文第三句话中"民间"和"坊间"表达的意义相同，可译为 among the common people。

3）原文包括许多文学术语，应注意这些术语的翻译。例如："五言律诗和七言律诗"可以合译为 the regulated verse in five or seven-character lines；也可以分别将"五言律诗"译为 penta-syllabic regulated verse 或者 five-character regulated verse，"七言律诗"译为 heptasyllabic regulated verse 或者 seven-character regulated verse。"小令"译为 Short Lyrics，"中调"译为 Medium Tune，"长调"译为 Long Tune。

4）"婉约派"可译为 the school of lyricism 或者 Soft and Tuneful School，"豪放派"可译为 the school of heroism 或者 Powerful and Free School。

5）"以……为特点"可用 be characterized by、feature 或 be characteristic of 来表达。

5.《红楼梦》

明清时期，中国古典小说达到了顶峰。《红楼梦》无疑是其中最具代表性的小说之一。曹雪芹基于自己痛苦的个人经历，讲述了贾宝玉和林黛玉之间悲剧性的爱情故事。书中有大约三十个主要人物和四百多个次要人物，每个人物都刻画得栩栩如生，具有鲜明的个性。小说详尽地描述了四个贵族世家兴衰的历程，反映了封建社会隐藏的种种危机和错综复杂的社会冲突。《红楼梦》融合了现实主义和浪漫主义色彩，具有很强的艺术感染力。

难点讲解：

1）《红楼梦》有许多外语译本，其中杨宪益、戴乃迭（Gladys Yang）夫妇的 *The Dream of Red Mansions* 和大卫·霍克斯（David Hawkes）与约翰·敏福德（John Minford）合译的 *The Story of the Stone* 影响广泛。

2）翻译"曹雪芹基于自己痛苦的个人经历，讲述了贾宝玉和林黛玉之间悲剧性的爱情故事"一句时可以将第一个分句处理为分词短语作伴随状语，第二个分句在翻译时添加主语"曹雪芹"。

3）"详尽地描述"可译为 elaborate on、describe in detail 或 narrate with detail。

4）"贵族世家"可译为 noble families 或 aristocratic families。

5）"反映了"可译为 mirror 或 reflect。

6.《水浒传》

《水浒传》是中国文学四大经典小说之一。施耐庵创作的这部小说讲述了北宋末年宋江及其伙伴反抗封建帝王的故事，数百年来一直深受中国读者的喜爱。毫不夸张地说，几乎每个中国人都熟悉小说中的一些主要人物。这部小说中的精彩故事在茶馆、戏剧舞台、广播电视、电影屏幕和无数家庭中反复讲述。事实上，这部小说的影响已经远远超出国界。越来越多的外国读者被这部小说里生动感人、趣味盎然的故事所打动。直到今天，《水浒传》仍然是众多电影、电视节目和视频游戏的灵感源泉。

难点讲解：

1）《水浒传》的英译本有多种版本，其中影响较大的有四个译本：一是赛珍珠（Pearl S. Buck）翻译的 *All Men Are Brothers*（1933），取"四海之内皆兄弟"之意，表明了梁山好汉之间的兄弟情谊；二是英国人杰克逊（J. H. Jackson）翻译的 *The Water Margin*（1937）；三是沙博礼（Sydney Shapiro）的译本 *Outlaws of the Marsh*（1981）；四是英国汉学家登特·杨父子（John Dent-Young 和 Alex Dent-Young）的译本 *The Marshes of Mount Liang*（1994–2002）。

2)第二句话为一个长句，可采用分译法将其译为两句。其中"封建帝王"可译为 the feudal emperor。

3)"毫不夸张地说"是习惯用语，可译为"It's no exaggeration to say that…"。这里列出了一些汉语中常用的习惯用语的翻译：

可以有把握地说……	It may be safely said that…
大家普遍认为……	It is generally considered that…
专家们普遍认为……	It is generally agreed among experts that…
据说……	It is said that…
据报道……	It is reported that…
据发现……	It is found that…
众所周知……	It is well-known that…
必须承认……	It must be admitted that…
必须指出……	It must be pointed out that…
有人宣称……	It is claimed that…
有人主张……	It is asserted that…
有人相信……	It is believed that…

4)在翻译"这部小说中的精彩故事在茶馆、戏剧舞台、广播电视、电影屏幕和无数家庭中反复讲述"这句话时，可使用被动语态，另外也要注意正确使用介词。

5)"远远超出了国界"可译为 go far beyond the national borders 或者 be far beyond the national boundary。

7.《西游记》

《西游记》是明代吴承恩撰写的一部优秀的神话小说。它可能是中国文学四大经典小说中最有影响力的一部，在海内外广为人知。这部小说描写了唐朝著名僧侣玄奘在三位弟子的陪同下穿越中国西部地区以及中亚和南亚的几个国家，经历八十一难，战胜各种各样的妖魔鬼怪，最终抵达印度取到佛经(Buddhist scripture)的艰难历程。虽然故事的主题基于佛教，但这部小说加入了大量的中国民间故事和神话的元素，创造了各种栩栩如生的人物和动物形象。1986年，这部小说被改编为电视剧，受到广大观众的喜爱。

难点讲解：

1)第一句中的定语"是明代吴承恩撰写的"较长，翻译时可将其处理为后置定语，用过去分词短语表被动，译为 written by Wu Cheng'en in the Ming Dynasty。

2)第三句话较长，可采用分译法将其译为两句。在翻译时要先确定句子的主干部分，弄清楚句子间的逻辑关系。很显然，此句的主干为"这部小说描写了……的艰难历程"，其中出现了"描写""穿越""经历""战胜""抵达"和"取到"等多个动词。在翻译时，注意采用合理的方式处理这些动词。

3)"栩栩如生"可译为 vivid and lifelike 或者 true to life。

4)"受到广大观众的喜爱"含有被动意义，但在翻译时可以处理为主动形式，译为 become popular among the large number of audiences 或者 gain popularity among massive audiences。

8.《三国演义》

罗贯中的《三国演义》是中国古代第一部章回历史小说。该小说写于14世纪，描写的是从东汉末年到西晋初年之间的历史风云，尤其是魏、蜀、吴三国的兴衰以及这一时期复杂的政治、军事和外交斗争。《三国演义》的基本表现手法是写实主义，但情节安排和对历史人物的刻画充满了浪漫主义色彩。这部小说用清晰生动的语言写成。小说中的对话在揭示人物性格方面发挥了重要作用。刘备被描绘成一个奉行仁政的理想统治者，诸葛亮被描绘成一位杰出的政治家和一位高瞻远瞩的战略家，张飞的勇敢和直率、关羽的忠诚、曹操的狡猾也被巧妙地刻画出来。《三国演义》是一部公认的文学杰作。自出版以来，这部小说吸引着一代又一代读者，对中国文化产生了广泛而持久的影响。

难点讲解：

1)"章回小说"可译为 chapter-by-chapter novel 或者 chapter-styled novel。

2)"这部小说用清晰生动的语言写成"以及后文"《三国演义》是一部公认的文学杰作"在形式上是主动的，但意义却是被动的，因此在翻译这两个句子时宜使用英语中的被动结构。其中"清晰生动的语言"可译为 clear, concise and vivid language。

3)第五句很长，各分句是并列关系，在翻译时可采用分译法将它们译为三句。其中"奉行仁政的理想统治者"可处理为定语从句形式，译为 an ideal ruler who adheres to benevolent policies，"一位高瞻远瞩的战略家"同样可以处理为定语从句形式，译为 a strategist whose foresight is god-like、a strategist who shows great foresight 或者 a strategist who can stand high and see far。

9. 京剧

2010年11月，京剧被列入人类非物质文化遗产代表作名录。作为中国三大国粹之一，京剧来源于18世纪晚期安徽和湖北的当地剧种。京剧高雅且表现力强，因而也很受欢迎。京剧的表演形式很有特色，它既不同于歌剧，又不同于舞剧，更不同于话剧，而是一种唱、念、做、打并重的艺术。京剧演员分生、旦、净、丑四个行当。京剧还赢得了许多外国戏迷的青睐，被视为东方艺术的杰出代表。京剧同西方歌剧的相似之处在于它们都有唱段和道白，有悲剧也有喜剧，但它们毕竟是很不一样的戏剧。京剧大量采用象征手法，对时空变化的表现极其自由。京剧的另一特色是脸谱，京剧脸谱象征着人物的性格，不同的颜色表示不同的性格。例如，黑色代表正直，白色表示背叛和狡诈，红色则常用来表示忠诚。

难点讲解：

1)三大国粹可译为 three quintessential forms of Chinese culture。中国三大国粹为京剧、中医和国画。

2)"京剧同西方歌剧的相似之处在于它们都有唱段和道白，有悲剧也有喜剧，但它们毕竟是很不一样的戏剧。"此句的后半句语意有转折，因此在翻译时可在转折处断句，采取分译的方法译为两句。"京剧同西方歌剧的相似之处在于……"可译为"The similarity between Beijing Opera and western opera lies in the fact that…"或者"Beijing Opera is similar to Western opera in that…"，其中"唱段和道白"可译为 arias and dialogues。

3)"京剧的另一特色是脸谱，京剧脸谱象征着人物的性格，不同的颜色表示不同的性格。"这句话由三个分句组成，每个分句有不同的主语。第一个分句的主语是"京剧的另一特色"，第二个分句的主语是"京剧脸谱"，第三个分句的主语是"不同的颜色"。翻译时可在第二个分句和第三个分句之间断句，第一个分句和第二个分句合译成一句，第二个分句处理为定语从句，第三个分句单译为一句话。

4)"背叛和狡诈"可译为 treachery and cunning。

10. 文艺需要人民

我国久传不息的名篇佳作都充满着对人民命运的悲悯、对人民悲欢的关切，以精湛的艺术彰显了深厚的人民情怀。《古诗源》收集的反映远古狩猎活动的《弹歌》，《诗经》中反映农夫艰辛劳作的《七月》、反映士兵征战生活的《采薇》、反映青年爱情生活的《关雎》，探索宇宙奥秘的《天问》，反映游牧生活的《敕勒歌》，歌颂女性英姿的《木兰诗》等，都是从人民生活中产生的。屈原的"长太息以掩涕兮，哀民生之多艰"，杜甫的"安得广厦千万间，大庇天下寒士俱欢颜"、"朱门酒肉臭，路有冻死骨"，李绅的"谁知盘中餐，粒粒皆辛苦"，郑板桥的"些小吾曹州县吏，一枝一叶总关情"，等等，也都是深刻反映人民心声的作品和佳句。世界上最早的文学作品《吉尔伽美什》史诗，反映了两河流域上古人民探求自然规律和生死奥秘的心境和情感。《荷马史诗》赞美了人民勇敢、正义、无私、勤劳等品质。《神曲》、《十日谈》、《巨人传》等作品的主要内容是反对中世纪的禁欲主义、蒙昧主义，反映人民对精神解放的热切期待。因此，文艺只有植根现实生活、紧跟时代潮流，才能发展繁荣；只有顺应人民意愿、反映人民关切，才能充满活力。

难点讲解：

1) 此段节选自习近平于2014年10月15日在文艺工作座谈会上的讲话，此段的翻译难点在于讲话中引用了大量的中外名篇佳作，这些作品的英文翻译对照如下：

《古诗源》	Origin of Ancient Poet	《敕勒歌》	Song of the Chile
《弹歌》	The Pellet Song	《木兰诗》	The Ballad of Mulan
《诗经》	The Book of Songs	《吉尔伽美什》	Epic of Gilgamesh
《采薇》	Gathering Thorn-ferns	《荷马史诗》	The Epics of Homer
《关雎》	Crying Ospreys	《神曲》	The Divine Comedy
《天问》	Asking Heaven	《十日谈》	Decameron
《巨人传》	The Life of Gargantua and Panagruel		

2) 原文中第二句话非常长，提到了许多作品，因为该句的主语很长，为避免句子头重脚轻，英译时可采用分译法进行处理，将"都是从人民生活中产生的"单译为一句话，同时添加主语。由于这个长句的主语都是带有定语的名词，因此可将它们处理为五句有主语、谓语和宾语的句子，并且英译完成后依然保持并列关系。

3) 第三句话的主语也非常长，为避免句子头重脚轻，也可采用分译法进行处理。原文中分别引用了屈原、杜甫、李绅和郑板桥的诗句，这些诗句的翻译对照如下：

长太息以掩涕兮，哀民生之多艰　I sigh and cry, how hard life is for my countryman

安得广厦千万间，大庇天下寒士俱欢颜　Where to find decent homes? To shelter all poor scholars on earth and bring a smile to their face

朱门酒肉臭，路有冻死骨　The rich wine and dine, the poor starve and die

谁知盘中餐，粒粒皆辛苦　Every grain on the plate comes from hard labor

些小吾曹州县吏，一枝一叶总关情　For petty country officials like us, every concern of the people weighs in our heart

4) "两河流域"指的是底格里斯河和幼发拉底河流域，译为 the Tigris-Euphrates area。

5) "中世纪的禁欲主义、蒙昧主义"译为 medieval asceticism and obscurantism。

6) "植根现实生活"译为 be firmly grounded in reality。

拓展阅读

Reading A

Chinese Poetry: The Birth of Literature

Poetry is the earliest form of Chinese literature that originated from folk songs before the written Chinese language even existed. The earliest anthology of ancient poems, *Shi Jing*（*The*

Book of Poetry), which is prized by scholars for its literary and historic significance, dates back to between the 11th and 6th century BCE. Conventionally, Chinese poetry is divided into four classes—shi or poetry, ci, ge or songs, and fu.

History of Poetic Culture

Rhyming has always been an essential part of Chinese poetry. The shi verse form (poetry) evolved from *Shi Jing*—a collection of poems written in four-word verses. Instead of glorifying gods and heroes as was the case in early poems of other cultures, these poems expressed the daily lives of the peasants: their sorrows and joys, occupations and festivities. Characterized by simplicity of language and emotion, they marked the beginning of Chinese poetry.

Qu Yuan, a poet of the Chu State, wrote *Elegies of Chu*, pioneering a unique form of classical Chinese poetry, both romantic and mythological. Next came yuefu folk songs, a general term for folk songs and ballads of the Han Dynasty (206BCE – 220CE).

The heyday of poetry, like so many other Chinese art forms, came in the Tang Dynasty (618 – 907)—a period of general peace and prosperity. More than 50,000 poems written by 2,200 poets during these 300 years are still known today. Li Bai (701 – 762), the Poet Immortal, and Du Fu (712 – 770), the Poet Sage, are the twin pinnacles of Chinese poetry.

In the Song Dynasty (960 – 1279), while poetry in five and seven-character lines and other classical forms was generally regarded as somewhat inferior, ci flourished. Sorrows of widows and divorced women or others who have been separated from their husbands comprised the main theme of ci in its initial stages of development. In time, themes became increasingly diverse along with changes in society.

In modern Chinese arts, politics and patriotic sentiment inevitably took precedence. The May 4th Movement of 1919 called on science and democracy to give birth to "new poetry"—an entirely new genre that broke out of the rigid form, language and meter of classical poetry. *The Goddess* by Guo Moruo (1892—1987)—an ardent call for social reform and rebellion against the decadent, old regime—is identified as the beginning of the movement from classical poetry to new poetry. By the early 1940s a whole generation of powerful poets had emerged.

Classification

Gushi (old poetry) is arranged in five, six or seven-syllable lines, or long and short verses. As a rule, the rhymes can be changed in almost any place—from even tone to inflected tones, or vice versa. Much more liberty is permitted with the tonal order within a line, which is decided by individual temperament.

Lüshi (regulated verse) appeared in the Tang Dynasty and must contain two or more of so-called parallel couplets. In addition to parallelism in content there is also a phonetic parallelism or a parallelism of tones. Even tones are combined with inflected ones, and vice versa.

Jueju (curtailed verse) only has four lines of five or seven characters, each with the least word's way and a high tone.

The Tang Dynasty produced a new poetic form called ci that was written to music with strict tonal patterns and rhyme schemes in fixed numbers of lines and characters. Ci can be defined as "a song without a tune." Ci, which reached its greatest popularity in the Song Dynasty, is an intricate tonal pattern to which the writer sets characters.

The third class of poetic literature is ge (songs and poems written to folk melodies) which differs from poetry only in its musical or melodic origin. The difference between ge and ci is insignificant: instrumental music always accompanies ci, but ge was mostly vocal.

The fu verse form is a prose poem or descriptive poem. Often it is simply a cluster of parallel couplets of varying lengths.

Exercises

1 **Match the English expressions in Column A with the Chinese translations in Column B.**

Column A		Column B	
1	four-word verses	a	《楚辞》
2	simplicity of language	b	诗歌的全盛时期
3	*Elegies of Chu*	c	押韵格式，韵格
4	heyday of poetry	d	五言和七言
5	five and seven-character lines	e	朴素的语言
6	even tones	f	语音平行
7	phonetic parallelism	g	四字诗
8	rhyme schemes	h	散文诗
9	prose poem	i	平声
10	tonal pattern	j	声调模式，平仄

2 **Answer the following questions.**

1) Why was poetry so popular in Tang Dynasty?

2) What are the main themes of Song ci poetry in its initial stages of development?

Reading B

The Chinese Novel

—Nobel Lecture (an excerpt), December 12, 1938

By Pearl S. Buck

The Chinese say: "The young should not read *Shui Hu* and the old should not read *San Kuo*." This is because the young might be charmed into being robbers and the old might be led into deeds too vigorous for their years. For if *Shui Hu Chuan* is the great social document of Chinese life, *San Kuo* is the document of wars and statesmanship, and in its turn *Hung Lou Meng* is the document of family life and human love.

The history of the *San Kuo* or *Three Kingdoms* shows the same architectural structure and the same doubtful authorship as *Shui Hu*. The story begins with three friends swearing eternal brotherhood in the Han Dynasty and ends ninety-seven years later in the succeeding period of the Six Dynasties. It is a novel rewritten in its final form by a man named Lo Kuan Chung, thought to be a pupil of Shih Nai'an, and one who perhaps even shared with Shih Nai'an in the writing, too, of *Shui Hu Chuan*. But this is a Chinese Bacon-and-Shakespeare controversy which has no end.

Lo Kuan Chung was born in the late Yuan Dynasty and lived on into the Ming. He wrote many dramas, but he is more famous for his novels, of which *San Kuo* is easily the best. The version of this novel now most commonly used in China is the one revised in the time of K'ang Hsi by Mao Chenkan（毛宗岗）, who revised as well as criticized the book. He changed, added and omitted material, as for example when he added the story of Suan Fu Ren（孙夫人）, the wife of one of the chief characters. He altered even the style. If *Shui Hu Chuan* has importance today as a novel of the people in their struggle for liberty, *San Kuo* has importance because it gives in such detail the science and art of war as the Chinese conceive it, so differently, too, from our own. The guerillas, who are today China's most effective fighting units against Japan, are peasants who know *San Kuo* by heart, if not from their own reading, at least from hours spent in the idleness of winter days or long summer evenings when they sat listening to the storytellers describe how the warriors of the Three Kingdoms fought their battles. It is these ancient tactics of war which the guerillas trust today. What a warrior must be and how he must attack and retreat, how retreat when the enemy advances, how advance when the enemy retreats—all this had its source in this novel, so well-known to every common man and boy of China.

Hung Lou Meng, or *The Dream of the Red Chamber*, the latest and most modern of these three greatest of Chinese novels, was written originally as an autobiographical novel by Ts'ao Hsüeh Ching, an official highly in favor during the Manchu regime and indeed considered by the Manchus as one of themselves. There were then eight military groups among the Manchus, and Ts'ao Hsüeh Ching belonged to them all. He never finished his novel, and the last forty chapters were added by another man, probably named Kao O（高鹗）. The thesis that Ts'ao Hsüeh Ching was telling the story of his own life has been in modern times elaborated by Hu Shih（胡适）, and in earlier times by Yuan Mei（袁枚）. Be this as it may, the original title of the book was *Shih T'ou Chi*, and it came out of Peking about 1765 of the Western era, and in five or six years, an incredibly short time in China, it was famous everywhere. Printing was still expensive when it appeared, and the book became known by the method that is called in China, "You-lend-me-a-book-and-I-lend-you-a-book."

The story is simple in its theme but complex in implication, in character study and in its portrayal of human emotions. It is almost a pathological study, this story of a great house, once wealthy and high in imperial favor, so that indeed one of its members was an imperial concubine. But the great days are over when the book begins. The family is already declining. Its wealth is being dissipated and the last and only son, Chia Pao Yü, is being corrupted by the decadent influences within his own home, although the fact that he was a youth of exceptional quality at birth is established by the symbolism of a piece of jade found in his mouth. The preface begins, "Heaven was once broken and when it was mended, a bit was left unused, and this became the famous jade of Chia Pao Yü." Thus does the interest in the supernatural persist in the Chinese people; it persists even today as a part of Chinese life.

This novel seized hold of the people primarily because it portrayed the problems of their own family system, the absolute power of women in the home, the too great power of the matriarchy, the grandmother, the mother, and even the bondmaids, so often young and beautiful and fatally dependent, who became too frequently the playthings of the sons of the house and ruined them and were ruined by them. Women reigned supreme in the Chinese house, and because they were wholly confined in its walls and often illiterate, they ruled to the detriment of all. They served men and children and protected them from hardships and strife to an unnecessary degree. Such one was Chia Pao Yü, and we follow him to his tragic end in *Hung Lou Meng*.

　　I cannot tell you to what lengths of allegory scholars went to explain away this novel when they found that again even the emperor was reading it and that its influence was so great everywhere among the people. I do not doubt that they were probably reading it themselves in secret. A great many popular jokes in China have to do with scholars reading novels privately and publicly pretending never to have heard of them. At any rate, scholars wrote treatises to prove that *Hung Lou Meng* was not a novel but a political allegory depicting the decline of China under the foreign rule of the Manchus, the word Red in the title signifying Manchu, and Ling Tai Yü, the young girl who dies, although she was the one destined to marry Pao Yü, signifying China, and Pao Ts'ai, her successful rival, who secures the jade in her place, standing for the foreigner, and so forth. The very name *Chia* signified, they said, falseness. But this was a farfetched explanation of what was written as a novel and stands as a novel and as such a powerful delineation, in the characteristic Chinese mixture of realism and romance, of a proud and powerful family in decline. Crowded with men and women of the several generations accustomed to living under one roof in China, it stands alone as an intimate description of that life.

　　...

　　But I can mention only a small fraction of the hundreds of novels which delight the common people of China. And if those people knew of what I was speaking to you today, they would after all say "tell of the great three, and let us stand or fall by *Shui Hu Chuan* and *San Kuo* and *Hung Lou Meng*." In these three novels are the lives which the Chinese people lead and have long led, here are the songs they sing and the things at which they laugh and the things which they love to do. Into these novels they have put the generations of their being and to refresh that being they return to these novels again and again, and out of them they have made new songs and plays and other novels. Some of them have come to be almost as famous as the great originals, as for example *Ching P'ing Mei*, that classic of romantic physical love, taken from a single incident in *Shui Hu Chuan*.

Exercises

 Answer the following questions.

　　1) Why do Chinese say "The young should not read *Shui Hu* and the old should not read *San Kuo*"? To what extent do you agree or disagree, and why?

　　2) According to Pearl S. Buck, the tragic ending in *The Dream of the Red Chamber* is partially attributed to too great power of the women in the Chinese house. Do you agree with her? What do you think is the major reason that led to the decline of the Jia Family?

Translate the following sentences into English.

　　1)《三国演义》中对战争科学和艺术的详细描写使古代战争策略在中国为许多人所熟知。

　　2)《红楼梦》通常被称为《石头记》，前八十回由曹雪芹所写，高鹗续写了后四十回。

　　3) 曹雪芹以自己对人生的理解为基础，以严肃的思想和高超的写作技艺，创作了《红楼梦》。《红楼梦》被誉为中国古典小说的巅峰之作。

4）曹雪芹如果没有对当时的社会生活进行全景式的观察和显微镜式的剖析，就不可能完成《红楼梦》这部百科全书式巨著的写作。

翻译佳作赏析

望庐山瀑布

李白

日照香炉生紫烟，遥看瀑布挂前川。
飞流直下三千尺，疑是银河落九天。

译文：

Cataract on Mount Lu

By Li Bai

The sunlit Censer peak exhales a wreath of cloud,
Like an upended stream the cataract sounds loud.
Its torrent dashes down three thousand feet from high,
As if the Silver River fell from azure sky.

（许渊冲 译）

赏析：

这首风景诗是唐代诗人李白 50 岁左右隐居庐山时所写。诗人通过香炉、紫烟、瀑布、银河意象的描写将瀑布的动与静、虚与实生动地展现出来，形象地描绘了庐山瀑布雄奇壮丽的景色。

原诗第一句中一个"生"字赋予静止的香炉峰以灵性，同样，许渊冲的译文采用 exhale（"散发出""呼出"）也将香炉峰人格化。用 a wreath of cloud 形容"紫烟"，其中 wreath 为名词，意为"花环"，有"缭绕"及"色彩绚丽"的生动意味。

原诗第二句中"挂"字将瀑布飞流而下的动态意象转化为静态意象，遥望中的瀑布像一条巨大的白练从悬崖直挂到前面的河流上，而许渊冲使用动词 upended（"被倒置"）来形容远望中的瀑布像"倒挂"的飞流，使人惊叹大自然的神奇力量。此外许渊冲还添加了 sound loud 这一听觉意象，使读者身临其境，仿佛听到了轰然巨响，译出了诗词的弦外之音和意境之美。

原诗第三句中一个"飞"字将瀑布凌空飞泻的气势描绘了出来，译作中 dash down 既译出了瀑布的走向，又传达出瀑布凌空而落的气势，与原诗中"飞流直下"的意象具有同等的效果。

诗人发挥想象，在最后一句中把瀑布想象成自九天而下的"银河"，一个"疑"字用得空灵活泼，引人遐想，增添了瀑布的神奇色彩。许渊冲将"银河"直译为 the Silver River，用 fell 译"落"的意象，生动地突出了庐山瀑布的磅礴气势，同时使用虚拟语气，把现实中的瀑布和想象中的银河自然地联系起来。总之，许渊冲的译文很好地将原诗的韵味传达了出来。

翻译练习

1. 中国人在日常生活中经常要使用印章。印章最初是一种政治权力的象征。在古代，印章被用来验证签名，也用于任免官吏的文件；官府文告和公文都要加盖公章。后来，文人和士大夫也视印章为其社会地位的佐证。印章有雕琢、浇铸和陶土烧制三种主要制作方法。材料有金、银、铜、铁、玉、石、骨、木、瓷等。三千多年来，随着汉字的发展演变，印章上的字体也在不断演变，反映出汉字各个时代的不同特征。还有人把书法、绘画、图章三种艺术结合于一体。

2. 传统的中国画不是模仿自然的工具，而是表达情感、彰显气质的艺术形式。绘画中的意象就像书法中的文字一样，是一种概括抽象的象征符号，与之相伴的是传统的程式表现技巧。古代的大师们创造了独特的意象及程式，风格迥异，生机勃勃。后来许多画家惯于模仿古人的程式，所作之画千人一面。现代的艺术家从原始形式中找寻自我，建立现代的意象和格局，却一直不曾背离高雅的传统。

3. 李白是中国文学史上伟大的浪漫主义诗人，被人称为"诗仙"。他生活在社会繁荣稳定的盛唐时期。李白有远大的政治抱负，但由于他不愿意迎合权贵，屡遭排挤。但是李白在诗歌创作上获得了巨大的成就。他的诗歌内容广泛，想象丰富，具有强烈的艺术魅力，对后世影响极深。他以叛逆的思想和豪放的风格，展现了盛唐时代乐观的精神以及不满封建秩序的潜在力量。李白的诗歌在一定程度上是浪漫主义和现实主义的结合，他的诗篇留存至今的有一千多首，其中有许多脍炙人口的诗篇被译为各种语言在世界各地传诵。

4. 杜甫是中国文学史上伟大的现实主义诗人，被誉为"诗圣"。杜甫出生在一个传统的崇尚儒家价值观的家庭，这使他充满了强烈的使命感，努力为国家服务。同时他也深切担忧着国家和人民的命运。他的诗是对安史之乱前后生活的真实记录，因此被称为"诗史"。他的"三吏""三别"以强烈的抒情笔触描绘了重大的历史事件，深得民心。杜甫的律诗，尤其是他的七言律诗，广受好评。他善于运用技巧来营造一种自然、轻松的印象。杜甫在充分吸收当代和历代诗歌特点的同时，也在盛唐和中唐诗歌之间架起了一座桥梁。

5. 元曲分为两类——杂剧和散曲，但元杂剧也可以单独称为"元曲"。杂剧是有音乐背景的诗体戏剧，剧本与舞台表演相结合。散曲是以民间音乐曲调为蓝本创作的诗歌，因此不需要舞台。在这两种形式中，杂剧是最早繁荣起来的。杂剧经历了两个发展阶段：一是元初，这一时期杂剧主要流行于中国北方。关汉卿以其无与伦比的角色创造和朴素的语言使元曲走向成熟。《窦娥冤》是他的杰作。其他著名的北方杂剧作家还包括：王实甫，以《西厢记》而闻名；白朴，以《梧桐雨》而闻名；马致远，以《汉宫秋》而闻名。二是元代中后期，中国南方取代北方成为杂剧创作的中心。受南方文化的影响，杂剧的主题主要是传奇故事和神仙故事。南方杂剧创作所使用的语言精练而优雅，与北方截然不同。郑光祖是当时南方著名的杂剧作家，以《倩女离魂》而出名。

6. 昆曲是"中国戏曲之母"。昆曲又称昆山腔、昆腔，起源于长江三角洲下游的苏州和昆山一带，它是中国最古老的戏曲形式之一。元代后期，南戏中的元素与昆山方言以及地方音乐形式相融合。明代以后，杂剧衰落，而南戏吸收了杂剧的音乐形式，开始被称为昆曲。京剧、川剧、越剧和黄梅戏都是由昆曲发展而来的。最著名的昆曲作家是明朝的汤显祖(1550—1616)。他的代表作有《牡丹亭》《邯郸记》《南柯记》和《紫钗记》。这四部剧被称为"临川四梦"，在中国流行至今。2001年5月，联合国教科文组织将昆曲列为"人类口头和非物质遗产代表作"。

7. 秦腔是中国戏曲中最具影响力的剧种之一，历史悠久。目前，秦腔在陕西、甘肃、宁夏、青海、新疆等西北地区的省份和自治区最为流行。秦腔起源于今天的陕西、甘肃一带，是在宋、金、元时期的铙鼓杂剧(Cymbals Drama)和陕西、甘肃民歌的基础上发展起来的。在清朝，秦腔在全国各地广为流传，对各种戏曲产生了巨大的影响。京剧就吸收了秦腔的部分剧目(repertoire)、曲调和表演方法。秦腔的唱腔激越高亢、节奏鲜明。所用的乐器以板胡为主，辅以笛子、京胡、月琴、唢呐等。艺人们用梆子以及锣、鼓、铙钹之类的打击乐器打拍子。秦腔演员不仅注重唱功，也重视表演技巧，如趟马、担水、担柴、喷火等。

8. 鲁迅，原名周树人，是著名的作家、思想家、革命家、教育家，中国现代文学的创始人之一。鲁迅在中国现代文学中犹如一座大山，在思想文化领域有着十分重要的地位和影响。他是五四新文化运动中的领军人物之一，对中国文学和社会思想文化的发展产生了深远的影响。1918年，鲁迅出版了中国现代文学史上第一部白话文小说《狂人日记》，这部小说的出版具有开创性意义。鲁迅的小说有两个主题，一是观察和反思中国农民的思想和命运以达到改造国民性的目的，如《阿Q正传》《祝福》等小说；另一个是思考和揭示变革时期知识分子的困境和性格，如《孔乙己》《伤逝》等小说。鲁迅的散文在反映现实时尖锐、深刻而具有批判性。他希望能用文学艺术来推动历史的发展。

9. 茅盾，原名沈德鸿，是现代著名作家、五四运动先驱者之一。茅盾倡导"文学为生活"的艺术观，强调文学要反映和服务于人民的生活，文学创作要广泛描写中国社会现象，作家要担负起动员群众、赋予群众以力量的重任。作为中国现代文学史上伟大的现实主义者，茅盾喜欢用大场景的描写来反映时代的全貌和发展。他成功地塑造了许多在特殊环境中的独特人物，开创了城市题材小说的先河。茅盾文学奖就是以他的名字来命名的。茅盾文学奖是中国小说领域的最高奖项，每四年评选一次。

10. 还有，国际社会对中国的关注度越来越高，他们想了解中国，想知道中国人的世界观、人生观、价值观，想知道中国人对自然、对世界、对历史、对未来的看法，想知道中国人的喜怒哀乐，想知道中国历史传承、风俗习惯、民族特性，等等。这些光靠正规的新闻发布、官方介绍是远远不够的，靠外国民众来中国亲自了解、亲身感受是很有限的。而文艺是最好的交流方式，在这方面可以发挥不可替代的作用，一部小说，一篇散文，一首诗，一幅画，一张照片，一部电影，一部电视剧，一曲音乐，都能给外国人了解中国提供一个独特的视角，都能以各自的魅力去吸引人、感染人、打动人。京剧、民乐、书法、国画等都是我国文化瑰宝，都是外国人了解中国的重要途径。文艺工作者要讲好中国故事、传播好中国声音、阐发中国精神、展现中国风貌，让外国民众通过欣赏中国作家艺术家的作品来深化对中国的认识、增进对中国的了解。要向世界宣传推介我国优秀文化艺术，让国外民众在审美过程中感受魅力，加深对中华文化的认识和理解。

Unit 9

节日民俗

> **Unit Goals**
>
> In this unit, you are going to
> - grasp words and expressions concerning Chinese festivals and customs;
> - acquire knowledge about Chinese festivals and customs;
> - know how to translate sentences from Chinese into English by adjusting word order;
> - grasp translation skills of paragraphs on Chinese festivals and customs.

Related Words and Expressions

春节 **Spring Festival; Chinese New Year**

元宵节 **Lantern Festival**

清明节 **Tomb-Sweeping Day; Qingming Festival; Pure Brightness Festival**

端午节 **Dragon Boat Festival**

七夕节 **Double Seventh Day; the Qixi Festival**

中秋节 **Mid-autumn Festival**

重阳节 **Double Ninth Festival; Chongyang Festival**

除夕 **Chinese New Year's Eve**

那达慕大会 Nadam Festival

火把节 Torch Festival

泼水节 Water Splashing Festival; Water Sprinkling Festival

开斋节 Kaizhai Festival; Eid al-Fitr

古尔邦节 Corban Festival; Eid al-Adka

酥油花灯节 Butter Lamp Festival

雪顿节 Shoton Festival; Sho Dun Festival

三月节 March Fair

花山节/跳花场 Jumping Flower Festival

达努节 Danu Festival

三月三歌节 Antiphonal Singing Day

春联 **Spring Festival couplets**

红包 **red envelope; red packet**

压岁钱 **gift money; lucky money**

放烟花爆竹 **set off firecrackers and fireworks**

团圆饭 family reunion dinner

年画 Chinese New Year paintings

倒着贴"福"字 paste Fu character upside down

拜年 pay a New Year call; pay a New Year visit; extend New Year greetings

猜灯谜 guess lantern riddles

舞龙舞狮 dragon-dancing and lion-dancing

灯会 the Lantern Fair

扫墓 tomb sweeping

踏青 spring outing

祭祖 worship ancestors; offer sacrifices to one's ancestors

赛龙舟 dragon boat racing

艾草 Ay Tsao; Chinese mugwort

戴香包 wear sachet; wear scent bag

赏月 appreciate the moon

月饼 moon cake

牛郎 the Cowherd

织女 the Weaver Girl

鹊桥 the magpie bridge

赏菊 appreciate chrysanthemums

佩茱萸 wear cornels; wear dogwood

雄黄酒 realgar wine

二十四节气 the 24 solar terms

立春 Start of Spring; Beginning of Spring

雨水 Rain Water

惊蛰 Awakening of Insects; Waking of Insects

春分 Spring Equinox; Vernal Equinox

清明 Pure Brightness

谷雨 Grain Rain

立夏 Start of Summer; Beginning of Summer

小满 Grain Buds; Slight Fullness

芒种 Grain in Ear

夏至 Summer Solstice

小暑 Minor Heat; Slight Heat

大暑 Major Heat; Great Heat

立秋 Start of Autumn; Beginning of Autumn

处暑 End of Heat

白露 White Dew

秋分 Autumn Equinox

寒露 Cold Dew

霜降 Frost's Descent

立冬 Start of Winter; Beginning of Winter

小雪 Minor Snow; Slight Snow

大雪 Major Snow; Heavy Snow
冬至 Winter Solstice
小寒 Minor Cold; Slight Cold
大寒 Major Cold; Great Cold

Lead-in Activities

1 Answer the following questions.

1) What traditional Chinese festivals do you know? Which is your favorite one? Why?

2) How do Chinese people celebrate the Spring Festival? Could you introduce some traditional customs about it?

3) Do you know some special food eaten during traditional Chinese festivals? Give some examples.

2 Listen to a brief introduction to the Mid-autumn Festival and fill in the blanks with the words you hear.

The Mid-autumn Festival takes place on the 15th day of the eighth month according to the _____, which usually falls between early September and early October based on the Western calendar. Interestingly, on almost every Mid-autumn day, the weather is fine and the full moon is bright and beautiful in the sky. To Chinese people, the full moon is _____. And family is always the _____. Because of this, there is a tradition of having a family reunion on this day that _____ all the Chinese people. Sons and daughters working far away go back home for the Mid-autumn Festival and spend time with their families. That is why the festival is also known as the "day of reunion" and _____ Chinese people's lives. After the _____, the family will get together out of doors to enjoy the beautiful moon and _____ and delicious food, including, of course, the traditional moon cake. The moon cake is a staple dessert during the Mid-autumn Festival and _____. The most popular fillings are egg yolk, lotus paste and _____. Eating lots of tasty food seems particularly appropriate since the festival is also associated with _____, as many different crops are harvested at that time.

3 Read the following passage and then do the exercises.

Chinese Festivals

Every nation in the world has its own traditional festivals, so does China. China is a multi-ethnic country with many festivals shared by all people. And most of the traditional festivals are related to historical development, religious practice and moral principles of the Chinese culture. They had appeared before Qin Dynasty, but they evolved slowly in the later times. The earliest festival was related with primitive worshipping. Tales added romance to the festivals. Religion influenced festivals greatly and famous people went to them as well. These factors made Chinese traditional festivals seem more attractive. Of those festivals, some are kept to commemorate certain historical events so as to inspire the people to succeed and carry out some lofty spirit or fine traditions; others to sing the praise for the outstanding persons, express people's grief for them and cherish their memory. Traditional festivals are created by the people themselves, radiating with their wisdom and ideals.

Traditional festivals are precious treasure in Chinese culture. China's major traditional festivals include the Spring Festival, the Lantern Festival, the Qingming Festival, the Dragon Boat Festival, the Mid-autumn Festival, and the Double Ninth Festival. Ethnic groups have also retained their own traditional festivals including the Water Sprinkling Festival of the Dai people, the Nadam Fair of the Mongolian people, the Kaizhai Festival of Hui people and the Torch Festival of the Yi people, etc.

Chinese traditions and festivals are closely related to complex, mystical concepts of time, similar to those found in Western astrology. The traditional lunar calendar makes it difficult to set dates, so in modern China there are two calendars, the solar calendar and the lunar calendar in use. The solar calendar is the same calendar as used in Western countries. This is the official calendar and all holidays and festivals that began in modern times are celebrated on days of this (Gregorian) calendar. The lunar calendar is the one that the Chinese have used throughout most of their history. It is also known as the Farmer's Calendar.

Months in the traditional Chinese year are known as moons and they have either 29 or 30 days. The calendar is arranged so that the first day of each month coincides with a new moon and the 15th day corresponds to a full moon. However, the 12 lunar months are not equal to a real (solar) year, so an extra, intercalary month is added every third year. This 13rd month is inserted anywhere between the 2nd and 11th month.

Combining the two calendars presents a few problems, so the Chinese use almanacs to determine the Gregorian dates of lucky or unlucky days. Chinese people like to refer to such almanacs when setting dates for marriages, opening business or having children. Traditionally, the calendar was critical to the timing of events, both on a personal and social level. Almost all the great Chinese festivals, except the Qingming Festival which is based on 24 solar terms, occur at special times in the traditional calendars.

1) Answer the following questions.
   (1) According to the passage, some festivals are kept to commemorate certain historical events or historical figures so as to inspire people to succeed and carry out some lofty spirits or fine traditions. Can you give some examples of such events or figures?
   (2) What are the differences between lunar calendar and solar calendar?
   (3) Apart from what have been mentioned in the article, do you know other ethnic minority festivals?
2) Translate the following words or phrases into English.
   农历
   闰月
   年历
   纪念历史事件

3) Match the festival in Column A with the food eaten in certain festival in Column B.

Column A	Column B
1 Spring Festival	a yuanxiao
2 Lantern Festival	b zongzi
3 Mid-Autumn Festival	c fish
4 Dragon Boat Festival	d moon cake

4) Please translate the following paragraph into English based on what you have learned from the above article.

中国的传统节日内容丰富多彩，是中国文化的重要组成部分。传统节日的形成过程也是传统文化发展的过程。从这些节日中，可以清楚地看到古代中国人的生活方式。节日是人类社会的产物。中国的传统节日可以追溯到很久以前。节气为节日提供了前提条件。大多数传统节日在秦朝之前就已经出现，但之后的演变进程比较缓慢。最早的节日与原始的崇拜有关，民间传说和故事为节日增添了浪漫色彩，宗教对节日的影响同样很大，而名人也会对节日的形成产生影响。这些都使中国的传统节日颇具吸引力。

翻译技巧：调整语序（Adjusting Word Order）

语序是指句子成分的排列顺序，它是词语和句子成分之间关系的体现。汉语和英语的语序，在表达模式上有相同点也有不同点。相同之处在于二者都是以"主语＋谓语＋宾语"(SVO)或"施动者＋动作行为＋受动者"为基本语序；不同之处在于两种语言句内语序的灵活性，以及定语、状语等次要成分的位置。在翻译的过程中，译者需要进行适当的语序调整，以使译文符合译入语的表达习惯。

Ⅰ. 句内主要成分位置的调整

从形态学角度来看，语言有分析型和综合型两种。分析型语言的一个主要特征是语序较固定，而综合型语言语序灵活性较高。英语是以综合型为主的语言，有丰富的形态和语法手段，语序灵活。汉语则是以分析型为主的语言，形态变化少，语序较固定。汉译英时，译者需要根据不同的语言特点来调整语序。例如：

原文 早晨的公园里，遛鸟者随处可见。

译文 A Early in the morning, in every corner of the parks we often can see people walk with caged birds in hand.

译文 B Early in the morning, people with caged birds in hand can be seen everywhere in the parks.

译文 C Taking a walk with caged birds in hand is a common scene in every corner of the parks in the early morning.

评析 原文省略施动者，处在主语位置的"遛鸟者"实际上是受动者，"随处可见"则是动作行为。也就是说原文中受动者在前，而动作在后。这三种译文都对语序进行了调整：译文 A 增添了人称代词 we 作主语，补充了施动者，将句子按照英文习惯以"施动者＋动作行为＋受动者"的语序进行排列。译文 B 利用了英文中被动语态的特点，直接省略了句中较模糊的施动者，这是一种比较常见的翻译方法。译文 C 调整比较大，将受动者"遛鸟者"转化为表示现象的短语 taking a walk with caged birds in hand 作为句子的主语。同时将动作行为"随处可见"转化为名词短语 a common scene 跟在系动词 is 之后，句子结构变为"主语＋系动词＋表语"的结构。相比较而言，译文 C 的表达更加地道，更加符合英语的表达习惯。

句内主要成分位置的调整还指谓语动词位置的变化。汉语句子经常会出现多个谓语动词一起使用的现象；而英语中动词的连用现象并不多见。翻译时要考虑到两种语言的区别，从而进行相应的调整。例如：

原文 刘四爷搭茬儿，想了想，问道："话匣子呢？唱唱！"。

译文 A Fourth Master Liu did not answer—he was thinking and asked presently, "Where's the gramophone? Let's have a song!"

译文 B Fourth Master Liu did not answer—he was thinking. "Where's the gramophone?" he asked presently. "Let's have a song!"

评析 原文中连着使用了三个动词"搭茬儿""想"和"问道"。这种动词的连用是汉语句子的一大特点，读起来很有节奏感，生动且画面感强。但在英语中就不同了——比较上面A、B两种译文，译文A把三个动词放在了一起，表述不够简洁，且逻辑关系不清，而译文B把"问道"巧妙地放在两个问句之间，避免了动词连用的重复之感，使得整个译文层次更加分明，逻辑关系更加清晰。

Ⅱ. 定语位置的调整

汉语的定语位置比较固定，总是出现在其修饰的中心词前，英语的定语位置则比较灵活。单个单词作定语的时候，除了少数情况（比如形容词修饰不定代词或作表语的形容词作定语时需后置），一般都放在中心词前。而较长的定语，如词组、介词短语或者定语从句则一般放在中心词之后。当一个中心词的定语是几个单词时，这些单词的排列顺序也不是随机的。在英语中，越能表示事物基本性质的定语越要靠近它所修饰的中心词，而在汉语中越能表示事物基本性质的定语往往放在最前面，离中心词较远。

例1 原文 一九四九年解放以前，中国人民曾经遭受世界罕见的恶性通货膨胀的灾祸。

译文 Before liberation in 1949, the Chinese people suffered from some of the worst inflation the world had ever known.

评析 原句的两个定语"世界罕见的"和"恶性通货膨胀的"都在中心词"灾祸"之前。译者根据英语的表达习惯省略了"灾祸"一词，由名词 inflation（通货膨胀）取而代之。两个定语的位置则变为一前一后，其中"世界罕见的"被翻译为一个定语从句，故后置。

例2 原文 鲁迅先生是在文化战线上，代表着全民族的大多数，向着敌人冲锋陷阵的、最正确、最勇敢、最忠诚、最热忱的空前的民族英雄。

译文 Representing the great majority of the nation on the cultural front, Lu Xun breached and stormed the enemy citadel; he was the bravest and most correct, the firmest, the most loyal and the most ardent national hero, a hero without parallel in our history.

评析 原句的中心词"民族英雄"前有数个定语。为了使句子意思表述更清楚、更有层次，在译文中拆分为两个句子。定语"代表着全民族的大多数"被翻译为一个现在分词短语，放在了第一句句首。"最正确""最勇敢""最忠诚""最热忱"作为前置定语，根据重要性依次排序，最后的定语"空前的"翻译为介词短语，放在中心词之后。

Ⅲ. 状语位置的调整

在状语的位置上，汉英两种语言也存在着较大的差异。当表示时间、地点、方式的状语同时出现时，在汉语中排列顺序通常为先时间状语，再地点状语，最后是方式状语；在英语中的排序则是先方式状语，再地点状语，最后才是时间状语。例如：

原文 大会将于明年三月在上海隆重开幕。

译文 The conference will begin ceremoniously in Shanghai the next March.

评析 原文状语的排列顺序是时间状语（明年三月）在前，紧接着是地点状语（上海），然后是方式状语（隆重），后接动词（开幕）。而按照英语表达习惯，应先译方式状语（ceremoniously），然后译地点状语（in Shanghai），最后是时间状语（the next March）。所修饰的动词则放在所有状语之前（begin）。

若句中含有一系列表示时间或地点的状语，这些状语在汉语句子中的顺序通常是从大到小、由远及近，而在英语中的顺序则恰恰相反。例如：

原文 毛主席是1893年12月26日在湖南韶山出生的。

译文 Chairman Mao was born in Shaoshan, Hunan Province on December 26, 1893.

评析 原文中时间状语在前，地点状语在后，时间状语按年、月、日排序，而地点状语按省、市排序。当翻译成英语时，按照英语表达习惯，地点状语一般置于时间状语前，具体地点和时间的排序也与汉语表达习惯完全相反。

段落翻译

1. 春节

中国人认为，春天是一年的开始，是一年中最重要的季节。由于中国新年通常在二十四节气的第一个节气"立春"之后，中国新年也被称为春节，它标志着寒冷冬天的结束。春节是举国欢庆、阖家团圆的重大节日，蕴含着深刻的文化内涵，承载着丰厚的历史文化底蕴，凝聚着中华传统文化的精华。2006年，春节民俗经国务院批准列入第一批国家级非物质文化遗产名录。

难点讲解：

1)第一句"是一年的开始"可以处理为同位语，使层次性更强。

2)"祈年、庆贺、娱乐"可翻译为 worshiping, celebrating and entertainment。

3)"蕴含着深刻的文化内涵"可以直译为 present/imply profound Chinese culture，或者意译为名词短语 a symbol of profound Chinese culture。

4)第三句很长，可以考虑进行拆译。

5)"承载""凝聚"可分别译为 inherit 和 embody。

6)"国务院"译为 the State Council；"非物质文化遗产"译为 Intangible Cultural Heritage。

2. 清明节

清明节是中国的一个传统节日，在冬至后的第104天，或者春分后的第15天，通常在阳历4月5日前后。与清明节临近的还有纪念介子推的寒食节。清明节时人们会祭祖、扫墓。清明节是草木吐绿、万物复苏的时节。这一天有外出春游的传统习俗。在中国南方，人们会在清明节吃青团。青团是一种时令小吃，皮由糯米粉和绿色植物汁混合制成，内里填充豆沙、肉松或蛋黄等馅料。

难点讲解：

1)"冬至""春分"分别译为 the Winter Solstice 和 the Spring Equinox。

2)第一句比较长，可用现在分词 usually occurring around April 5th of the Gregorian/Solar calendar 作定语进行翻译。

3)"寒食节"可以直译为 Hanshi Day 或者 the Cold Food Day；"纪念"在翻译的时候可以进行词

性转化，译为 memorial day。

4)"春游"可译为 spring outings。

5)"青团""糯米粉""豆沙""肉松"和"蛋黄"可分别翻译为 Sweet Green Rice Balls、glutinous rice flour、sweetened bean paste、meat floss 和 egg yolk。

3. 重阳

重阳节，也叫重九节，在每年农历九月初九。在《易经》中，"九"为阳数，因而得名"重阳节"。重阳节适合外出活动，人们常在这一天去野外郊游或者登山。吃重阳糕、观赏菊花也是重阳节的重要活动。随着现代社会的发展，重阳节被赋予"敬老节"的含义，因为在中国文化中，重九象征着长寿。

难点讲解：

1)"重阳节"可以翻译为 Chongyang Festival 或 Double Ninth Festival，但根据原文第二句对节日名称"阳"字的解释，在这里译为 Chongyang Festival 会更加合适。

2)第一句中"也叫重九节"可以使用过去分词短语 also named the Double Ninth Festival 来翻译。

3)"去野外郊游或者登山"可译为 go hiking and climbing in the countryside。

4)"观赏菊花"可译为 enjoy the flourishing chrysanthemum。

4. 中秋节

中秋节是中国仅次于春节的第二大传统节日，庆祝时间为每年的农历八月十五。根据中国传统历法，一年分春、夏、秋、冬四季，每季分为三个阶段，农历八月为秋季的第二个月，而农历八月十五在月中，故称为中秋。中秋节源于古人对月亮的崇拜。西汉的文献中便有嫦娥奔月、吴刚伐桂的记载。明清时期，中秋节已成为重要的节日。满月象征着家庭团聚，会让人们想起家乡和亲人。赏月是一项古老的传统，古时人们会举行仪式来迎接满月。而如今，在吃完团圆饭之后，很多人会选择在中秋节晚上到户外赏月。

难点讲解：

1)第一句较长，可在逗号处进行拆译。

2)"中国传统历法"可译为 traditional Chinese calendar。

3)"崇拜"可翻译为 worship。

4)"嫦娥奔月、吴刚伐桂"可译为 Chang'e flying to the moon and Wu Gang cutting an osmanthus。

5)"象征"一词可以翻译为动词 symbolize，也可转换词性翻译为 a symbol of；"让人们想起……"则可以使用现在分词短语"reminding people of…"作为定语进行翻译。

5. 除夕

除夕是农历年最后一天晚上，即春节前一天晚上。在中国，除夕是极为重要的，因为它是辞旧迎新的夜晚。除夕之夜，合家团聚，一家人在一起吃年夜饭，叙旧话新，畅谈未来。人们常常彻夜不眠，围坐守岁，足见除夕对中国人的重要性。如今，除夕之夜观看春晚节目已经成为重要活动。吃团圆饭、燃放烟花爆竹、给晚辈发压岁钱等都是除夕的重要习俗。除夕的团圆饭对中国人来说非常重要。家人聚在一起，分享快乐的时光。团圆饭的传统菜肴在中国的不同地区会有所不同。

难点讲解：

1)"辞旧迎新的夜晚"可译为 the night connects the past year and the new year。

2)"彻夜不眠，围坐守岁"可译为 stay up all night to welcome the coming new year together。

3)"春晚"即 Spring Festival Gala。

Unit 9　节日民俗

4）第六句主语很长，可形式主语 it 代替，即"it has become an indispensable part of New Year's Eve celebration to…"。

5）"团圆饭""燃放烟花爆竹""压岁钱"可翻译为 reunion dinner、set off fireworks and firecrackers、lucky money。

6）"对……非常重要"可以翻译为 be very important for sb，也可翻译为 matter a lot for sb，后者表述更加贴切一些。

6. 冬至

每年 12 月 22 日（或前后一天）是中国的二十四节气之一——冬至。冬至又称冬节，是二十四节气中最早被确定的一个节气，常被看作我国二十四节气的起点。由于冬至标志着一年中最大的气候变化，古人对冬至极为重视。在过去，冬至甚至相当于中国的新年，告诉人们冬天已经正式来临。冬至节起源于汉代，兴盛于唐宋，是一个有两千多年历史的古老节日。如今，冬至庆祝方式上的差异主要体现在南、北地区各不相同的饮食习俗方面。在冬至这天，北方地区的人们大多会吃饺子或者馄饨，而南方地区的人们则有冬至吃汤圆、米团和长面线的习俗，这些习俗都表达了人们的美好愿望。

难点讲解：

1）在翻译第一句的时候可以根据英文的习惯调整语序，即以"冬至"为主语来进行翻译。

2）"起源于……，兴盛于……"可译为"originated from…, and reached its peak in glory in…"。

3）"体现在……方面"可译为"be reflected in…"。

4）"馄饨""汤圆""米团""长面线"可分别翻译为 wonton、sweet dumpling、rice ball、long noodles。

7. 中式婚礼装饰

在婚礼上，装饰非常重要，而在中国的传统婚礼习俗中，一些装饰是必须的。中式婚礼装饰经常使用"双喜"，即"囍"字。事实上，"囍"字只与结婚有关。婚礼上也会有很多写着祝福语的喜帐。中式婚礼使用的传统颜色与西式婚礼有很大的不同。红色是中式婚礼的主要颜色，因为它在中国文化中被认为是一种非常幸运的颜色，象征着快乐、繁荣和幸福。在中式婚礼上，人们还会看到很多金色的装饰物，因为金色象征着财富。在中式婚礼上，餐桌上还会装饰鲜花。在中国，百合花是婚礼上最受欢迎的花。这是因为在汉语中，百合花有美好的寓意，祝福新人百年好合、幸福美满。

难点讲解：

1）第一句中的"必须的"可以直接翻译成形容词 necessary，也可以通过词性转化翻译成名词短语 a must。

2）在翻译"囍"这个字的时候，除了解释其意思，即 double happiness，最好也保留原来的汉字，使读者更直观地理解这个字的文化含义。

3）第六句比较长，可以翻译成一个由 because 引导的原因状语从句，"象征着……"则可以翻译为现在分词作定语，修饰"幸运的颜色"。

4）第六句和第七句中都使用了"象征"这一表达，为了避免语言使用的重复，可以分别使用 symbolize 和 signify 这两个词来翻译。

5）百合之所以在中式婚礼上受欢迎是因为它的发音和"百年好合"相似，所以在翻译的时候，最好将其汉语发音标注出来，帮助读者更好地理解百合花的寓意。

8. 礼尚往来

赠送礼物是世界各国通用的社交礼仪，是一种维系感情的社交活动。中国是礼仪之邦，十分重视礼尚往来。礼尚往来以达到和谐平衡的人际关系为目标。和谐指互利互惠、互助合作；平衡主要指礼品赠送是双向行为，有送有回才是相处之道。中国人在礼品选择和送礼场合方面都十分讲究。中国有句古话叫作"礼轻情意重"，赠送礼品的目的是要表达心意和友好，而不是为了炫耀自己的富有，故而在礼品的选择上要考虑到对方的需求和喜好，以实用性为先。另外，中国普遍有"好事成双"的说法，送的礼物无论是金钱还是实物往往为双数。中国人一直非常重视给老人过寿，在老人的生日上送的礼物往往与"健康长寿"相关，比如寿桃、寿糕等。在婚丧嫁娶等重要场合，应邀参加的亲朋好友往往赠送礼金。慰问病人时，携带的礼物通常是食品，如水果、营养品等。在参加朋友的聚会、庆祝乔迁之喜等普通场合，常送的礼物有水果、酒类、茶叶、土特产等。中国人在接受礼物方面也有礼仪之道。收到礼物时，收礼人往往谦让婉拒，而送礼人则会一再坚持。当收礼人收下礼物时，通常不会当着送礼人的面拆看礼物。有些场合收礼人会在分别时回赠一个小礼物，表示礼尚往来。

难点讲解：

1) 标题"礼尚往来"可以翻译为 reciprocal courtesy。

2) "社交礼仪"的英语表达为 social etiquette。

3) 翻译第二句和第三句时，可根据逻辑关系可以进行重新断句。第二句的前半句"中国是礼仪之邦"可单独成句，后半句和原文的第三句都是关于"礼尚往来"的内容，可以使用介词短语 with the purpose of 合并为一句。

4) "互惠互利、互相合作"可以翻译为 mutual benefit and cooperation，这一句可以拆出来单独翻译。

5) 在翻译"礼轻情意重"这句中国俗语时，可以使用意译的翻译方法，即用英语具体解释这句话的意思，译为"It's not the gift that counts, but the thought behind it."。

6) "好事成双"可译为 good things should be in pairs。

7) "送礼人"和"收礼人"可分别翻译为 gift giver 和 the recipient。

拓展阅读

Reading A

China's 24 Solar Terms

Solar terms, also called Jieqi in Chinese, are days marking one of the 24 time buckets of the solar year in traditional Chinese calendar, and were used to indicate the alternation of seasons and climate changes in ancient China. It is a unique component and creative invention of Chinese traditional calendar.

China's 24 solar terms was added to the United Nations Educational, Scientific and Cultural Organization's (UNESCO) World Intangible Cultural Heritage List on November 30, 2016. The announcement was made during the 11th session of UNESCO's Intergovernmental Committee for the Safeguarding of Intangible Cultural Heritages in Addis Ababa, Ethiopia's capital.

Origin of 24 Solar Terms

The Yellow River Basin, in northern China, is believed to be the cradle of the solar terms system. Ancient Chinese farmers used astronomical signs, changes in temperature and precipitation as the basis to create the calendar, which was later adopted by multiple ethnic groups in different regions across China.

As early as the Spring and Autumn Period, Chinese ancestors had already established two major solar terms, ri nan zhi (日南至 "Sun South Most") and ri bei zhi (日北至 "Sun North Most").

As of the end of the Warring States Period, eight key solar terms (Start of Spring, Spring Equinox, Start of Summer, Summer Solstice, Start of Autumn, Autumn Equinox, Start of Winter and Winter Solstice) marking the four seasons, were established according to the different positions of the sun and changes in natural phenomena.

The rest of the solar terms were initiated in the Western Han Dynasty. Hence most terms refer to the climate of Xi'an, capital of the Han Dynasty.

General Introduction

China's 24 solar terms is a knowledge system and social practice formed through observations of the sun's annual motion, and cognition of the year's changes in season, climate and phenology.

Ancient Chinese divided the Sun's movement through the sky into 24 segments, with each segment equaling one roughly two-week-long "solar term."

The 24 solar terms each suggests the position of the sun, every time it travels 15 degrees on the ecliptic longitude. The 24 solar terms include Start of Spring, Rain Water, Awakening of Insects, Spring Equinox, Pure Brightness, Grain Rain, Start of Summer, Grain Buds, Grain in Ear, Summer Solstice, Minor Heat, Major Heat, Start of Autumn, Limit of Heat, White Dew, Autumn Equinox, Cold Dew, Frost's Descent, Start of Winter, Minor Snow, Major Snow, Winter Solstice, Minor Cold and Major Cold.

Classification of 24 Solar Terms

The 24 solar terms known as Start of Spring, Start of Summer, Start of Autumn, and Start of Winter are used to reflect the change of seasons, dividing the year into four seasons of exactly three months.

The solar terms of Spring Equinox, Autumn Equinox, Summer Solstice and Winter Solstice are divided from an astronomical aspect, reflecting the turning point of the variation of the altitude of the sun.

Minor Heat, Major Heat, Limit of Heat, Minor Cold, and Major Cold reflect the changes of temperature in different periods.

Rain Water, Pure Brightness, Grain Rain, Minor Snow, Major Snow, White Dew, Cold Dew, and Frost's Descent reflect the phenomenon of precipitation, indicating the time and intensity of rainfall, snowfall, dew, and frost.

Grain Buds and Grain in Ear reflect the maturity and harvest time of crops, while Awakening of Insects reflects observed insect activity.

Application of 24 Solar Terms

Based on the sun's position in the zodiac, the 24 solar terms, were created by farmers in ancient China to guide the agricultural affairs and farming activities. The 24 solar terms reflect the changes in climate, natural phenomena, agricultural production, and other aspects of human life, including clothing, food, housing, and transportation.

They serve as an instruction manual of sorts for farmers, allowing them to know what conditions to expect or what agricultural activities to carry out during certain periods of the year.

Besides its role as an almanac, many of these solar terms have become associated with Chinese customs over the centuries, such as honoring one's ancestors for Qingming (Pure Brightness) in April or eating dumplings for Lidong (Start of Winter).

For example, the solar term Qingming, or Pure Brightness, is deeply tied to China's tradition of paying respects to one's ancestors and visiting the family tomb. For this reason, in English the Qingming Festival is often known as the Tomb-Sweeping Day.

Contemporary Significance

In the current time of technology-based modern farming, traditional solar terms remain relevant. It is also an important cultural existence in modern Chinese social life, serving as a reference in daily life, ancestor worship and others around seasons. Although in modern times it is not regarded as the major guiding knowledge in agriculture production, it remains the symbol of the evolving farming civilization relationship between people and nature. It can recall our memories and remind us that the nature is changing at its own pace. 24 solar terms is the crystallization of Chinese people in the relationship between human and nature.

To sum up, it is an indispensable component of the traditional Chinese calendars and its living applications, serving as a timeframe for agricultural activities and daily life. In international circle of meteorology, this cognitive system has been honored as the "fifth great invention" of China.

"This legacy reflects the Chinese people's respect for nature and tradition, their unique understanding of the universe, their wisdom to live in harmony with nature, and the world's cultural diversity," said Zhang Ling, an official with the Ministry of Culture, who attended the UNESCO meeting in Addis Ababa.

Exercises

 Match the English expressions in Column A with the Chinese translations in Column B.

Column A   Column B
1 ecliptic longitude   a 文化多样性
2 UNESCO   b 降雨强度
3 intensity of rainfall   c 联合国教科文组织
4 cognitive system   d 黄经
5 cultural diversity   e 认知系统

 Answer the following questions.

1) What are the four key solar terms which can mark the four seasons?

2) How can people classify the 24 solar terms?

3) Why are 24 solar terms often called China's "fifth great invention" in international circle of meteorology?

4) List some special customs which can be associated with the solar terms.

Reading B

Chinese Ethnic Minority Festivals

China has 55 minority groups except for the Han people. Every minority has some unique festivals to celebrate every year. For example, Dai people's Water Splashing Festival in Xishuangbanna, Tibetan Shoton Festival, and Mongolian Nadam Fair are the best time to experience and study Chinese minorities' culture and life. If travelers want to experience some special minority festivals, you should not miss Chinese minority festivals when you are in China.

Mongolian Nadam Fair

Nadam Fair means entertainments to celebrate the happiness of harvest. It is widely celebrated by Mongol in Inner Mongolia, Gansu, Qinghai, and Xinjiang area. The Nadam Fair is on June 4th in the Chinese lunar calendar (around July or August). The fair is celebrated by physical games and matches for 7 to 10 days. The entertainments consist of traditional Mongolian horseracing, wrestling, archery, tug-of-war and other performances.

Travelers can go to Ordos near the south edge of Inner Mongolia to see the grand Nadam Fair. The Nadam Fair is also known as a festival of agricultural and livestock goods. Herdsmen get together to exchange daily goods during the festival.

Shoton Festival

The Shoton Festival is one of the most important and the grandest holidays in the Tibetan area. Usually, it is celebrated in late June and early July in the Tibetan calendar, and around August or early September in the Gregorian calendar. Shoton in the Tibetan means "yogurt banquet" as Tibetan families bring yogurt to welcome Buddhists. Nowadays, there are a lot of celebrations including magnificent "Buddha Displaying," Tibetan Opera, and musical and orchestic performances. Besides, there are yak competitions and horsemanship performances.

Corban Festival

Chinese Muslims such as the Uygur in Xinjiang and Hui People in Qinghai and Ningxia Provinces celebrate the Corban Festival. The festival, also known as Eid al-Adha, is one of the top 3 important festivals for Muslims. It is a festival of sacrfice with a 3-day celebration. There are some celebrations during the Corban Festival such as making tasty cakes and killing some prepared livestock.

Water Splashing Festival

Water Splashing Festival is the most important and ceremonious festival for Dai people. It is widely celebrated by the largest number of people among 25 ethnic minorities in Yunnan Province. The festival is Dai people's New Year celebrated around mid-April for 3 to 7 days. The first day is called Mairi in Dai language, a similar festival like Chinese New Year's Eve. The second day is Laori and the third day is Dai's New Year which is the most glorious and the luckiest day.

In the morning, Dai people dressed in festive costumes come to wash Buddha in the temple and then start to splash each other with best wishes. Xishuangbanna in the southwest corner of Yunnan Province is the best place to experience the Dai people's Water Splashing Festival and their culture.

Sisters Meals Festival

March 15th in the Chinese lunar calendar is the Miao people's Sisters Meals Festival. Miao women cook colorful glutinous rice and change gifts for luckiness during the festival. The rice is made of glutinous rice and wildflowers and leaves selected by Miao girls. At the same time, there are bullfighting, lusheng performances, singing, dancing, and other celebrations. Travelers can experience the festival in Taizhou County and other parts of the southeast of Guizhou Province. Other famous large-scale festivals of Miao people consist of Lusheng Festival and Bullfight Festival. The Kaili International Lusheng Festival is the most spectacular among the Lusheng festivals. Miao people's Bullfight Festival lies on April 8th in the Chinese lunar calendar. Miao girls who are not married prepare some food and get together and Miao boys bring their water buffaloes to take part in the festival.

March Fair

March Fair is Bai people's traditional festival to change goods. It is celebrated in the west of Dali Ancient Town in Yunnan Province from March 15th to 21st in the Chinese lunar calendar (around Mid-April) with a celebration of singing, dancing, and horseracing.

Nowadays, March Fair extends 5 to 10 days. Xu Xiake, a famous geographer and traveler praised the large-scale March Fair in the Ming Dynasty. It is not only a great chance to enjoy the Bai people's unique culture, but also an excellent time to select some amazing souvenirs. Travelers can also enjoy great nightlife and wander around the ancient town. Besides, Erhai Lake, Cangshan Mountain, and Butterfly Spring are hot destinations in Dali.

Torch Festival

Although Bai and Naxi people celebrate the Torch Festival, the Yi people's Torch Festival is the most famous and the grandest. The festival is held on June 24th or 25th in the Chinese lunar calendar (around August in the Gregorian calendar), with a three-day celebration popular in Yunnan, Guizhou, and Sichuan Provinces. Xichang in Sichuan Province has the largest-scale celebration of the Torch Festival.

The Yi People thought the fire can help the Yi hero to prevail over the evil God who sent numerous grasshoppers to destroy agriculture. Therefore, the Yi people held a lot of torches in order to fight the evil. The Yi people will get together with torches and held a series of celebrations including horseracing, bullfight, wrestling, music, and dance. Travelers can view a sea of fire in the evening and take part in the exciting bonfires.

Exercises

 Answer the following questions.

1) Do you know how minority people celebrate their New Year? Please give some examples.

2) From this passage, we have learnt something about seven famous ethnic minority festivals in China. Could you introduce any other ethnic minority festivals?

 Translate the following terms into English.

那达慕大会

雪顿节

古尔邦节

泼水节

苗族姐妹节

三月节

火把节

翻译佳作赏析

九月九日忆山东兄弟

王　维

独在异乡为异客，每逢佳节倍思亲。
遥知兄弟登高处，遍插茱萸少一人。

译文：

Thinking of My Brothers on Mountain Climbing Day

By Wang Wei

Alone, a lonely stranger in a foreign land,
I doubly pine for kinsfolk on a holiday.
I know my brothers would, with dogwood spray in hand,
Climb up mountain and miss me so far away.

（许渊冲　译）

赏析：

这首诗是唐代诗人王维的一首七言绝句。诗一开始先写到诗人独自身在异乡，倍感孤独，接下来将思绪拉回到故乡的亲人，遥想亲人们在按照重阳风俗登高的时候，是否也曾想念起自己。全诗含蓄深沉，既朴素自然，又蕴含巧思，其中"每逢佳节倍思亲"更是流传千古的名句。

许渊冲的翻译采用了隔行押韵的形式。第一行的 land 和第三行的 hand，以及第二行的 holiday 和第四行的 away 构成了两组巧妙的押韵。

原文第一句中，"异"字重复了两遍，"异乡""异客"皆表达了诗人在他乡的孤独寂寥。许渊冲的译文使用了 alone 和 lonely 两个近义词和原文相呼应，有异曲同工之妙。

原文第二句中的"倍"字是"更加，加倍"的意思，许渊冲很贴切地选取了 doubly 一词，即"双重地，加倍地"。"思亲"就是"思念亲人"，这里译者没有简单地用 miss 这样的词来翻译，而是选用了 pine for 这个短语。pine for 在字典里有两种含义：一是苦苦思念；二是渴望得到某样不容易得到的东西。这两层含义恰巧和原诗的意境贴合。

对于"遥知兄弟登高处，遍插茱萸少一人"，许渊冲并未如前两句一样逐句翻译，而是用浅显的语言描述了想象中远方亲人登高庆祝节日时的场景。他用了 I know 和 would 来体现诗人在远方感知到了亲人们对自己的思念。原诗中这两句并未直接表明兄弟们之间的思念之情，而是通过提到"登高""插茱萸"这样的传统民俗，让读者自己去体会隐含的意义，而许渊冲直接将其译为 miss me so far away，符合英文比较直白的表达习惯。

翻译练习

1. 传说中国古时候有一种凶猛的怪兽叫"年"，一年四季都在深海里。但逢新旧之交，"年"就出来糟蹋庄稼，伤害人畜，百姓们叫苦连天。有一次，它又跑到村庄里为非作歹，被一家门口晾着的大红衣服吓跑了。到了另一处，又被火光和院子里传出的噼里啪啦的响声吓得抱头鼠窜。于是人们掌握了"年"怕红色、怕火光、怕声音的弱点。每至年末岁首，人们就在门口贴红联、放鞭炮、挂红灯，在院子里烧柴火、拢旺火，用菜刀剁菜肉发出声音，把"年"吓得逃回海里，不再危害人畜。久而久之，这些活动就变成了过年的种种习俗。

2. 春节期间走访拜年是年节传统习俗之一，是人们辞旧迎新、互相表达美好祝愿的一种方式。

在新年的第一天或之后不久，人们与亲朋好友见面时都会互道祝福，希望彼此在新的一年里收获好运和幸福。年轻一辈拜访长辈，祝他们健康长寿。拜年的意义在于亲朋好友互相走访，联络感情、互贺新年。随着时代的发展，拜年的习俗亦不断增添新的内容和形式。除了传统的拜年方式，电话拜年、短信拜年、网络拜年等也非常流行。

3. 农历正月十五日是中国传统节日元宵节。农历里正月为元月，古人称夜晚为宵，而正月十五日又是一年中第一个月圆之夜，所以被称为元宵节。按照中国传统民俗，在元宵节的夜晚，人们合家团聚、观灯、猜灯谜、吃元宵，其乐融融，这充分体现了元宵节的文化内涵。从唐代起，元宵张灯成为法定之事。猜灯谜是元宵节期间一项非常受欢迎的活动。谜语通常是有关好运、家庭团圆、丰收和爱情的内容。在古代，单身人士可以通过这种猜谜游戏来吸引其心仪之人的注意。直到今天，中国人还会举行愉快的猜谜比赛来庆祝元宵节。2008年6月，元宵节入选第二批国家级非物质文化遗产。

4. 七夕节，也叫乞巧节，是中国传说中牛郎织女相会的日子。七夕节在每年农历七月初七，是中国传统节日中最浪漫的节日，也被称为中国的情人节。在古时，女孩是这个节日的主要参与者，节日期间的主要活动是祈求自己有一双巧手，因此这一天也被称为"乞巧节"或"女儿节"。

5. 端午节（农历五月初五）是中国的传统节日。端午节在中国所有传统节日中叫法最多。虽然名称不同，但各地区过节的习俗近似。端午文化在世界上影响广泛，世界上一些国家和地区也有庆贺端午节的活动。2009年9月，联合国教科文组织正式批准将端午节列入《人类非物质文化遗产代表作名录》，端午节成为中国首个入选世界非遗的节日。端午节是集祈福消灾、欢庆娱乐和饮食为一体的民俗大节，在传承发展中杂糅了多地多种民俗，内容丰富。赛龙舟与食粽是端午节的两大节俗主题，这两大传统主题在中国传承至今。赛龙舟源于民间传说。据说，在战国时期屈原投江自尽后，许多渔民在河上划着船试图找到他的尸体。他们尽力寻找这位受人尊敬的大臣，但是当他们到达洞庭湖时，屈原的尸体已经找不到了。自那以后，当地人每年都会划船来纪念屈原，希望通过这种方式来驱赶河底的怪物。

6. 在海外华人聚集的地区，每逢重大节日或庆典，人们总能看到喜庆的舞狮表演。这种表演不仅很好地烘托了节日气氛，也成为外国人了解中国文化的一个窗口。舞狮是一项历史悠久的民间表演艺术，南北朝时期就开始流行，至今已有一千五百多年的历史。"点睛"是舞狮前的一项重要活动，嘉宾把红色颜料涂在狮子的眼睛上，象征给狮子以生命。"点睛"之后，真正的舞狮表演就开始了。舞狮者身披形似狮子的道具，踏着音乐的节奏，模拟狮子的看、站、走、跑、跳、滚、睡、抖毛等动作，形态逼真，惹人喜爱。舞狮是一项集武术、舞蹈、音乐于一体的综合艺术。如今它已经走出国门，迈向更大的世界舞台。

7. 中国人创造了许多烹饪技术，并把食物视为日常生活中重要的一部分。食物的重要性甚至在某些方面影响了汉语。例如，人们见面打招呼时习惯问"你吃了吗"，这种问候通常并不是说打招呼的人真的想知道对方是否吃过饭，而是表达友好与亲密。筷子是华夏饮食文化的标志之一。在中国餐桌礼仪中，重要的不仅是使用筷子，而且要知道如何正确地使用筷子，否则会被视为不礼貌。许多传统的餐桌礼仪被沿用至今。

8. 在许多文化中，新生儿的出生总是一件重要而快乐的事，这在中国文化中也不例外。中国文化中为庆祝新生儿诞生有丰富的仪式和活动。通常，庆祝活动在婴儿一个月大、一百天大和一岁生日时举行。当婴儿满一个月大的时候，家人会为新生儿举办一个盛大的聚会。红色作为幸运和富有的象征，在庆祝活动中扮演着重要的角色。客人们会送各种各样的礼物，例如婴儿衣服或婴儿玩具。新生儿百日又称"百岁"，带有健康长寿的美好寓意。百日的一个习俗是父母让理发师给孩子剃头，然后在后脑勺上留一撮头发。这撮头发被称为"百岁辫"。婴儿一岁时，最常见庆祝仪式是"抓周"。在这一天，父母会在孩子面前放置一些有象征意义的东西供其选择，以便预测孩子未来的职业。

Unit 10

生活方式

> **Unit Goals**
>
> In this unit, you are going to
> - grasp words and expressions concerning lifestyle;
> - acquire knowledge about Chinese lifestyle;
> - know how to translate sentences without subject from Chinese into English by changing sentence pattern;
> - grasp translation skills of paragraphs on Chinese lifestyle.

Related Words and Expressions

中国功夫 Chinese Kung Fu
太极 Tai Ji
围棋 go chess
红眼航班 red-eye flight
泡沫经济 bubble economy
牛市 bull market
智库 think tank
亚健康 sub-health
底线 bottom line
街舞 street dancing
破冰之旅 ice-breaking trip
主题公园 theme park
虚拟现实 virtual reality
网络犯罪 cybercrime
电子商务 e-business
应试教育 exam-oriented education
第三产业 third industry
峰会 summit
空巢 empty nest
微信 WeChat
八大菜系 eight Chinese cuisines
《舌尖上的中国》 *A Bite of China*
回头率 head turning

车展 auto show
猎头 head-hunting
不折腾 no trouble-making
零容忍 zero tolerance
给力 gelivable; givingpower; awesome
胶囊公寓 capsule apartment
团购 group purchase; teambuying
秒杀 seckilling; instant killing
围观 circusee

Lead-in Activities

 Answer the following questions.

1) What is a healthy lifestyle in your eyes? How should we cultivate a healthy lifestyle?

2) Do you like travelling? Where do you want to travel in the future and what do you think travelling can bring you?

3) Do you have similar lifestyles with your parents? If not, what are the differences? And what do you think are the reasons behind them?

② **Listen to a brief introduction to the recent changes in Chinese lifestyles and fill in the blanks with the words you hear.**

Since the adoption of the _____, life in China has been changing _____ _____. The lives of young people are different from those of their parents and grandparents. Great changes _____ have taken place, for instance. People now have more money to spend and more products and services to purchase, which has contributed to _____ in China. People now spend more money on luxuries, including entertainment and food. Furthermore, some Chinese young people now prefer to spend their time singing Karaoke during Chinese New Year _____ in traditional ways. And the number of people who celebrate Chinese New Year in novel ways is _____. However, this does not mean that people have stopped _____. The increase in wealth is making it possible for the average person to become a _____. They may buy antique furniture or even old houses which _____. This consumer aspect of the new lifestyle is also resulting in a growing desire to see the beautiful Chinese countryside. _____ has also increased as a result of the expansion of the Chinese middle class, who desire to search for their roots.

 Read the following passage and then do the exercises.

Martial Arts and Chinese Life

Martial arts are a genuine native sport of China. The Chinese people take pride in it, both because of its age and many aspects of Chinese culture and life that it reflects. Martial arts incorporate traditional Chinese philosophies, aesthetic sense, ethics and medical science.

Martial arts were developed under the great influence of ancient Chinese culture and borrowed widely from various academic studies, such as ancient philosophy, aesthetics, ethics and medicine.

Chinese martial arts have benefited from ancient Chinese philosophy. The Spring and Autumn Period was a golden age of academic study and resulted in different schools of philosophical thinking that would lay a solid foundation for the subsequent formation of Chinese culture. The period also nourished the theoretical aspect of martial arts and supplying inspiration and insight for its continued development. Chinese martial arts have adapted aspects of Confucianism, Taoism, Mohism, and schools of ancient military strategists and geomancers.

Ancient Chinese philosophy advocated the theory of Dao, or the Way, and held that the Dao was connected with both the heaven and the earth and was the source of everything. Martial arts practitioners begin with the irregularity and infinity of Dao and seek to reach a stage in which he or she blends harmoniously with nature. The arts teach practitioners to train the inner spirit and mind as well as the external muscles, bones and skin. Martial arts stress the combination of the physical being with the mental being and emphasize a close relationship between physical exercises and the surrounding environment. Practitioners are advised to use different methods of exercises according to the changes of natural environment and the conditions of the body. These practices reflect martial arts' understanding of the ancient philosophy, let the mind swim freely in Dao and the oneness of man and nature.

Ancient Chinese aesthetics advocated a balance between hardness and softness, voidness and solidness, motion and stillness, and negative and positive, as well as the expression of the spirit of an object through its form. Under this influence, Chinese martial arts have formed their own aesthetic standards that incorporate a stage of conceptual contentment, harmony, and nature, as well as beauty and elegance. For example, Changquan or Long Boxing features fully extended, elegant and unrestrained movement; Nanquan or South Boxing demonstrates steadiness and momentum of movements; Shaolin Boxing expresses resolution and strength in its quick and rhythmical movements; and the beautiful and smoothly stringed movements of Taijiquan remind viewers of floating clouds and flowing streams.

A distinct aspect of Chinese martial arts is the advocacy of morals and emphasis on benevolence, fidelity and sincerity. As a result, practicing martial arts not only implies building health and strength, but also purifying one's soul. Benevolence is the core of Confucianism. It includes love, generosity and leniency. Chinese martial arts work for those who are benevolent, brave, and courageous. Those who are brave and courageous but morally inferior will finally be rendered to a stage of disorder and incompetence. The arts stress that the moral level of a practitioner is as important as his or her martial arts skills.

Martial arts practices are closely related to those of traditional Chinese medicine. Besides improving people's health, cultivating their minds and souls and bringing out the potential of the human body, martial arts are also believed to be able to help cure diseases. Such health benefits are achieved through breathing exercises and improved circulation.

While carrying on the tradition of this ancient art, specialists today are trying to turn martial arts into a scientific sport that combines fighting skills with health building. They hope that one day, martial arts will become an event at the Olympic Games.

1) Answer the following questions.

   (1) What philosophy schools' theories are accepted by Chinese martial arts and how do they contribute to martial arts?

   (2) What is the core of Confucianism according to the text? How does Confucianism relate to martial arts?

   (3) What attracts to you to Chinese martial arts?

2) Translate the following words or phrases into English.

   武术套路

   习武者

   天人合一

   中国哲学

3) Translate the following paragraph into English.

   功夫（Kung Fu）是中国武术（martial arts）的俗称。中国武术也是中国传统体育运动的一种，无论是年轻人还是老年人都可以练习。中国武术已成为中国文化的独特元素。中国武术中有些招式模仿了动物的动作，还有一些则是受到中国哲学思想、神话和传说的启发。

翻译技巧：无主句（Sentences without Subject）

无主句，即只有谓语部分而没有主语的句子。汉语注重意合，无主句较为常见，而英语注重形合，句子一般都不能缺少主语。英译汉语无主句时，一般可采取两种策略：一是寻找主语并改变句式，基本做法是增译隐藏主语；二是进行句型的转换。由于汉英两种语言在思维方式、句法结构等方面存在诸多差异，译者的工作就是运用相关技巧对原文进行适当调整。在翻译无主句时，一定要灵活处理句子结构，以求达到最佳的翻译质量。

例 1　原文　据说文明总是在进步。

　　　译文　It is said that civilization is always on the move.

　　　评析　"据说……"可用固定句型"It is reported/said/believed that…"进行翻译。

例 2　原文　他的脸上闪现出一丝淡淡的微笑。

　　　译文　A faint smile lights up his face.

　　　评析　原文中的宾语在翻译时转换为谓语动词的动作发出者。

例 3　原文　接着是一场激烈的战争。

　　　译文　A fierce war ensued.

　　　评析　该无主句为"是"字句，翻译时原文中的表语转换为译文的主语。

例 4　原文　有报道称该城市弥漫着不满的情绪。

　　　译文　There are reports of widespread discontent in the city.

　　　评析　"有……"是汉语无主句最常用的一种句型，可用 there be 句型译出。

例 5　原文　是篮球让我保持了好心情和好体型。

　　　译文　It is basketball that keeps me in good shape and mood.

　　　评析　表示原因的无主"是"字句，通常译为强调句型。

例 6　原文　不要光等待好事降临。

　　　译文　Do not wait for good things to happen to you.

评析　对于一些表示一般要求的无主句，建议译为祈使句。

例7　原文　近处是深灰色的屋顶，远处是层层叠叠的楼群。
　　　译文　Nearer in sight are dull grey rooftops, and farther on stand row upon row of buildings.
　　　评析　对于表示"……地方有……"的句式，可按照原文直接译出。

段落翻译

1. 太极

太极是古代中国自有武术体系的一部分，融合了深刻的理论和武术技能。太极始终流动的招式表面上看起来很神秘。它能提升内部能量，对身体进行调理，独特而富有挑战性。太极需要放松，练习太极需要全神贯注、思想集中，使思想能够引领身体的能量。太极不仅是一门武术，还一直被视为一种健康运动。无论是出于健康的目的练习太极，还是将其视为竞技运动项目和武术，掌握太极的内在特点都需要时间、耐心和高质量的练习。要达到很高的太极水平，必须经历一个相当复杂的训练过程。

难点讲解：

1) 第一句和第三句均包含对太极的描述，描述部分可采用定语从句组织翻译。

2) "使思想能够引领身体的能量"可译为分词短语 allowing the mind to lead and guide the body's energy。

3) "掌握太极的内在特点都需要时间、耐心和高质量的练习"可译为形式主语为 it 的句式。

4) "要达到很高的太极水平，必须经历一个相当复杂的训练过程"一句无主语，翻译时可用不定式短语作主语。

2. 互联网

随着互联网时代的快速发展，互联网技术正在改变企业的经营方式和管理手段。电子商务平台的建立为企业的营销和推广提供了新的渠道。电子商务市场的不断扩大，使得一些传统企业也开始进行电子商务平台的搭建与使用，这些企业有效地利用了电子商务平台，开拓出新的领域。互联网在中国被广泛使用，已经渗透到中国人生活的各个方面。中国使用较多的互联网业务包括电子邮件、新闻、搜索引擎、网页浏览、在线音乐、即时消息、在线娱乐等。互联网正逐步改变着人们的消费理念、娱乐方式、社交模式及思维方式。现在互联网信息技术比人类历史上的任何一项科学发明都更加深刻地影响着人们的生活。互联网的日渐流行带来了重大的社会变化。随着中国电子商务的繁荣和发展，网络团购如今已非常流行。它方便、快捷、价格低、不受地域限制。据了解，网络团购的主要群体是中国大中城市的年轻人。

难点讲解：

1) "互联网在中国被广泛使用"中的"在中国被广泛使用"可以译为分词短语 being widely used in China，将"已经渗透到生活的各个方面"作为句子的主句。也可以将这两个分句译为并列句，用 and 连接。

2) "中国使用较多的互联网业务包括……"，可译作"The Internet businesses frequently used by Chinese Internet users include …"，使用过去分词短语作定语，放在所修饰的名词 the Internet businesses 之后，其意义相当于定语从句 which are used frequently by Chinese Internet users。

3) 翻译"互联网正逐步改变着……"一句时注意使用连接词 and 或 as well as 等增强逻辑性；另

外,"正逐步改变着"暗示时态要用现在完成进行时。

4)"现在互联网信息技术比人类历史上的任何一项科学发明都更加深刻地影响着人们的生活"这句话较长,主干结构为"互联网信息技术影响着人们的生活"。句中的"现在比人类历史上……"等词提示该句的时态应为现在完成进行时;此外,句中还包含一个比较结构"更深刻地",比较的是影响的程度,可译为"more deeply than…"。

5)"日渐流行"可译为 increasingly popular/prevalent 或 increasing popularity。

6)"方便、快捷、价格低、不受地域限制"可译为 convenient, fast, low in price and unrestrained by regions。此外,该句也可以译为"It has the characteristic of convenience, efficiency, inexpensiveness and no territory restriction"。

7)最后一句中的"据了解……"可使用"It is known that…"的结构,后跟 that 引导的主语从句。

3. 旅游

越来越多的中国年轻人开始对旅游产生兴趣,这是近年来的新趋势。年轻游客数量的不断增加,可以归因于年轻人探索外部世界的好奇心。随着旅行多了,年轻人在大城市和著名景点花的时间少了,他们反而更为偏远的地方所吸引。有些人甚至选择长途背包旅行。最近有调查显示,很多年轻人想要通过旅行体验不同文化、丰富知识、扩展视野。居家度假(staycation)是指一个人或一家人待在家里休息,或者在离家不远的景点度过一段时光。人们居家度假的原因有很多,如家庭预算紧张、出游成本不断攀升,或者孩子太小。节假日期间景区人山人海,高速公路和城市道路拥堵(congestion),这也是促使人们居家度假的主要原因。常见的居家度假活动包括在家里招待朋友、游览当地的公园和博物馆或参与当地一些节日活动等。居家度假也可以丰富多彩,它将成为一种新的度假趋势。

难点讲解:

1)第一句中"这是近年来的新趋势"是对前半句的解释,可采用定语从句译出。

2)第二句中"年轻游客数量的不断增加"可采用直译法翻译。

3)"最近有调查显示,很多年轻人想要通过旅行体验不同文化、丰富知识、扩展视野"中的并列短语可采用平行结构译出,再现原文的修辞效果。

4)"居家度假是指一个人或一家人待在家里休息,或者在离家不远的景点度过一段时光"中的主干结构为"居家度假是指……一段时光",因为定语过长,可将定语处理成 which 引导的定语从句。

5)"如家庭预算紧张、出游成本不断攀升,或者孩子太小"具体列举人们在家中度假的原因,翻译"紧张""攀升"和"太小"时可采用"形容词+名词"的结构,即 like tight family budgets, rising travel costs or having very young kids,比较符合英文表达习惯。

6)在"节假日期间景区人山人海,高速公路和城市道路拥堵,这也是促使人们居家度假的主要原因"一句中,"景区人山人海"和"高速公路和城市道路拥堵"都是主谓短语,可理解成"人山人海的景区"和"拥堵的高速公路和城市道路",分别译作 overcrowded tourist sites 和 congestion on expressways and city roads,符合英文中多用名词表达的语言特点。

7)最后一句由两个分句组成,可译为两个并列句,用连接词 and 连接。

4. 生活方式

近年来,中国传统的家庭规模和结构发生了明显变化,家庭结构呈现出小型化(miniaturization)趋势,传统的大家庭逐渐被核心家庭取代。家庭规模与结构的变化,使家庭中的人际关系变得简单。

难点讲解：

1）翻译"家庭结构呈现出小型化趋势，传统的大家庭逐渐被核心家庭取代"一句时可将"家庭结构呈现出小型化趋势"处理成句子主干，"传统的大家庭逐渐被核心家庭取代"可处理成 which 引导的非限制性定语从句，进一步说明"家庭结构的小型化趋势"，同时使句式富于变化。

2）翻译"家庭规模与结构的变化，使家庭中的人际关系变得简单"一句时，可将"家庭中的人际关系变得简单"处理成名词短语，译作 simple family relationship，这样处理符合英文中多用名词表达的语言特点，也使译文表达更简洁。

5. 智能手机

由于通信网络的快速发展，中国智能手机用户数量近年来以惊人的速度增长。这极大地改变了许多人的阅读方式。现在，人们经常在智能手机上阅读新闻和文章，而不再像以前那样经常购买传统报刊。大量移动应用程序（Apps）的开发使人们能用手机读小说和其他形式的文学作品。因此，纸质书籍的销售也受到了一定影响。但一项调查显示，尽管智能手机阅读市场稳步发展，超半数成年人仍喜欢阅读纸质书。

难点讲解：

1）"这极大地改变了许多人的阅读方式"与前文句意紧密，可采用定语从句，与前一句合译为一句。

2）"而不再像以前那样经常购买传统报刊"可采用介词短语直接译出。

3）"稳步发展"可译为"grow steadily"。

6. 广告消费

公益广告（public service advertisement）指为社会公众的利益和社会风尚服务的广告。它不以营利为目的，属于非商业性广告，是社会公益事业（cause of the public good）的重要组成部分。公益广告的主题一般取材于老百姓的日常生活，如健康、安全和环保等。它的目的是提高公众的道德意识，引导公众用正确的态度关注社会问题。中国最早的公益广告出现在1986年。随后，公益广告的社会影响力逐渐增强。2013年，中央电视台举办了首届电视公益广告大赛，呼吁社会各界关注并参与公益事业。

难点讲解：

1）第一句的主干结构为"公益广告指……广告"，即"Public service advertisement refers to the advertisement…"。"为社会公众的利益和社会风尚服务的"是"广告"的定语，由于定语较长，可将其处理为 that 引导的定语从句，修饰"广告"。

2）第二句由三个分句构成，可将"它不以营利为目的，属于非商业性广告"处理成主句，即 it is noncommercial and does not aim at making profit；"是社会公益事业的重要组成部分"可采用"as+名词短语"结构，译作 as a significant part of the cause of the public good，置于句首。这样翻译比译为并列句或定语从句更加简洁明了。

3）翻译"它的目的是提高公众的道德意识，引导公众用正确的态度关注社会问题"一句时，可用"Its objectives are…"作为句子主干结构。

4）对于最后一句的翻译，"中央电视台举办了首届电视公益广告大赛"可处理为译文句子的主干。"呼吁……"可采用现在分词"appealing to…"作伴随状语来翻译。

7. 社会服务

大学生社会实践活动是引导学生走出校门、接触社会、了解国情，并使理论与实践相结合的良好形式；是大学生投身祖国建设、向社会学习、锻炼自身能力的重要渠道；是提高思想觉悟、增强大学生服务社会的意识、促进大学生健康成长的有效途径。社会实践活动有助于大学生更新观念，树立正确的世界观、人生观、价值观。同时，大学生参加社会实践对社会主义物质文明建设和精神文明建设也可起到积极的作用。

难点讲解：

1)"大学生"可译为 college students，也可译为 undergraduates。

2)"引导学生走出校门"可译为 to guide undergraduates out of the university。

3)"接触社会"可译为 get in touch with the society。get in touch 意为"接触，联系"。

4)"投身祖国建设"可译为 devote to the construction of the country。其中 devote to 意为"投身于，奉献"，to 为介词。

5)"更新观念"可译为 renew ideas。其中 renew 意为"更新"。

6)"同时"可译为 meanwhile 或 at the same time，也可译为 in the meantime。

7)"起到积极的作用"可译为 have a positive effect on 或 have a positive impact on。

拓展阅读

Tuina and Your Emotional Health

In Traditional Chinese Medicine the body, mind and spirit cannot be divided and so the unique whole-body treatment in Tuina can also be a useful treatment correcting any imbalances in the body's energy before symptoms and disease can develop. It also works to restore emotional harmony as well as physical health. This is why after a Tuina treatment many people feel good. Many people in China use Tuina regularly to keep health and to deal with some specific illnesses.

Tuina is performed on the clothed body and the patient is either lying on a couch or sitting on a chair. Therapists using a variety of strokes or movements will control the intensity and direction of pressure in an exact way. The unique rolling movement in Tuina is one of the most difficult strokes to learn and students have to practice sometimes for many months on a rice bag before they are allowed to practice on the human body.

Stress

Tuina is of course very useful for treating stress.

Not only is it very relaxing for the muscles, but also by working on the meridians, it distributes the energy around the whole body. It is believed that Tuina moves the strong energy in the tense muscles to the weaker areas, thus making a more balanced body. When your Qi, or energy flow in the body is balanced you feel relaxed and comfortable. Tuina is especially useful for stiff shoulders and tense neck muscles.

Emotions

In Traditional Chinese Medicine each major organ is linked to an emotion. By balancing the energy in the organ, the relevant emotion will be calmed.

When your emotions are out of control you would usually turn to your doctor or perhaps a psychotherapist. But perhaps some people would not like to be seeing a psychotherapist or feel nervous about discussing their problems with others. With Tuina one does not need to tell the therapist anything one does not want to. The treatment of Tuina can deal with the problem itself—although if one does need to talk, then the safe space is there to do so. An active dialogue between the therapist and the patient will help to get a better effect.

How the major organs rule your emotions?

Each major organ—the heart, the stomach, the spleen, the liver, the bladder, the kidneys, the lungs, etc. —is linked to a relevant emotion.

The heart is linked to joy, excitement and sadness. If the heart is out of balance, the patient may dream a lot at night and often forget something important in the day.

The stomach and spleen are connected with too much thinking or worrying—over anxiety. When the stomach is out of balance there is often a lack of energy. The patient often feels very tired and has no interest in doing anything at all.

The liver and gall bladder are linked to anger. In Chinese Medicine the eyes are connected with the liver, and many people who suffer from anger often suffer from eye problems. The gall bladder rules decision-making and too much energy here can lead to rashness, while if there is too little it can bring about indecision. Where there is a history of depression, the therapist would look to the liver.

The bladder and kidneys are linked to fear of all kinds, from simple anxieties and phobias to vague fears and worries.

The lungs are connected with feelings of grief and sadness. When there is a history of grief, the therapist would look to the lungs.

Tuina is used in almost all the hospitals in China and very popular among Chinese people. It is a useful and valuable method of restoring Qi balance, when emotional and physical health is out of balance. Tuina is one of the remaining secrets of Chinese Medicine.

Exercises

 Match the English expressions in Column A with the Chinese translations in Column B.

Column A   Column B

1 traditional Chinese medicine therapy   a 调节机体平衡
2 therapy movements   b 疏通经络
3 the balance of yin and yang   c 治疗手法
4 maintain good health   d 中医学
5 correct imbalance in body's energy   e 中医治疗
6 full of energy   f 阴阳调和
7 restore physical health   g 养生
8 work on the meridians   h 恢复生理健康
9 emotions out of control   i 情绪紊乱
10 traditional Chinese medicine   j 精力充沛

2 Answer the following questions.

1) How can the emotion be calmed from the perspective of Tuina?

2) What does the last paragraph tell us about Tuina?

翻译练习

1. 改革开放以来，中国人民生活水平不断提高，这在人们的饮食变化上得到充分体现。如今，人们不再满足于吃得饱，而是追求吃得更加安全、更加营养、更加健康，食物也愈来愈丰富多样，不再限于本地的农产品。物流业(logistics industry)的发展使人们很容易品尝到全国各地的特产。毫无疑问，食品质量的提高与饮食结构的改善为增进人们健康提供了有力的保障。

2. 越来越多的中国人现在离不开手机。他们中的许多人，包括老年人，都使用手机应用程序(Apps)与亲朋好友保持联系并拓宽朋友圈。他们也用手机购物、查找信息。然而，这种新趋势可能导致人们在社交时过度依赖手机，容易使人们忽视与家人和朋友面对面的交流。

3. 随着生活水平的提高，度假在中国人生活中的作用越来越重要。近年来中国旅游业发展迅速。经济的繁荣使国内旅游市场蓬勃发展，出国旅游也越来越普遍。2019年国庆节假日期间，旅游消费总计超过4,000亿元。据世界贸易组织估计，在未来几年里中国将成为出境旅游支出增长最快的国家。

4. 自行车曾经是中国城乡最主要的交通工具。如今，随着人们生活方式的改变，骑自行车又开始流行起来。近年来，中国企业家将移动互联网技术与传统自行车结合在一起，发明了共享单车商业模式。共享单车的出现使骑车出行更加方便，人们仅需一部连接了网络的手机就可以随时使用共享单车。为了鼓励人们骑车出行，很多城市修建了自行车道。现在，越来越多的中国人也喜欢通过骑自行车健身。

5. 过去，拥有一辆私家车对大部分中国人而言是件奢侈的事。如今，私家车在中国随处可见。汽车成了人们生活中不可或缺的一部分，为人们的出行提供了便利。然而，汽车数量日益增长也使交通拥堵和停车位不足的问题日益严峻。出于环保考虑，现在越来越多的人选择购买新能源汽车，中国政府也采取了一些措施，支持新能源汽车的发展。

6. 随着人们环境保护意识的增强，"低碳"这个词变得非常流行。这个词出现在许多领域，如低碳产品、低碳消费、低碳旅游等。低碳生活是一种新型生活方式，旨在尽量减少生活中的二氧化碳排放。例如，一些上班族不再开私家车通勤，而是骑车或乘坐公共交通工具。

7. 中国城市化将会充分释放潜在内需。一些经济学家指出，在中国，城市化进程使得越来越多的人向城市迁徙。住房及城市基础设施建设，包括水、天然气等能源的供应将会成为城市发展的焦点问题。商品的快速自由流通是城市化社会的一项基本特征。

8. 近年来，中国老龄人口持续增长。中国政府正采取各种措施，推进养老服务体系建设，使老年人晚年生活健康幸福。全国各地兴建了各类养老服务机构。为了提升养老机构的服务质量，政府颁布了一系列标准，加强对养老机构的监管。许多城市为方便老年人用餐，开设了社区食堂，为他们提供价格实惠的饭菜。行动不便的老年人还能享受上门送餐服务。同时，中国还在积极探索居家和社区养老等其他养老模式。

Unit 11

风景名胜

> **Unit Goals**
>
> In this unit, you are going to
> - grasp words and expressions concerning scenic spots and historical sites in China;
> - acquire knowledge about scenic spots and historical sites in China which attract tourists all over the world;
> - know how to use the skills of word conversion in the translating process;
> - grasp translation skills of paragraphs on scenic spots and historical sites in China.

Related Words and Expressions

世界文化和自然遗产 World Cultural and Natural Heritage
名胜古迹 scenic spots and historical sites
旅游胜地 tourist attraction
自然保护区 nature reserve; nature preservation zone
自然景观 natural attraction; natural scenery; natural landscape
人文景观 places of historic figures and cultural heritage
历史人文 history and human culture
历史文物 historical relics
文物 cultural relics
书法真迹 calligraphic relics
度假胜地 holiday resort
避暑胜地 summer resort
蜜月度假胜地 honeymoon resort
奇峰异石 picturesque peak and rocks
奇花异草 exotic flowers and herbs
青山绿水 green hills and clear waters
依山傍水 nestling under a mountain and near river; lie at the foot of a mountain and beside a river
名山大川 famous mountains and great rivers
湖光山色 landscape of lakes and hills
景色如画 picturesque views
险峰 perilous peaks
雪峰 snow-topped peaks

极目远眺 look as far as the eyes can see
一览无余 hold all views in sight/in a single glance
尽收眼底 have/command a panoramic view
十三陵 Ming Tombs
颐和园 Summer Palace
承德避暑山庄 Chengde Mountain Resort
莫高窟 Mogao Grottoes
拙政园 Humble Administrator Garden
狮子林 Lion Grove Garden
留园 Lingering Garden
网师园 Master of Nets Garden
沧浪亭 Surging Waves Pavilion
孔庙 Confucian Temple
孔府 Confucius Family Mansion
都江堰水利系统 Dujiangyan Irrigation System
乐山大佛 Leshan Giant Buddha
曲径 winding path
亭台楼阁 pavilions, terraces and towers
走廊 corridor
泉水 spring water; spring
假山 rockeries
怪石 rock formations
行宫 a temporary imperial palace
御花园 imperial garden
外朝 the Outer Court
内廷 the Inner Court
文渊阁 the Pavilion of Literacy Profundity
太庙 Imperial Ancestral Temple
养心殿 Hall of Mental Cultivation
乾清宫 Palace of Heavenly Purity
坤宁宫 Palace of Earthly Tranquility
太和殿 Hall of Supreme Harmony
西湖 The West Lake
日月潭 Sun Moon Lake
象鼻山 Elephant Trunk Hill
石林 Stone Forest
黄鹤楼 Yellow Crane Tower
外滩 the Bund
人民英雄纪念碑 Monument to the People's Heroes
人民大会堂 the Great Hall of the People

Unit 11 风景名胜

武汉长江大桥 Wuhan Changjiang River Bridge
鼓浪屿 Gulangyu Island; Gulangyu Islet
居庸关 Juyongguan Pass
蓬莱阁 Penglai Pavilion
雍和宫 Yonghegong Lamasery
中山陵 Dr Sun Yet-sen's Mausoleum
华清池 Huaqing Hot Spring

Lead-in Activities

 Answer the following questions.

1) Do you like traveling? What will be your first concern when you decide where to go?

2) Have you ever visited any famous tourist attractions in China? Which place impressed you most?

3) Why does China attract so many foreign tourists every year? Could you explain the reasons?

2 **Listen to a brief introduction to the Huangguoshu Waterfall and fill in the blanks with the words you hear.**

The Huangguoshu Waterfall, _____ in China and also the largest waterfall in Asia, is located on the Baishui River in the Buyei Miao _____, in southwest China's Guizhou province. The Huangguoshu Waterfall cascades over a rocky cliff face and _____ _____.

There are 18 more waterfalls _____ of the Baishui River, where the Huangguoshu Waterfall lies. These waterfalls form _____ in the world and were listed in the Guinness World Records in 1999. The best time to visit the Huangguoshu Waterfall is from May to October. As early as 300 years ago, the famous Chinese _____ Xu Xiake wrote, "the foams rise from the rocks _____. The waterfall has such momentum that even 'a screen of pearl _____ hooks' or 'silk that hangs on faraway peaks' cannot describe to the full its majesty."

 Read the following passage and then do the exercises.

The Five Famous Mountains

The Five Famous Mountains are collectively called "Wuyue." They are the East Mountain Taishan (located in Shandong Province), the West Mountain Huashan (located in Shaanxi Province), the South Mountain Hengshan (located in Hunan Province), the North Mountain Hengshan (located in Shanxi Province), and the Central Mountain Songshan (located in Henan Province).

The East Mountain Taishan is the first of the Five Famous Mountains and the highest mountain in the eastern part of the Central Plains. The ancient people believed that the east side represented spring and was also a place where the auspicious purple gas came from, so Taishan became an ancient worship ground of the people and emperors. There is a saying, "If Taishan is at peace, all the seas are safe." The mountain body of Taishan is heavy and contrasts with the changing of clouds on the mountain. The scenery is beautiful and magical. The Jade Emperor's Peak at an altitude of more than 1,500 meters is the highest peak of Taishan. In ancient times, many emperors climbed to worship. Along the steps from the foot of the mountain to the Jade Emperor's Peak, the majestic mountain walls of Taishan have many ancient inscriptions, which confirmed the glorious history of the Taishan culture.

The West Mountain Huashan, which is opposite from the East Mountain, is part of the Qinling Mountains. The five peaks of the east, west, south, north and center look like five petals. In ancient times, the words "花(flower)" and "华(splendid/China)" were interchangeable, so it was called "Huashan." Huashan has a turbulent climate for it is surrounded by clouds, and it is like a fairyland. Although Huashan is not the highest in the Five Famous Mountains, it is the steepest and reputed as "the world's most dangerous mountain." There are many dangerous places on the mountain. The narrowest ridge is only one meter wide and there are cliffs on both sides. Visitors can only pass slowly while holding a rope, and those who do not have courage should not go.

The North Mountain in Hengshan (恒山) is the first natural barrier to the plains of Inner Mongolia. Legend has it that more than 4,000 years ago, when Emperor Shun arrived at this place, he found that the mountain was majestic; he liked it so much that he sealed it as "North Mountain." The scenery of Hengshan is beautiful. The pine trees, cypress trees, Buddhist temples, Taoist temples, pavilions, beautiful flowers and plants, rock formations and caves make up the famous "18 sceneries." There are also many cultural relics and historic sites, such as the Hanging Temple and the Pure Sun Palace, which occupy an important position in the history of ancient Chinese architecture. Especially the Hanging Temple: looking from afar, it seems like a huge rock wall carving, so that visitors cannot help but admire the superb architectural skills of the ancients.

The South Mountain Hengshan (衡山) is a famous Taoist and Buddhist holy place in China. There are 72 large and small mountain peaks, among which Zhurong Peak is the highest peak. Legend has it that the fire god Zhurong lives here. The climate of Hengshan is warm and humid, and the plants on the mountain are dense, so it is called "the Natural Botanical Garden."

The Central Mountain Songshan has a unique geological structure and was selected as a World Geology Park by UNESCO. Songshan has many places of interest in the surrounding area, and China's rich cultural traditions combine here. In addition to Confucian culture, Songshan sees the thriving of Buddhist and Taoist culture, the most representative of which is the Shaolin Temple. During the Tang Dynasty, the Shaoling Temple was called the "First Pagoda in the World" and is the birthplace of Zen Buddhism in China. Shaolin martial arts have been famous all over the world, and there is still a constant stream of people who come here to learn Kung Fu at the temple.

1) Answer the following questions.

   (1) What are the Five Famous Mountains in China?

   (2) What are the characteristics of the Five Famous Mountains respectively?

   (3) Who is Emperor Shun? Do you know anything about him?

   (4) Among the five mountains, which one is the most attractive one for you? Why?

2) Translate the following words or phrases into English.

   紫气东来

   泰山安，四海皆安

   天下第一险

   天然植物园

   世界地质公园

   禅宗佛教

3) Match the mountains in Column A with the information in Column B.

Column A		Column B	
1	the East Mountain	a	the Hanging Temple and the Pure Sun Palace
		b	The Jade Emperor's Peak
2	the West Mountain	c	a unique geological structure
		d	Zhurong Peak
3	the South Mountain	e	18 sceneries
		f	The Shaolin Temple
4	the North Mountain	g	the five peaks of the east, west, south, north and center
		h	the first of the Five Famous Mountains
5	the Central Mountain	i	part of the Qinling Mountains

4) Please translate the following paragraph into English.

   位于中国东部安徽省的黄山是中国十大著名景点之一。它的特点是"四奇"，即奇松、怪石、云海和清澈的温泉。黄山以山景俱全而闻名，有"天下第一山"之称，1,000米以上的山峰77座，石柱林立，松树长青。黄山的风景特色还包括奇形怪状的岩石，其中许多都是单独命名的，此外还有瀑布、水池和温泉。由于雾和云的存在，黄山的自然景观常会发生意想不到的变化。

翻译技巧：词性转换（Word Conversion）

词性转换是指在翻译的过程中为了使译文保持通畅，在不改变原文内容的前提下，按照译入语的规范，把原文中某些词的词性进行转换。英语和汉语的词类大部分是重合的，但是在汉语中一个词可以充当的句子成分要比英语中一个词能充当的句子成分更多。例如：英语中充当主语的只能是代词、名词或是相当于名词的动名词或不定式，充当谓语的则只有动词；而在汉语中，名词、动词、形容词都可以作主语、谓语、宾语及表语。因此在进行翻译的时候，可以采取灵活处理的策略，不拘泥于原文所使用的词性，在必要的时候可以对一些词的词性进行适当转换。汉语和英语作为两种完全不同的语言，词汇之间并不存在完全对应的关系，语言的表达习惯也不尽相同，在汉译英时，译者常常需要进行词性转换。

Ⅰ. 汉语动词的转换

汉语和英语句子在动词使用方面区别很大：汉语动词使用很频繁，一个句子中会出现好几个动词连用的情况，除了大量的动宾结构还有连动式和兼语式；英语中一个句子通常只有一个动词作为谓语。所以在翻译过程中，汉语动词经常要转换成其他词性的词，如名词、形容词、介词等。

1. 汉语动词转换为英语名词

例1 原文 选择朋友，越谨慎越好。
译文 One can never be too careful in the choice of friends.
评析 原文中"选择"为动词，为了更加符合英语的构句特点，在翻译时转换成了名词 choice。

例2 原文 屋顶需要特别考虑一下，以确保能经受住日晒雨淋。
译文 Roofs require special consideration to ensure adequate durability in relation to the exposure to the sun and rain.
评析 原句中"需要"和"考虑"都是动词，如果对应翻译成英语的动词，即 require to be considered，则太过啰唆。把"考虑"翻译成英语的名词，译文则会更加紧凑、自然。此外"确保"和"经受"也同为动词，翻译的时候同样需要把其中之一转换为名词。按照英语表达习惯，可将"经受"翻译为名词 durability。

2. 汉语动词转换为英语形容词

例1 原文 对于一个二十岁的女孩来说，很难抵制住这样的诱惑。
译文 For a girl aged 20, such temptation is irresistible.
评析 原文中的"很难抵制"在翻译的时候可以直接译为"is difficult to resist…"，也可以像译文这样用其同根词 irresistible，语言更加精练，也更符合英语的表达习惯。

例2 原文 他热爱科学研究，但对升职完全不感兴趣。
译文 He is keen on scientific research but indifferent to promotion.
评析 原文中"热爱"和"不感兴趣"都是动词，但根据英语的表达习惯，翻译成了形容词 keen 和 indifferent。

3. 汉语动词转换为英语介词或介词词组

例1 原文 他一想到这场灾难，就两腿僵硬得一步都挪动不了。
译文 At the thought of the disaster, his legs stiffened under him and he couldn't move a step further.
评析 原文中"一想到"是谓语动词，在翻译成英语时译成 at the thought of 这一介词短语引导的时间状语，译文句子结构更加紧凑、精练。

例2 原文 我谨代表公司全体员工，感谢你所提供的帮助。
译文 On behalf of all staff of the company, I would like to thank you for all your help.
评析 "代表"在原文中是谓语动词，在翻译时用 on behalf of 引导的介词短语作状语放在句首，使译文句子结构更加清晰。

Ⅱ. 汉语名词的转换

当汉语的名词作主语、表语或宾语时，一般会译为相应的英语名词。但有时为了符合英语表达习惯，汉语句子中的名词会转译为英语的动词、形容词或者副词。

1. 汉语名词转换为英语动词

例1 原文 雄伟的人民大会堂给我们留下了深刻的印象。

译文 The magnificent Great Hall of the People impressed us tremendously.

评析 原文中"留下深刻印象"既可翻译为"make a deep impression on…"，即不改变原文名词的词性，又可以用动词短语"impress … tremendously"来翻译，其中原文中作定语的形容词"深刻的"需转译为英语的副词 tremendously。

例2 原文 诚实与勤奋是他成功的原因。

译文 Honesty and diligence have contributed to his success.

评析 原文中"原因"这个名词并没有直接被翻译成英语中对应的名词 reason，而是用更符合英语表达习惯的动词短语 contribute to 来翻译。

2. 汉语名词转换为英语形容词或副词

例1 原文 钢的碳含量越高，硬度就越大。

译文 The more carbon the steel contains, the harder it is.

评析 原句中的"越……越……"可以用"the more … the more …"结构来翻译。原句中的"硬度"是名词，翻译成英语时转换成形了容词 hard，并使用其比较级形式。

例2 原文 氧是物质世界的重要元素之一，它的化学反应非常强烈。

译文 Oxygen is one of the important elements in the physical world; it is very chemically active.

评析 原文中的"化学反应"是名词短语，但是在翻译的时候为了符合英语的表达习惯使用了形容词 active，原文中"化学"这个词作为"反应"的定语，也需要相应地转换为修饰形容词 active 的副词 chemically。

Ⅲ. 汉语形容词或副词的转换

有时为了使译文更为流畅和地道，汉语的形容词或副词也需要进行词性的转换，译为英语的名词、介词或介词短语。

1. 汉语形容词或副词转换为英语名词

例1 原文 我很荣幸地得到了他的帮助。

译文 I had the fortune to get his help.

评析 在这个例子中，"荣幸地"这个副词在翻译的时候转译为名词 fortune，使用了 have the fortune to do sth 这样的结构，更符合英语表达习惯。

例2 原文 我们应该使受教育者成为有社会主义觉悟的、有文化的劳动者。

译文 We must enable everyone who receives an education to become a laborer with both socialist consciousness and culture.

评析 原句中的两个形容词"有社会主义觉悟的""有文化的"在翻译成英语的时候转换成了名词 socialist consciousness 和 culture，由 with 引导作定语修饰名词 laborer。

2. 汉语副词转换为英语形容词或汉语形容词转换为英语副词

例1 原文 她急切地希望解决这个棘手的问题。

译文 She has a strong desire to solve this thorny problem.

评析　原文中的"急切地"是一个副词，但因为原文中的动词"希望"在翻译时被转译为名词 desire，所以修饰语也需要由副词转换为形容词 strong。

例 2　原文　(卢沟桥的狮子)生动活泼，坐卧起伏，姿态各不相同。

译文　They are all vividly and lively depicted in different postures—sitting, lying, standing or crouching.

评析　原句中的"生动活泼"本是形容词，在译文中为了更清晰地表达句子含义使用了副词 vividly and lively 用来形容动词 depict。

3. 汉语形容词或副词转换为英语介词或介词短语

例 1　原文　他放弃了这次难得的机会，我很惊讶。

译文　To my surprise, he gave up the precious opportunity.

评析　在这个例子中，"惊讶"这个形容词在翻译成英语时转换成了介词短语 to one's surprise，使译文更加自然、地道。

例 2　原文　我们必须广泛利用现代科学技术的新发明和新成就。

译文　We have to utilize the new inventions and achievements of modern science and technology on a wide scale.

评析　原文中的"广泛"是副词，但是在翻译成英语的时候转换成了介词短语 on a wide scale，这样翻译既能准确地表达出原文的含义，又使译文更加地道。

段落翻译

1. 世界遗产

自 1987 年以来，经联合国教科文组织审核被批准列入《世界遗产名录》的中国世界遗产共有 57 项。北京拥有 7 处世界遗产，是世界上拥有遗产项目最多的城市。中国的世界遗产包括文化和自然遗产。既有泰山、黄山、武陵源、九寨沟等自然遗产地，又有著名的石窟、古城和村落等文化遗产地。这些景点是中国宝贵而丰富的旅游资源中重要的组成部分，吸引着大量国内外游客前来旅游参观。中国还有丰富的非物质文化遗产。昆曲是中国最具影响力的传统戏剧之一，被联合国教科文组织列入人类口头和非物质文化遗产代表作名录。

难点讲解：

1)《世界遗产名录》应译为 World Heritage List；联合国教科文组织英语全称为 United Nations Educational, Scientific and Cultural Organization，简称 UNESCO。

2) 第一句中的"经……审核被批准列入……的"可以译为 by 引导的介词短语，即"… put on the … by …"，"审核被批准"无须翻译出来。

3) 第二句"是世界上……最多的城市"可用 ranks first 来表达，也可直译为 owns the most heritage sites。

4) "石窟""古城"可分别译为 grottos 和 old/ancient cities。

5) "国内外游客"可译为 tourists at home and abroad。

6) "人类口头和非物质文化遗产代表作名录"应译为 Masterpieces of the Oral and Intangible Heritage of Humanity。

2. 长城

中国长城是古代的军事防御工事，由石头、砖头、夯实土、木材和其他材料建成。长城基本上是沿中国历史上的北部边界线从东到西建造的，以保护中原地区免遭游牧民族的入侵。现在所看到的长城多为明长城。明长城东起鸭绿江，西至嘉峪关，长达8,000多千米，是历史上最令人印象深刻的建筑之一。自20世纪起有一种说法流行起来，即长城是地球上唯一可以从太空用肉眼观测到的人造建筑物。中国长城，不仅是文化古迹，也是独一无二的自然景观，是人类的奇迹。

难点讲解：

1)第一句和第二句可以分别翻译，也可合译成一句，即将第二句翻译为过去分词形式作为第一句的状语。

2)"防御工事"和"夯实土"可译为 fortification 和 tamped earth。

3)"游牧民族"可译为 nomadic groups。

4)"鸭绿江""嘉峪关"可用音译与直译相结合的方式翻译为 the Yalu River 和 Jiayuguan Pass。

5)第五句可以用 emerging since 20th century 作定语来修饰 a popular claim。

6)"文化古迹"和"自然景观"可分别翻译为 cultural relic 和 natural landscape。

3. 珠穆朗玛峰

在青藏高原南部边缘，耸立着高大、雄伟的喜马拉雅山，"喜马拉雅"在藏语中意为"雪的故乡"。它的主峰珠穆朗玛峰终年积雪，是世界最高峰，因此成了登山爱好者的圣地。2020年，经测量，珠穆朗玛峰的高度为8,848.86米。每年的4月至6月是游览珠穆朗玛峰的最佳时节，对登山爱好者来说也是绝佳的时机。每年都有大批英勇强健的登山爱好者从世界各地前来参观和攀登珠穆朗玛峰。他们希望通过登上世界最高峰俯瞰世界，实现毕生的梦想。

难点讲解：

1)第一句比较长，"'喜马拉雅'……'雪的故乡'"可以处理为定语从句。

2)第二句的"是世界最高峰"与后一分句存在因果关系，故可以拆译；"圣地"可译为 holy place。

3)"最佳时节"可以直译为 the best season，也可译为 the optimum weather。

4)最后一句"通过……实现毕生的梦想"可以用介词 by 引导的短语作方式状语来翻译，即"fulfill a life-long dream by…"。

4. 九寨沟

九寨沟位于中国四川省北部的阿坝藏族羌族自治州。常年积雪覆盖的山峰，苍翠繁茂的森林，连绵的湖泊，各种各样的鸟兽，构成了九寨沟独特的景观。一进入景区，你就会发现自己漫步在仙境中。这是一个水的世界。水是九寨沟的灵魂，为它带来了最迷人的景色。无论是宁静的湖泊，还是奔腾的瀑布，都会使人沉浸其中，流连忘返。九寨沟的当地人称这些湖为"海子"。九寨沟共有108个大小不一、形状各异的"海子"，但每一个都清澈见底。一些湖泊隐匿在山谷中，而另一些则镶嵌在原始森林中。"五花海"是九寨沟的著名景点之一，意为"五彩的海"，在阳光明媚的日子里，湖底的藻类和沉积物会发出五彩缤纷的光芒。

难点讲解：

1)"阿坝藏族羌族自治州"译为 Aba Tibetan and Qiang Autonomous Prefecture。

2)第二句可以用现在分词短语作定语来进行翻译，即"contributing to…"，也可译为定语从句"which contribute to…"。

3)"苍翠繁茂的森林，连绵的湖泊"可译为 verdant and lush forest, stretches of serene lakes。

4)"漫步在仙境中"可译为 strolling in a fairyland。

5)"清澈见底"可译为 limpidity to the bottom of the lake。

6)"藻类和沉积物"可翻译为 algae and sediments。

5. 孔庙

孔子是中国儒家学派的创始人,他是中国伟大的哲学家、道德家、政治家和教育家。人们建立了数千座孔庙来纪念他,现今保存比较好的孔庙有 300 余座。其中规模最大、最著名的要数孔子的故乡山东曲阜的孔庙。历代帝王不断对其进行扩建,使它成为一处规模宏大的古建筑群,前后共有九进院落。曲阜孔庙是世界人民朝拜孔子的重要场所,也是中国、日本、越南、印度尼西亚、新加坡、美国等地 2,000 多座孔庙的典范。曲阜孔庙极高的历史文化艺术价值也使其发展成一处著名的旅游胜地。

难点讲解:

1)"孔子"和"儒家学派"为专有名词,译为 Confucius 和 Confucianism。

2)"纪念"可译为 to commemorate。

3)第二句和第三句可根据句子之间的逻辑关系拆解再重新合并翻译,即第二句前半句独立成句,后半句和第三句合译。

4)"规模宏大的古建筑群"可译为 a grand ancient building complex。

5)"朝拜孔子"在翻译的时候可进行词性转换,转译为名词词组 worshippers of Confucius。

6. 秦始皇陵兵马俑

秦始皇陵兵马俑被誉为世界第八大奇迹。1987 年,秦始皇陵和兵马俑被联合国教科文组织批准列入《世界遗产名录》。秦始皇陵是我国规模最大、结构最奇特、内涵最丰富的帝王陵寝。事实上,它是一个豪华的地下宫殿。秦兵马俑无论从数量、质量还是考古发现上都是举世罕见的。它为深入研究公元前 2 世纪秦朝的军事、政治、经济、文化、科学和艺术提供了非常珍贵的资料。它不仅是中国人民的艺术瑰宝,也是世界人民的共同文化遗产。秦兵马俑是一种真实的主题艺术。其艺术表现手法细腻、明快、生动。每个兵马俑的手势和面部表情都不尽相同,具有鲜明的个性和强烈的时代特征,显示出当时极高的泥塑艺术水平。

难点讲解:

1)"秦始皇陵"译为 Emperor Qinshihuang's Mausoleum Site,"帝王陵寝"一般不用 tomb,要用 mausoleum。

2)"规模最大、结构最奇特、内涵最丰富"可译为 with 引导的介词短语作定语,即 the largest imperial mausoleum with most peculiar structure and abundant connotation。

3)第五句和第六句可按照中文断句分开翻译,也可把第六句处理为一个非限制性定语从句。

4)第八句较短,且和第九句逻辑关系紧密,故第十句可处理为 with 引导的介词短语。

5)"细腻、明快、生动"可译为 delicate, lucid and lively。

6)"泥塑"可翻译为 clay sculpture。

7. 杭州

在中国流传着这样一句话:"上有天堂,下有苏杭。"杭州的名气主要在于风景如画的西湖。西湖一年四季都美不胜收,宋代诗人苏东坡用"淡妆浓抹总相宜"的诗句来赞誉西湖。在杭州,游客不仅可以饱览西湖的秀色,还可以漫步街头闹市,品尝一下杭州的名菜名点,买上几样名特土产。苏堤和白堤把西湖一分为二,仿佛两条绿色的缎带,飘逸于碧波之上。湖中心有三个小岛:阮公墩、湖心亭和小瀛洲。湖水泛着涟漪,四周山林茂密,点缀着亭台楼阁,美丽的景致使西湖成为我国著名的旅游景点之一。杭州是中国六大古都之一,已有两千多年的历史。杭州不仅以自然美景闻名于世,还有着传统的文化魅力;不仅有历代文人墨客的题咏,还有美味佳肴和漂亮的工艺品。

难点讲解：

1）"上有天堂，下有苏杭"的翻译方式比较多，可译为"Just as there is paradise in heaven, there are Suzhou and Hangzhou on earth." "Up above there is paradise, down here there are Suzhou and Hangzhou."等。

2）"风景如画"可以直接用 picturesque 这个形容词来翻译。

3）"赞誉"这个词可以直接翻译出来，也可以借鉴许渊冲对"欲把西湖比西子，淡妆浓抹总相宜"这句诗的翻译"West lake may be compared to Lady of the West, whether she is richly adorned or plainly dressed."，将其翻译为 be compared to。

4）"漫步"这个词比较贴切的表述是 stroll along。

5）第五句中"一分为二"可以使用 bisect 这个词来表述，这里用被动语态会比较合适；后半句"飘逸于碧波之上"可以用现在分词短语来进行翻译。

6）"涟漪"可以翻译为 ripple，"点缀"可以表述为 be dotted by。

7）在翻译"传统文化的魅力"的时候可以省略"魅力"一词，直接翻译为 traditional culture，前文的"自然美景"可译为 natural beauty，二者在表达形式上相对应。

8）"文人墨客"可翻译为 scholars and men of letters。

8. 苏州园林

明清时期，苏州是中国最繁华的地区之一，有许多私家园林，但现在保存较好的只有十几处。著名的园林有拙政园、狮子林、留园、沧浪亭等。这些私家园林与颐和园、承德避暑山庄等皇家园林相比，规模要小得多，但它们是中国南方地区民间建筑的典型代表。苏州园林很像中国的山水画，也像唐诗宋词，在有限的空间内放置了假山树木、亭台楼阁、池塘小桥等多种景观。在园林中游览，好像在读诗赏画。园林中有图案精致的花窗、弯弯曲曲的小路、清澈的池塘，到处都能看出中国人在美化居住环境方面的创造力。1997年，苏州园林被列入《世界遗产名录》。

难点讲解：

1）原文第一句过长，可以在转折处将其拆为两句，即用一句引出苏州园林，另一句介绍具体数量。

2）拙政园、狮子林、留园、沧浪亭的英语名称分别为 Humble Administrator Garden、Lion Grove Garden、Lingering Garden、Surging Waves Pavilion。

3）颐和园、承德避暑山庄的英语名称分别为 Summer Palace 和 Chengde Imperial Summer Resort。

4）第四句也比较长，可以在意思变化处将句子拆开。"像"一字可以翻译为 looks like 或者 can be compared to，"唐诗宋词"可以简略地翻译为 Chinese classical poetry，和前面的 Chinese landscape paintings 对应；"在有限的……景观"可以单独成句，但需添加主语。

9. 乌镇

乌镇，地处中国浙江桐乡市北部，位于上海、杭州、南京三大城市中间。乌镇被纵横交错的河流分为四个区域，京杭大运河穿镇而过，是中国唯一与运河毗邻的水乡古镇。乌镇位于杭州-嘉兴-湖州淤积平原，无山丘，河流纵横交错，气候温和湿润，雨量充沛，光照充足，物产丰富，素有"鱼米之乡、丝绸之府"之称。镇内19世纪晚期的原建筑占地面积达40多亩[①]，有100多座形状各

[①] 1亩约为 666.667 平方米。

异的古石桥。乌镇好比一座古建筑的自然博物馆。当地居民就像他们的祖先一样，在古老的房子里过着安宁的生活。乌镇由于其悠久的历史、深远的文化、美丽的水乡风景、独特风味的美食、多种多样的民俗和节日，成为东方古代文明的活化石。这是自然赋予的美。乌镇向我们展示了中国古代文化的独特魅力和东方生活的灵魂，是中国传统文化的传播者和促进中外交流的使者。

难点讲解：

1)"位于上海、杭州、南京三大城市中间"按字面可以翻译成 at the center of Shanghai, Hangzhou and Nanjing，但是这样翻译对地理位置的描述并不清晰，翻译为 at the center of the triangle formed by Shanghai, Hangzhou and Nanjing 更好。

2)第二句有三个分句，三个动词"被分为""穿镇而过"和"是"分别可以处理为谓语动词、介词短语和现在分词短语；"京杭大运河"的英语是 the Beijing-Hangzhou Grand Canal；"毗邻"可以翻译为 adjacent to。

3)第三句过长，可从句子意思变化处分为两句，即先说地理位置，再说气候物产。

4)"淤积平原"的英语名称为 alluvial plain；文中出现的两处"纵横交错"可以用不同的方式翻译，比如 cross-shaped rivers 和 interlaced rivers。

5)"鱼米之乡、丝绸之府"可以简略地翻译为 the town of fish, rice, and silk。

6)"亩"可翻译为 acre，注意单位换算。

7)文中第七句需要调整语序，此句可以用原因状语从句进行翻译，但是由于从句过长，所以需要把主句放在前面，即先翻译"乌镇成为东方古代文明的活化石"，再翻译"由于……"；句中"活化石"可以翻译为 living fossil。

8)"传播者"和"使者"可分别翻译为 disseminator 和 emissary。

拓展阅读

Reading A

The Forbidden City

The Forbidden City was formerly known as the Imperial Palace, which covers an area of over 720,000 m^2, has more than 70 palaces and construction area of 150,000 m^2. Forbidden City was the imperial palace of the Ming and Qing dynasties, and is the existing China's largest and most complete ancient buildings. It was first built in 1406 and finished in 1420. There were 24 emperors living here. Experiencing several times renovation and expansion during the Ming and Qing dynasties, the Forbidden City still maintains its original layout.

The Forbidden City is known as the world's five major palaces (Forbidden City in Beijing, the Palace of Versailles in France, Buckingham Palace in UK, the White House in America, and the Kremlin Palace in Russia). In 1961, the State Council announced the Forbidden City as the first batch of national key cultural relics protection units. In 1987, the Forbidden City was listed as World Cultural Heritage by the UNESCO. Juries evaluated: "The Forbidden City is the supreme power center in China over five centuries. With its landscape architecture, and huge buildings which accommodate 9,000 rooms of furniture and crafts, it has become a priceless historical witness of the Chinese civilization of Ming and Qing era."

The Forbidden City is also a treasure trove of movable cultural relics; it is the seat of the Palace Museum. It has over 1.8 million movable cultural relics, including more than 1.68 million pieces of precious relics. In 2012, the highest single-day passenger flow volume of Forbidden City exceeded 180,000 people, and annual passenger flow volume exceeds 15 million people. It can be regarded as the busiest museum in the world.

Palace of Earthly Tranquility

Palace of Earthly Tranquility (Kunning Palace), the internal construction of the Forbidden City in Beijing, is one of the queen's palaces. Since Emperor Yongzheng of the Qing Dynasty, Kunning palace was nominal main palace, but the actual use was the shamanic's ritual spaces and the emperor's wedding bridal chamber. Palace of Heavenly Purity represents masculine gender, and Kunning palace represents feminine gender, combining them means combination of masculine and feminine.

Palace of Heavenly Purity

Palace of Heavenly Purity (Qianqing Gong), one of three imperial harems, is the main hall of the imperial palace in Beijing Forbidden City. It is the place for the residence and the day-to-day public affairs of Ming and Qing emperors in the Forbidden City. It is the first of the three imperial harems located inside the Gate of Celestial Purity. "Qian" means "Heaven," and "Qing" means "Purity;" the name of this palace means lucid sky—a symbol of national stability, also a symbol of the emperor's clear and magnanimous behavior.

Hall of Supreme Harmony

The Hall of Supreme Harmony, also known as the Hall of Golden Chime, is one of the "three main palaces" in Beijing Forbidden City, and it is China's existing largest wood structure palace. It is located in a powerful and influential position of the north-south main axis in the Forbidden City. It was first built in 1420, experienced many times of damage by fire and rebuilding.

This hall is the largest and chief building inside the Forbidden City. It has 11 rooms outwardly and 5 rooms deeply; it is 64.24 meters in length, 37 meters in width and 26.92 meters in height, covering a building area of 2,377 m^2. In front of the hall, there is a broad platform with one sundial and grain measure, a pair of copper tortoise and a pair of copper crane as well as 18 bronze tripods.

Treasure Museum

Treasure Museum (Zhenbaoguan Museum) is located in the eastern part of the Forbidden City in Beijing, inside Hall of Huangji, Hall of Mental Cultivation, Hall of Happiness and Longevity and Yihe Xuan Pavilion. Treasure Museum is a treasure trove with a variety of colored gemstones, sparkling gold and silver vessels, jade pearls, gold coronet, ivory and other kinds of unparalleled treasures. The most impressive treasure in the museum is a multi-layer tower, which is carved from a large jade, weighing 5,000 kg. The Treasure Museum in Beijing Forbidden City was originally opened in 1958. It is one of the important exhibition halls that are open in all year around in the Palace Museum. Together with the Hall of Watches and Clocks, it shows the imperial historical relics of Qing Dynasty, mainly with paintings, ceramics, bronzes, and curios etc.

Imperial Garden

The Imperial Garden is located in the middle of Beijing Forbidden City, back of the Palace of

Earthly Tranquility. It was used as a garden for resting and playing by the queen and the princess. Also, it was used to sacrifice and keep fit, collect books and read books. This garden was first built in 1420 and was expanded later but the original style has been kept to this day. It is 89 m from south to north, 135 m from east to west, covering an area of more than 12,000 m². The main building along with the surrounding pavilions, terraces and open halls, fresh and green pines, cypresses and bamboo, form an evergreen garden landscape. The arrangement of the garden is symmetrical but not rigid. The rare stone and luxuriantly green trees especially some old trees, adorn the garden and make it full of interest; the colorful path is primitive and special.

Exercises

 Match the English expressions in Column A with the Chinese translations in Column B.

Column A		Column B	
1	the Palace of Versailles	a	故宫博物院
2	Imperial Garden	b	坤宁宫
3	the Palace Museum	c	凡尔赛宫
4	the White House	d	乾清宫
5	Palace of Earthly Tranquility	e	珍宝馆
6	the Kremlin Palace	f	白金汉宫
7	Palace of Heavenly Purity	g	太和殿
8	Hall of Supreme Harmony	h	克里姆林宫
9	Buckingham Palace	i	白宫
10	Treasure Museum	j	御花园

 Answer the following questions.

1) What are "the three imperial harems" and "three main palaces" in the Forbidden City?

2) Among what have been introduced in the passage, which part of the Forbidden City attracts you most? Explain the reasons.

Reading B

Nanjing

Nanjing, the capital of Jiangsu province, is the second largest international trading port after Shanghai in the Yangtze River Delta. As an ancient capital, it is described as "a birthplace of southern beauties."

Important sights in Nanjing include the Nanjing Yangtze River Bridge, the Confucius Temple, Dr. Sun Yat-sen's Mausoleum, the Memorial Hall of the Victims in Nanjing Massacre by Japanese Invaders, Xiaoling Mausoleum of Ming Dynasty, Nanjing City Wall, etc.

Nanjing Yangtze River Bridge

Designed by Chinese and constructed with local materials, the Nanjing Yangtze River Bridge was opened to traffic in October 1968. It is a double-decked bridge with a four-lane, 4,589-meter-long highway and 6,772-meter-long double railroad tracks.

Confucius Temple

The Confucius Temple, lying in the south of Nanjing, is for consecrating and worshipping Confucius. The Confucius Temple was built during the Song Dynasty and expanded in the Eastern Jin Dynasty. The temple was ruined and rebuilt several times. It was again destroyed by fire when the Japanese invaders occupied the city in 1937. In 1984, the Chinese government restored the Confucius Temple to its former glory.

In the area surrounding the temple, residential houses, pavilions, teahouses and inns sprawl in picturesque disorder along the Qinhuai River. Many businessmen and men of letters gather there. In recent years, the Confucius Temple and its vicinity have been decorated with a sea of colorful lanterns and people flock here to enjoy the sight every year during the Spring Festival.

Dr. Sun Yat-sen's Mausoleum

Covering an area of about 80,000 square meters, Dr. Sun Yat-sen's Mausoleum is located in the Zhongshan Mountain Scenic Area (钟山风景名胜区) in the east suburb of Nanjing. It is the mausoleum of Dr. Sun Yat-sen, the father of the Republic of China. The mausoleum complex is composed of the memorial archway, the tomb passage, the mausoleum gate, the stele pavilion, the sacrificial hall and the coffin chamber, all located on the central axis. From the entrance of the mausoleum to the granite hall, there are 392 ascending steps with eight landings in between, covering a length of 700 meters and a height of about 70 meters. Built of white granite and surrounded by green mountains, the mausoleum is solemn and imposing.

Memorial Hall of the Victims in Nanjing Massacre by Japanese Invaders

In December 1937, Nanjing fell into the hands of Japanese invaders. The Japanese army launched a massacre (屠杀) that continued for six weeks. According to the records of several welfare organizations that buried the dead after the massacre, more than 300,000 people, mostly civilians and prisoners of war (POWs) were brutally slaughtered.

In order to commemorate the victims, the Memorial Hall was built in 1985. It is located in the southwestern corner of Nanjing, known as Jiangdongmen and occupies an area of about 28,000 square meters. Later in 1995, it was enlarged and renovated. The buildings in the complex are fashioned out of black and white granite blocks, looking spectacular and magnificent and rendering a feeling of solemnity and reverence. It is an exhibition site with historical records and objects as well as architecture, sculptures, and video and film projections to unfold a specific chapter of history concerning one of the ugliest experiences forced on mankind.

Xiaoling Mausoleum of Ming Dynasty

Xiaoling Mausoleum of Ming Dynasty (Ming Xiaoling) is one of the biggest imperial tombs in China. It lies in the eastern suburbs of Nanjing City at the southern foot of Purple Mountain. Emperor Chengzu, Zhu Yuanzhang, the first emperor of the Ming Dynasty (1368 - 1644) and Queen Ma were buried there. Xiaoling Mausoleum is renowned for its unique design, its eminent status, its amazing beauty and its magnificent scale. It's the milestone in the historical development of Chinese mausoleums. As an extension of the Imperial Tombs of the Ming and Qing dynasties, it is listed by

UNESCO as a world cultural heritage site. The construction of the Xiaoling Mausoleum of Ming Dynasty began in 1381 and was completed in 1405. In 1382, Queen Ma died and was buried there. Emperor Chengzu had bestowed upon her the title "Queen of Xiao Ci" which means "Queen of Filial Piety and Kindness." Hence, the name Xiaoling derives from her title.

Nanjing City Wall

Nanjing City Wall is one of the key historical and cultural remains of Ming Dynasty under state protection. It is a masterpiece of China's ancient architecture. With an original perimeter of about 35 kilometers, the City Wall has a height of 14–21 meters. The footing has a width of 14 meters. The present remains have a length of more than 21 kilometers. Nanjing is one of the few cities in China that still has its old city walls, and the City Wall is better preserved with most areas remained. Even though it has a history of more than 600 years, it is still spectacular and of great value in terms of cultural relics' protection.

The Nanjing City Wall is made up of four parts. From the outside first there is Outer City, Inner City, Imperial City and Palace City. In 1390, Outer City was built with a length of about 180 kilometers in a diamond shape to strengthen defenses though it does not exist anymore and only the names of the 13 gates are still used now. The Nanjing City Wall we can see today is mainly the relic of the Inner City.

The Nanjing City Wall is an important cultural relic for the inscriptions on the bricks. The inscriptions come in two forms. One is from scholars and officials, the other from the artisan or folk people. The characters of the former are beautiful and elegant and contain the major calligraphic styles; the origin of one of the characters styles even cannot be traced. From here, you can see how Chinese characters developed and understand the multi-culturalism of the Ming Dynasty. These inscriptions act like a historical scroll, recording the changes of the wall over dynasties. It provides an indispensable record for the study of Nanjing history.

Exercises

 Answer the following questions.

1) Nanjing, as one of the four great ancient capitals of China, is famous around the world. Do you know the other three ancient capitals? If you know, please introduce something about them.

2) Besides what have been introduced in the passage, do you know any other tourist attractions in Nanjing?

 Translate the following terms into English.

南京长江大桥

夫子庙

中山陵

侵华日军南京大屠杀遇难同胞纪念馆

明孝陵

南京城墙

翻译佳作赏析

登鹳雀楼

王之涣

白日依山尽，黄河入海流。

欲穷千里目，更上一层楼。

译文：

On the Stork Tower

By Wang Zhihuan

The sun beyond the mountain glows;

The Yellow River seawards flows.

You can enjoy a grander sight,

By climbing to a greater height.

（许渊冲 译）

赏析：

这首五言绝句是盛唐诗人王之涣的不朽之作，是一首典型的寓情于景、借物言志的作品。前两句诗描写的是登鹳雀楼所看到的雄奇壮观的景色，赞叹祖国的大好河山。后两句则表达了诗人不凡的胸襟抱负，体现了诗人无限进取与探索的精神，把人生哲理与自然景物融合得天衣无缝。诗的最后两句至今仍然被广为引用。

本诗的译者是翻译家许渊冲，这首诗的译本也是许渊冲翻译唐诗的代表作之一。许渊冲所提倡的"意美，音美，形美"在这首诗的翻译上体现得淋漓尽致。

"意美"是指在传达原文含义的基础上，要展现出原文的意境之美。许渊冲在译作中使用了 beyond 和 seawards 这两个词，点明了诗中几处意向的空间位置，充满了想象力。此外，"千里目"被译作 a grander sight，"更上一层楼"被译作 by climbing to a greater height，并非简单地把"千里"和"一层楼"直译出来，而是用意译的方式传达出原诗所蕴含的哲理。原诗实际上是想表达出诗人高瞻远瞩的气魄，许渊冲的翻译则能准确地将其表达出来。

"音美"是指借用英文中的押韵、格律，来尽量还原中文古诗中的韵律之美。在许渊冲的译作中，全诗以 AABB 的形式压了尾韵，即 flows 和 glows，sight 和 height；除此之外，grander 和 greater、sight 和 height 还分别压了头韵和腹韵，可见译者语言功底之深厚。

"形美"是指在诗句的长短对仗方面尽量做到形似。原诗为绝句，一共四行，译诗同样为四行。原诗中名词对名词，动词对动词，方位词对方位词；译文中 sun 对 yellow river，glows 对 flows，beyond 对 seawards，grander 对 greater，sight 对 height，对仗极其工整，能让目标语读者充分感受原诗的形式之美。

许渊冲正是以这种以诗译诗的形式展现出了中国古诗独有的魅力。

翻译练习

1. 中国广袤无垠的国土上点缀着无数绚丽多姿的自然景观。中国五千多年灿烂的历史和文明，为这片风景如画的土地增添了迷人的色彩。中国各地的名胜古迹大都成为热门的旅游目的地。外国人到中国旅游，常选择北京的长城和故宫、西安的秦始皇陵兵马俑、桂林的漓江。"购物天堂"上海、神秘的拉萨、"春城"昆明、享有"人间天堂"美誉的杭州、六朝古都南京也是他们经常游览的城市。中国的三亚、成都等许多城市，也都具有独特的魅力。

2. 少林寺位于河南省登封市,坐落于嵩山西面的少室山上。四周的丛林和高山构成了少林寺天然的屏障。据说少林寺由北魏孝文帝元宏所建,为安顿来朝传授小乘佛教(Hinayana Buddhism)的印度僧人跋陀。之后,菩提达摩(Bodhidharma),中国佛教禅宗(Zen Buddhism)的始祖,渡海途经广州、南京,来到少林寺,他广集信徒(disciples),传授禅宗。从此,少林寺逐渐成为禅宗祖庭。少林寺以少林功夫而享誉世界。少林功夫于隋唐时期声名远播。

3. 平遥古城是中国目前保存最完整的古代县城,位于山西省平遥县。19世纪到20世纪初,平遥曾经是中国的金融中心。一座座商铺和民居见证了平遥经济繁华的时期。平遥古城的面貌反映了500多年来中国古代建筑风格和城市布局的演变。平遥古城的遗产包括保存完好的古代城墙、街市、商铺、民居、寺庙,这些遗产反映了当时的文化、社会、经济及宗教的发展。

4. 海南岛是中国南海上的一颗璀璨的明珠,它是中国最大的热带资源宝库,拥有还未曾有人踏入的珍贵的热带林地、珍稀的动植物资源、各种各样的热带水果和丰富的地下矿产。海南岛处于热带地区,因此气候温暖,年平均气温在23~26℃之间。海南岛也是著名的度假胜地。水清沙白的海岸,宜人的阳光、壮丽的海底世界、丰富的热带景观使它成为一个绝佳的避寒地。

5. 张家界国家森林公园位于武陵源风景名胜区的南部。数千座石英山峰从地面拔地而起。小溪流经金鞭溪大峡谷,两侧是陡峭的悬崖。野生动物在原始森林里自由自在地玩耍。景区就像一个风景名胜区仙境,充满了野性的自然之美。1982年,它被认定为中国第一个国家森林公园。1992年,武陵源国家公园被联合国教科文组织正式认定为世界文化遗产。2004年,张家界国家森林公园被列入联合国教科文组织世界地质公园。这个公园一年四季景色优美。春天,万物复苏,花儿盛开,充满生机;冬天,白雪覆盖,公园也变成了一个神秘的仙境;而游览张家界国家森林公园的最佳时间是春末、夏季及秋季(4月至10月)。张家界是中国最好的避暑胜地之一,凉爽宜人,秋天的张家界天气温和舒适,游客们可以欣赏迷人的秋叶和山峰上萦绕不去的云雾。

6. 天坛位于紫禁城的东南方,占地273万平方米,约是紫禁城的4倍。天坛是明清两个朝代的皇帝在冬至祭神和在农历正月祈求丰收的仪式场所,是中国现存最大的祭天建筑。据史料记载,中国古代正式拜祭天地的历史可以追溯到公元前2000多年的夏朝。中国古代皇帝自称为"天子",他们极其敬重上天。朝拜建筑在帝都的建设中起着决定性作用。中国古代帝王会集中人力、物力和财力,建造最完善、技术水平最高的建筑。天坛建造于封建社会后期,是众多祭祀建筑中最具代表性的作品。天坛不仅是中国古代建筑中的一颗明珠,也是世界建筑史上的一块瑰宝。天坛始建于明朝永乐十八年(1420年),原名为"天地坛",明嘉靖九年(1530年),改名为"天坛"。后经清朝乾隆、光绪两代皇帝的重建,形成了现在的天坛公园的格局。

7. 青城山位于成都市都江堰市西南,是中国四大道教名山之一。青城山与都江堰灌溉系统,于2000年一同被列入《世界遗产名录》。青城山自古就有"青城天下幽"的美誉。全山终年被常绿森林覆盖,因此得名"青城山",字面意思是"绿色之山"。整个景区可分为两部分,前部分为前山,后部分为后山。前山面积约15平方千米,是青城山的主要景点。大部分历史文化遗迹位于前山,包括建福宫、天师洞、上清宫等。后山自然风光优美宁静,面积约100平方千米。后山的夏天非常凉爽,是一个避暑的好地方。青城山也是道教名山,它是中国道教的发祥地之一。青城山在研究中国道教哲学方面具有重要的历史和艺术价值。

8. 中山纪念堂位于广东省广州市越秀山南麓,由著名建筑师吕彦直先生设计,是广州人民和海外华侨为纪念孙中山先生集资兴建的。大厅采用中国传统的八角形(octagonal)建筑风格,至今仍然是一个重要的会议场所。1925年孙中山先生逝世后,为纪念这位伟大的革命先行者,广州人民于1931年在总统府原址上修建了这座孙中山纪念堂。纪念堂1929年奠基,1931年建成。1956年,孙中山先生的铜像被放置在纪念堂前。中山纪念堂建筑面积为8,700平方米,是目前世界上最大的孙中山纪念堂。

Unit 12

民间传说

Unit Goals

In this unit, you are going to
- grasp words and expressions concerning Chinese folk tales;
- acquire knowledge about Chinese folk tales which are the gems of Chinese culture and civilization;
- know how to translate the 是-Sentences into English;
- grasp translation skills of paragraphs on Chinese folk tales.

Related Words and Expressions

盘古开天辟地 Pangu separating heaven and earth
女娲补天 Nüwa patching the holes in the sky
伏羲画卦 Fuxi drawing the eight trigrams
神农尝草 Shennong tasting herbs
夸父追日 Kuafu chasing the sun
愚公移山 Yugong moving mountains
梁祝 The Story of Liang and Zhu; The Story of Butterfly Lovers
孟姜女哭长城 Meng Jiangnü weeping over the Great Wall
积劳成疾 fall ill through overwork; break down from constant overwork
木兰辞 *The Ballad of Mulan*
北方游牧民族 northern nomads
女扮男装 disguise as a man
孝敬父母 show one's filial respect to one's parents; treat one's parents with filial respect
随行人员 the accompanying staff
作出历史性贡献 make a historic contribution
增进关系 tighten the relationship
精卫填海 Jingwei trying to fill up the sea with pebbles; dogged determination to achieve one's purpose
乖巧活泼 clever and vivacious
掌上明珠 the pearl in the palm; apple of one's eye
波涛汹涌 surging waves; turbulent waves; stormy waves
悲伤不已 be prostrate with grief; be in sore distress; be very sad

滥竽充数 pass oneself off as one of the players in an ensemble; be there just to make up the number; fill a post without real qualifications

爱屋及乌 If you love someone, you'll love people and things related to him as well. /Love me, love my dog.

自食其力 support oneself by one's own labor; earn one's own living/bread; make a living for oneself

赏罚分明 be strict and fair in meting out rewards and punishments; be discriminating in one's rewards and punishments

通过道德和法律来治理国家 administer the country by morals and laws

按图索骥 look for a good steed according to its picture; deal with a matter in a mechanical way; handle a matter in a mechanical way

与……特征相符 match very well the characteristics of

牛郎织女 the Cowherd and the Weaving Girl

白蛇传 Legend of the White Snake

塞翁失马，焉知非福 Behind bad luck comes good luck. /Misfortune might be a blessing in disguise. /A loss sometimes spells a gain. /A loss may turn out to be a gain.

邯郸学步 imitate others slavishly only to lose one's own individuality; attempting to walk like a swan, the crow loses its own gait

不入虎穴，焉得虎子 without entering the tiger's den, one cannot capture the tiger's cub

才高八斗 be endowed with great/unusual talents

Lead-in Activities

Answer the following questions.

1) How many famous Chinese folk tales have you ever heard? What are your favorite ones?

2) Have you read any classical works of Chinese folk tales? What are they?

3) Have you finished reading four great classical Chinese folk tales? Which characters do you like best? Why?

2 Listen to a brief introduction to a Chinese folk tale and fill in the blanks with the words you hear.

After Pan Gu created the world, there were the sun, the moon and the stars in the sky, mountains, rivers, plants and trees on the earth, and even birds, animals, insects and fish, but no human beings existed. Then, there appeared a _____, called Nü Wa. One day, Nü Wa was walking _____, and looking around she felt very lonely. She felt that something should be put in between the heavens and the earth _____. So Nü Wa made human beings, _____, from yellow clay. From then on, man began to live in peace and happiness on the earth. Unexpectedly, one year, _____ supporting the heavens suddenly collapsed and the earth cracked. A great fire raged, torrential water flooded all the land, and fierce animals _____. Then Nü Wa melted five colored stones, using them _____ in the sky. To replace the broken pillars, she cut off

_____ and used them to support the fallen sky. Thus _____, its four corners were lifted, the flood was tamed, harmful animals were killed, and the innocent people were able to _____.

3 Read the following passage and then do the exercises.

Story of Meng Jiangnü

This story happened during the Qin Dynasty (221 – 206BCE). There was once an old man named Meng who lived in the southern part of the country with his wife. One spring, Meng sowed a seed of bottle gourd in his yard. The bottle gourd grew up bit by bit and its vines climbed over the wall and entered his neighbor Jiang's yard. Like Meng, Jiang had no children and so he became very fond of the plant. He watered and took care of the plant. With tender care of both men, the plant grew bigger and bigger and gave a beautiful bottle gourd in autumn. Jiang plucked it off the vine, and the two old men decided to cut the gourd and divide it by half. To their surprise, when they cut the gourd, a pretty and lovely girl was lying inside. They felt happy to have a child and both loved her very much, so they decided to bring the child up together. They named the girl Meng Jiangnü, which means Meng and Jiang's daughter.

As time went by, Meng Jiangnü grew up and became a beautiful young woman. She was very smart and industrious. She took care of old Meng and Jiang's families, washing the clothes and doing the housework. People knew that Meng Jiangnü was a good girl and liked her very much. One day while playing in the yard, Meng Jiangnü saw a young man hiding in the garden. She called out to her parents, and the young man came out.

At that time, Emperor Qinshihuang (the first emperor of Qin) announced to build the Great Wall. So, lots of men were caught by the federal officials. Fan Xiliang was an intellectual man and very afraid of being caught, so he went to Meng's house to hide from the officials. Meng and Jiang liked this good-looking, honest, and good-mannered young man. They decided to wed their daughter to him. Both Fan Xiliang and Meng Jiangnü accepted happily, and the couple got married several days later. However, three days after their marriage, officials suddenly broke in and took Fan Xiliang away to build the Great Wall in the north of China.

It was a hard time for Meng Jiangnü after her husband was taken away. She missed her husband and cried nearly every day. She sewed warm clothes for her husband and decided to set off to look for him. Saying farewell to her parents, she packed her luggage and started her long journey. She climbed over mountains and went through the rivers. She walked day and night, slipping and falling many times, but finally she reached the foot of the Great Wall at the present Shanhaiguan Pass.

Upon her arrival, she was eager to ask about her husband. Bad news came to her, however, that Fan Xiliang had already died of exhaustion and was buried into the Great Wall. Meng Jiangnü could not help crying. She sat on the ground and cried and cried. Suddenly, with a tremendous noise, a 400-kilometer-long section of the Great Wall collapsed over her bitter wail. The workmen and supervisors were astonished. Emperor Qinshihuang happened to be touring the wall at that exact time, and he was enraged and ready to punish the woman.

However, at the first sight of Meng Jiangnü, Emperor Qinshihuang was attracted by her beauty. Instead of killing her, the Emperor asked Meng Jiangnü, to marry him. Suppressing her feeling of anger, Meng Jiangnü agreed based on three terms. The first was to find the body of Fan Xiliang, the second was to hold a state funeral for him, and the last one was to have Emperor Qin Shihuang wear black mourning for Fan Xiliang and attend the funeral in person. Emperor Qin Shihuang thought for a while and reluctantly agreed. After all the terms were met, Emperor Qin Shihuang was ready to take her to his palace. When the guards were not watching, she suddenly turned around and jumped into the nearby Bohai Sea.

This story tells of the hard work of Chinese commoner, as well as exposes the cruel system of hard labor during the reign of Emperor Qing Shihuang. The Ten-Thousand-Li Great Wall embodied the power and wisdom of the Chinese nation. In memory of Meng Jiangnü, later generations built a temple, called the Jiangnü Temple, at the foot of the Great Wall in which a statue of Meng Jiangnü is located. Meng Jiangnü's story has been passed down from generation to generation.

1) Answer the following questions.
   （1）What's the origin of Meng Jiangnü's name?
   （2）Why did Fan Xiliang go to Meng's house to hide?
   （3）Why did a 400-kilometer-long section of the Great Wall collapse?
2) Translate the following words or phrases into English.
   告别
   跋山涉水
   累死
   举行国葬
   在……统治下
3) Translate the following paragraph into English based on what you have learned from the above article.
   孟姜女见范喜良知书达礼，忠厚老实，便芳心暗许。孟老汉对范喜良也很同情，便留他住了下来。孟姜女向爹爹言明心意，孟老汉非常赞成，便急忙来到前厅，对范喜良道："你现在到处流落，也无定处，我想招你为婿，你意如何？"范喜良急忙离座推辞道："我乃逃亡之人，只怕日后连累小姐，婚姻之事万不敢想。"无奈孟姜女心意已决，非范喜良不嫁，最后范喜良终于答应。孟老汉乐得嘴都合不上了，急忙和姜家商议挑选吉日，让他们完婚。

翻译技巧："是"字句（是-Sentences）

"是"字句在汉语中占有相当大的比例，但并非所有的"是"都是判断词，因此翻译"是"字句时必须结合具体语境，不能机械地用英语的系动词 be 来翻译。汉语中的"是"可表示等同、类属、特征、存在等意义。"是……的"常用来表示强调，含有被动意义。"是"与"才""就""正"等连用也表示强调。"是"字句可以表示一种直观表象或结果，也可以表示事物所处的状态。

例 1 原文 那年月,有钱人是天天过年。

译文 In those years, the rich people's extravagance was such that everyday was a Spring Festival.

评析 原文中的"是"表示事物所处的状态,用英语的系动词 be 来翻译。

例 2 原文 工业企业效益差是当前许多矛盾的症结所在。

译文 All the contradictions existing in industrial enterprises today boil down to scanty economic returns.

评析 原文中的"是"表示"存在",翻译中可以根据不同情况,按照英语的表达习惯灵活处理。

例 3 原文 革命者是杀不完的。

译文 Revolutionaries can never be wiped out.

评析 "是……的"结构表示强调,在翻译时通常转换成相应的强调句式,或译为被动语态。

例 4 原文 这是大势所趋,人心所向。

译文 This represents the general trend of development and the common aspiration of the people.

评析 原文中的"是"表示"确认",可根据"是"的实际意义进行翻译。

例 5 原文 这个故事好是好,就是长了点。

译文 It is a good story all right, but it's a bit too long.

评析 "就是"表示让步,这类句型中的"是"字在英译时往往通过适当的副词或让步句型来体现,如译为"but it is (was)…"。

例 6 原文 凡是重活,他都抢着干。

译文 Whenever there's a tough job, he is always the first to do it.

评析 "是"字用于"凡是",表示某一类事物中的每一个。这种句型的翻译要视英语的表达习惯而定,如用 there be 结构来翻译。

段落翻译

1. 引经据典——中国神话故事

在几千年历史长河中,中国人民始终心怀梦想、不懈追求,我们不仅形成了小康生活的理念,而且秉持天下为公的情怀。盘古开天、女娲补天、伏羲画卦、神农尝草、夸父追日、精卫填海、愚公移山等我国古代神话深刻反映了中国人民勇于追求和实现梦想的执着精神。中国人民相信,山再高,往上攀,总能登顶;路再长,走下去,定能到达。

难点讲解:

1)"心怀梦想、不懈追求"可译为 harbor dreams and pursue them relentlessly。

2)"小康生活"可译为 moderately prosperous life。

3)"秉持天下为公的情怀"可译为 upheld the spirit of serving the world for the common good。

4)"盘古开天、女娲补天、伏羲画卦、神农尝草、夸父追日、精卫填海、愚公移山"可译为 Pangu separating heaven and earth, Nüwa patching the holes in the sky, Fuxi drawing the eight trigrams, Shennong tasting herbs, Kuafu chasing the sun, Jingwei trying to fill up the sea, and Yugong moving mountains。

2. 梁山伯与祝英台

《梁山伯与祝英台》是中国人尽皆知的故事。故事发生在东晋时期，当时的社会只允许男性接受教育。作为一个女孩子，祝英台极力说服父亲让她女扮男装去杭州求学。在求学时，祝英台遇到了来自绍兴的书生梁山伯。三年的同窗生涯使他们成为挚友，祝英台逐渐爱上梁山伯。然而，梁山伯并不知道祝英台其实是女儿身。当他们完成学业回到家乡后，梁山伯终于得知他最好的朋友其实是个女孩儿。两人互诉衷肠，并承诺至死不渝。可当梁山伯想向祝英台求婚时，却为时已晚。祝英台的父母已经把她许配给一个叫马文才的富家子弟。得知真相后，梁山伯后悔不迭，从此一病不起，不久便离开人世。要嫁给马文才的那天，祝英台坐上花轿，去往新郎家，临近梁山伯的坟墓时，一阵强风突然迫使婚礼队伍停下了脚步。祝英台离开婚礼队伍，在梁山伯的墓前放声大哭。突然一声巨响，梁山伯的坟墓裂开了，祝英台趁机跳进了坟墓。出乎人们意料的是，就在祝英台投进梁山伯的坟墓后不久，一对美丽的蝴蝶从坟墓中飞出，在野花丛中翩翩起舞。

难点讲解：

1)《梁山伯与祝英台》可以采用直译法译为 the Story of Liang Shanbo and Zhu Yingtai，也可采用意译法，译为 the Story of Butterfly Lovers。

2)"女扮男装"可译为 in disguise of a man。

3)"互诉衷肠"可译为 confess their affection for each other。

4)"承诺至死不渝"可译为 promise that "till death do they part"。

5)"不久便离开人世"可委婉译为 succumb to disease。

6)"在梁山伯的墓前放声大哭"可译为 pay her mourn in front of Liang's grave。

7)"在野花丛中翩翩起舞"可译为 dance gracefully among the wild flowers。

3. 花木兰

花木兰是中国著名古诗《木兰辞》中描绘的一位替父从军的英雄。北魏时期，北方游牧民族不断南下骚扰，北魏当政者规定每家必须出一名壮丁上前线。花木兰的父亲年事已高又体弱多病，无法上战场，家中弟弟年龄尚幼，又没有兄长可以代替老父，于是花木兰决定女扮男装替父从军，从此开始了她长达十几年的军旅生活。去边关打仗，对于很多男子来说都是艰苦的事情，而花木兰既要隐瞒身份，又要与伙伴们一起杀敌，这就比一般从军的士兵更加艰难。幸运的是，花木兰最终完成了自己的使命，在数十年后凯旋回家。皇帝因为她的功劳很大，赦免其欺君之罪，同时认为她有能力在朝廷效力，可任得一官半职。然而，花木兰因家有老父需要照顾婉言拒绝，并请求皇帝能让自己返乡去孝敬父母。虽然这个故事是否真实不得而知，但是千百年来，花木兰的形象作为勇敢和孝顺的典范而深受中国人民的喜爱。花木兰的事迹屡屡被搬上舞台，长演不衰。

难点讲解：

1)《木兰辞》可译为 *The Ballad of Mulan*。

2)"不断南下骚扰"可译为 constantly invade the south。

3)"年事已高又体弱多病，无法上战场"可译为 too old and sick to go to war。

4)"花木兰既要隐瞒身份，又要与伙伴们一起杀敌，这就比一般从军的士兵更加艰难"中"既要……又要"可译为"not only … but also"，"这就比……"可译为一个非限定性定语从句。全句可译为"Hua Mulan not only had to conceal her identity but also had to fight alongside her pals. This made her task even more challenging than that of the average soldier."。

180

5)"赦免其欺君之罪"可译为 pardon her for the crime of deceiving the monarch。

6)"孝敬父母"可译为 show one's filial respect to one's parents，也可译为 treat one's parents with filial respect。

7)"花木兰的形象作为勇敢和孝顺的典范而深受中国人民的喜爱"可译为"the image of Hua Mulan has been deeply loved by the Chinese people as the model of bravery and filial piety."。

4. 文成公主进藏

　　唐朝时期有一位美丽的公主被皇上远嫁到了当时的吐蕃。这位公主就是历史上有名的文成公主。文成公主进藏留下了许多美丽的传说，一些传说至今仍然在藏族地区流传。关于她的传说有许多，其中一个是关于吐蕃使者在唐朝求娶公主联姻的故事，颇有趣味。传说中，除了吐蕃使者还有其他六位使者都想向唐太宗请婚。唐朝大臣们就出了三个考题来考验使者们。第一道题是考使者们如何让马匹辨认出自己的母亲。吐蕃使者因为对马性熟悉，所以很快就解开了难题。第二道题是给一块中间孔道弯曲的玉石穿线。这道题难倒了其他六位使者，可是吐蕃使者却非常聪明地利用了小蚂蚁将线穿过了孔道。第三道题是让使者们辨别木头的重量。这些木头大小粗细都相同，吐蕃使者把它们放到了水里，结果重的沉下，轻的浮起，就这样轻松把木头的轻重区分出来。三道难题都被吐蕃使者解开了，唐太宗只得同意了吐蕃的请婚。这位美丽的唐朝公主于641年离开长安到吐蕃和亲。除了大量的珠宝，文成公主还给当地带去了唐朝先进的科学和农业技术。随行的文士和乐师等人员极大地促进了藏族文化的发展。文成公主为促进唐朝和吐蕃经济文化的交流、增进汉藏两族人民之间的关系作出了历史性的贡献。

难点讲解：

1)"使者"可译为 envoy、messenger 或 emissary 等。

2)"第二道题是给一块中间孔道弯曲的玉石穿线"可译为"The second question was to thread a piece of jade with a curved hole in the middle."。

3)在翻译"第三道题是让使者们辨别木头的重量。这些木头大小粗细都相同，吐蕃使者把它们放到了水里，结果重的沉下，轻的浮起，就这样轻松把木头的轻重区分出来"翻译这两句时，要注意前后句的逻辑关系，同时还需要注意调整语序，可译为"The third question was for the envoys to determine the weight of pieces of wood which had the same size and thickness. The Tibetan envoy put them in water, and the heavier pieces sank while the lighter ones floated, which helped distinguish the weight of the wood."。

4)"离开长安到吐蕃和亲"可译为 leave Chang'an for Tubo to cement friendly relations through marriages。

5)"随行的文士和乐师等人员极大地促进了藏族文化的发展"可译为"The accompanying staff like scholars and musicians greatly promoted the development of Tibetan culture."。

6)在翻译"文成公主为促进唐朝和吐蕃经济文化的交流、增进汉藏两族人民之间的关系作出了历史性的贡献"一句时，可先译出此句主干 Princess Wencheng made a historic contribution，"作出……的贡献"可用介词 in 来表达，故"为促进唐朝和吐蕃经济文化的交流、增进汉藏两族人民之间的关系"可用"in promoting … as well as enhancing … between …"结构。整句可译为"Princess Wencheng made a historic contribution in promoting economic and cultural exchanges between the Tang Dynasty and Tubo, as well as enhancing the relationship between the Han and Tibetan peoples."。

5. 精卫填海

炎帝有一个女儿，她十分乖巧活泼，但喜欢冒险，炎帝视她为掌上明珠。一天，女孩没让父亲知晓，便一个人驾着一条小船向东海太阳升起的地方划去。女孩漫步东海边，看到碧波荡漾，便想去海里游泳。然而，当她游到离海岸很远的地方时，大海突然变得波涛汹涌。这时，女孩听到了龙形海神的咆哮。她惊恐万分，试图返回海岸，但她那瘦小的身体无法抵抗巨浪的力量，女孩不幸淹死了。当炎帝从女儿仆人那里得知这个噩耗时，他急忙赶到东海海岸。炎帝喊着小女儿的名字，突然看见一只小鸟从海里飞了出来。小鸟绕着炎帝飞来飞去，悲伤不已。那只鸟看起来像只乌鸦，花脑袋，白嘴壳，红脚爪。炎帝觉得这只鸟是他女儿灵魂的化身，他流下了痛苦的眼泪。这时，这只鸟突然叫了一声"精卫"，便迅速地飞向西山。它用嘴叼起一块小石头，扔进了东海。从此，这只鸟每天都会用嘴衔着小石子，往东海里扔。海神领悟了这只鸟的用意。他嘲笑小鸟："我的海是那么的宽广和深邃，你永远不可能把它填满。"然而，小鸟却回答："我会一直努力，我相信你的大海最终会被填满的"。几千年来，"精卫填海"的故事一直鼓励着人们终生为自己的理想而奋斗。

难点讲解：

1)"视……为掌上明珠"可译为"regard...as the pearl in the palm"，也可译为"regard...as apple of one's eye"。

2)"碧波荡漾"可译为 rippling with green wavelets。

3)"波涛汹涌"可译为 surging waves、turbulent waves 或 stormy waves。

4)"龙形海神的咆哮"可译为 the roar of the dragon-shaped Sea God。

5)"小鸟绕着炎帝飞来飞去，悲伤不已"可译为"The bird circled around Emperor Yan, filled with sorrow."。

6)"那只鸟看起来像只乌鸦，花脑袋，白嘴壳，红脚爪"可用增译法添加介词，译为"The bird looked like a crow, with a colorful head, a white beak, and red feet."。

6. 滥竽充数

战国时期，齐国的国君齐宣王爱好音乐，尤其喜欢听人吹竽。齐宣王喜欢热闹，讲究宏大排场，所以每次总是叫手下三百人一起合奏给他听，并给这些乐师们丰厚的报酬。有个叫南郭的人听说了齐宣王的这个爱好，心里痒痒的，他虽然对吹竽一无所知，但觉得这是个赚钱的好机会。于是南郭先生跑到齐宣王那里，吹嘘自己的竽吹得很好，请求为齐宣王吹竽，齐宣王欣然应允。事情按照南郭先生计划的那样顺利进行，他成功地成了一名乐师。此后，南郭先生就随这三百人一起合奏给齐宣王听，每逢演奏的时候，南郭先生就混在队伍中，人家摇晃身体他也摇晃身体，人家摆头他也摆头，脸上装出一副动情忘我的样子，居然没有被任何人看出破绽。但是好景不长，过了几年，齐宣王死了，他的儿子继承了王位。年轻的国君也爱听吹竽，可是他和齐宣王不一样，他认为独奏更加动听，一群人一起吹奏实在太吵。于是新国君要求乐师们一个一个地在他面前演奏。南郭先生得到这个消息之后吓出了一身冷汗。他想来想去，觉得这次再也混不过去了，只好连夜收拾行李逃走了。"滥竽充数"这个成语就是用来形容那些没有真才实干而混在内行人之中的人的。

难点讲解：

1)"喜欢热闹，讲究宏大排场"可译为 preferred lively and grand performances。

2)"吹嘘自己的竽吹得很好"可译为 boast about his exceptional Yu-playing skills，也可译为 brag about how well he played the Yu。

3)翻译"人家摇晃身体他也摇晃身体，人家摆头他也摆头，脸上装出一副动情忘我的样子"一句时，可采用减词法，省略"人家""样子"这两个词语。全句可译为"He would sway his body and nod his head along with others, putting on an impassioned and absorbed expression."。

4)翻译"居然没有被任何人看出破绽"时可采用增译法，添加 in his performance，译为"Surprisingly, no one could detect any flaws in his performance."。

5)"好景不长"可译为 good times don't last long，也可译为 pleasant hours fly fast。

6)"他认为独奏更加动听，一群人一起吹奏实在太吵"可译为"He believed that solo performances were more pleasing and group performances were too noisy."。

7)"吓出了一身冷汗"可译为 be terrified and break out in cold sweat。

8)"'滥竽充数'这个成语就是用来形容那些没有真才实干而混在内行人之中的人的"可译为"The idiom has been used to describe those who have no real talent or skill and only pretend to fill a role for personal gain."。

7. 爱屋及乌

中国历史上有一个王朝名"周"。一天，周王问他的官员，应该怎样处理战俘。一个官员说："我以前曾听说，如果喜欢某个人，就连停留在那人住的屋顶上的乌鸦都喜欢；如果厌恶某个人，就连那人家里的墙壁和围墙都厌恶。战俘是我们的敌人，和我们是对立的，我觉得最好把他们全部杀了。"周王认为这样做不妥。另外一个官员也提出了自己的意见："依我看应该把战俘区分对待，把有罪的和无罪的、好的和坏的区分开来。有罪的战俘要处死，不能留下祸患。"周王认为这样做也不大妥当。接着，又有一个官员说："大王，我认为应该把这些战俘全都放了，让他们回到自己的家里，耕种田地，自食其力。而大王对自己的亲人和朋友，也要赏罚分明，不能偏心。通过道德和法律来治理国家，人民肯定会对大王信服的。"周王听后觉得很有道理，就按这个办法去做，结果国家真的很快安定下来，变得越来越稳定和强大。成语"爱屋及乌"后来就用来比喻因为喜爱一个人而连带喜爱、关心和他有关的人或事物。

难点讲解：

1)"周王问他的官员，应该怎样处理战俘"可译为"The King of Zhou asked his officials how to handle prisoners of war."。

2)"如果喜欢某个人，就连停留在那人住的屋顶上的乌鸦都喜欢"可译为"If you like someone, you even like the crows that stay on the roof of their house."。

3)"如果厌恶某个人，就连那人家里的墙壁和围墙都厌恶"可译为"If you dislike someone, you even dislike the walls and fences of their home."。

4)"依我看应该把战俘区分对待，把有罪的和无罪的、好的和坏的区分开来"可译为"In my view, we should treat the prisoners of war differently, distinguishing the guilty from the innocent, the good from the bad."。

5)"我认为应该把这些战俘全都放了，让他们回到自己的家里，耕种田地，自食其力"可译为"I think we should release all these prisoners of war and let them return to their homes, cultivate the land, and support themselves."。

6)"赏罚分明"可译为 be strict and fair in meting out rewards and punishments 或 be discriminating in one's rewards and punishments。

8. 按图索骥

春秋时期，秦国有个名叫孙阳的人，善于鉴别马的好坏，因而他经常被人邀请去鉴定和挑选马匹。他把自己识马的经验写成了书，取名《相马经》。这本书图文并茂地介绍了各类好马，所以人们把孙阳称为"伯乐"。《相马经》上描述：良马有高高的额头，鼓起的眼睛，马蹄是圆圆的。孙阳的儿子熟读了这本书后，以为自己学到了父亲的本领，便拿着《相马经》外出去找好马。一天，他在路边看见一只癞蛤蟆，前额和《相马经》上好马的特征很相符，就以为找到了一匹千里马，马上跑回去告诉父亲："我找到的这个和你书上画的好马差不多，只是蹄子不太像。"孙阳听后，哭笑不得，开玩笑地说："这匹马太喜欢跳了，不好驾驭。"这就是我们所说的成语"按图索骥"的由来。后来，人们用它来比喻机械地照搬书本知识，不求事物的本质。

难点讲解：

1)"善于鉴别马的好坏，因而他经常被人邀请去鉴定和挑选马匹"一句可采用分译法进行翻译，译为"He was skilled at discerning the quality of horses. As a result, he was often invited to identify and select horses."

2)"良马有高高的额头，鼓起的眼睛，马蹄是圆圆的"可译为"A good horse has a high forehead, bulging eyes, and round hooves."。

3)"他在路边看见一只癞蛤蟆，前额和《相马经》上好马的特征很相符"可采用合译法进行翻译，译为一个含有定语从句的复合句，即"He saw a toad by the roadside that had similar features to the good horses depicted in the book, except for its hooves."。

4)"哭笑不得"可译为 do not know whether to cry or to laugh、be at a loss whether to cry or to laugh、be unable either to cry or to laugh 或 find sth both funny and annoying。

5)"按图索骥"可译为 look for a good steed according to its picture、deal with a matter in a mechanical way 或 handle a matter in a mechanical way。

6)"人们用它来比喻机械地照搬书本知识，不求事物的本质"可译为"People have used this set phrase to refer to mechanically following book knowledge without seeking the essence of things."。

拓展阅读

Overwhelming Popularity of a New Work Causes Shortage of Printing Paper

In the Jin Dynasty, there was a famous writer whose name was Zuo Si who, however, was very naughty and did not like to study when he was a small kid. His father often got angry, and yet young Zuo Si was as naughty as ever and would not study hard. One day, Zuo Si's father was chatting with his friends, who envied him his clever and lovely son. Hearing this, Zuo Si's father sighed and looked disappointed, "Please do not mention him. My son Zuo Si does not study as well as I did when I was young, although I did not study well enough myself. It appears that he is actually a good-for-nothing." All this was witnessed by young Zuo Si. He felt very sad, feeling intensely that he would not be able to have a bright future if he did not study hard. So, he was determined to study assiduously from then on.

Day after day, year after year, Zuo Si gradually grew up. Because of his unremitting efforts in studying hard, he became an erudite scholar and wrote excellent essays. "Ode to the Capital of the State of Qi," which took him one year to write, showed his brilliant literary talent and laid the foundation for his becoming an outstanding writer. Then he planned to write "Ode to the Capitals of the Three Kingdoms of Wei, Shu and Wu" with the local conditions and customs as well as the produce of the three capitals as its content. In order to achieve the desired effect in content, structure and language, he applied himself to research work with great concentration, and was so absorbed in creative writing as to forget food and sleep. It took him ten whole years to finish the writing of "Ode to the Capitals of the Three Kingdoms of Wei, Shu and Wu," a literary masterpiece.

"Ode to the Capitals of the Three Kingdoms of Wei, Shu and Wu" was well received by the broad masses of readers after it made its appearance to the public, and people considered it as superbly written as "Ode to the Western Capital and to the Eastern Capital" in Han Dynasty. As the art of printing had not been invented at that time, people who were fond of this "Ode" had to make handwritten copies of it themselves. As there were so many people who competed in making handwritten copies, the supply of writing paper fell short of the demand in Luoyang and therefore the price of writing paper went up greatly.

This story comes from "The life of Zuo Si" in the book *Literary Field of The History of the Jin Dynasty*. Based on this story, people have coined the set phrase "the price of writing paper went up greatly," meaning the overwhelming popularity of a new work causes shortage of printing paper, to show how popular an outstanding piece of literary work is.

Exercises

1 Match the English expressions in Column A with the Chinese translations in Column B.

Column A		Column B	
1	a good-for-nothing	a	学识渊博的人
2	study assiduously	b	《三都赋》
3	unremitting efforts	c	《齐都赋》
4	erudite scholar	d	风土、人情、物产
5	Ode to the Capital of the State of Qi	e	《两都赋》
6	lay the foundation for	f	没多大出息
7	Ode to the Capitals of the Three Kingdoms of Wei, Shu and Wu	g	供不应求
8	local conditions and customs as well as the produce	h	刻苦学习
9	Ode to the Western Capital and to the Eastern Capital	i	奠定基础
10	fall short of the demand	j	坚持不懈的努力

2 Answer the following questions.

1) Why did young Zuo Si feel intensely that he would not be able to have a bright future if he did not study hard?

2) Why did the price of writing paper go up greatly in Luoyang?

翻译佳作赏析

《嫦娥》

李商隐

云母屏风烛影深，

长河渐落晓星沉。

嫦娥应悔偷灵药，

碧海青天夜夜心。

译文：

To the Moon Goddess

By Li Shangyin

Upon the marble screen the candlelight is winking;
The Silver River slants and morning stars are sinking.
You'd regret to have stolen the miraculous potion;
Each night you brood over the lonely celestial ocean.

（许渊冲　译）

赏析：

此诗咏叹嫦娥在月中的孤寂情景，抒发了诗人的自伤之情。前两句分别描写室内、室外的环境，渲染空寂清冷的气氛，表现主人公怀思的情绪。后两句是主人公在一宵痛苦的思忆之后产生的感想，表达了一种孤寂感。全诗情调感伤，意蕴丰富，奇思妙想，真实动人。

第一句"云母屏风烛影深"，描绘了烛光越来越黯淡，云母屏风上笼罩着一层深深的暗影。许渊冲将"云母屏风"译为 marble screen，将"烛影深"译为 the candlelight is winking，即"烛影闪烁、摇曳"。

第二句"长河渐落晓星沉"，描绘了银河即将消失，点缀着空旷天宇的寥落晨星，也行将隐没。许渊冲将"长河渐落"译为 The Silver River slants，将"晓星沉"译为 morning stars are sinking。"沉"字逼真地描绘出晨星低垂、欲落未落的动态。"烛影深""长河落""晓星沉"，表明时间已到将晓未晓之际，透露出主人公在长夜独坐中的黯然心境。其中，第一句结尾处的 winking 和第二句结尾处的 sinking 押了尾韵，体现了许渊冲翻译中的韵律美。

对于第三句"嫦娥应悔偷灵药"，许渊冲采用第二人称的译法，将其译为 You'd regret to have stolen the miraculous potion。其中，miraculous potion 意思是"神奇的药水，灵药"。

第四句"碧海青天夜夜心"中的"碧海青天"表达了嫦娥孤清凄冷和不堪忍受寂寞的情绪，许渊冲将其译为 the lonely celestial ocean；"夜夜心"表达了嫦娥的忧思和焦虑，许渊冲将其译为 Each night you brood over。寂寞中的主人公，也面对着冷屏残烛、青天孤月，度过了一个个不眠之夜。同样，第三句结尾处的 potion 和第四句结尾处的 ocean 押韵，再次体现了许渊冲翻译中的韵律美。

翻译练习

1. 七夕节，也称为中国的情人节，适逢每年农历的七月初七。在这一节日背后，有一个非常著名的关于牛郎和织女的浪漫爱情故事。牛郎是一个年轻的放牛娃，只有一头老牛陪伴他，这头老牛是他的挚友。织女是一个仙女，住在天庭，她很擅长编织，可以织出美丽的彩虹和云彩，她也是王母娘娘的第七个孙女。一天，织女和她的姐妹们得到了王母娘娘的许可，来到了人间"度假"。织女和姐妹们在河里洗澡。牛郎路过，捡起一件衣服，这件衣服是织女的。两人相遇后，织女爱上了牛郎，牛郎也爱上了织女，并请求织女做他的妻子。随后的几年，牛郎和织女带着他们的两个孩子幸福地在人间生活。然而，王母娘娘发现她的孙女没有回来，甚至爱上了一个凡人，非常愤怒，派人把织女押送回天庭，并禁止这对恋人再见面。牛郎的牛（其实不是一头普通的牛）看到牛郎为他深爱的妻子难过，就告诉他的主人，在它死后用它的牛皮做成一双鞋。牛皮做成的鞋带着牛郎飞到天上去找他的妻子。然而，王母娘娘发现后，又用一条天河将这对恋人分开，这条天河就是现在的银河。天上的喜鹊被他们的坚贞爱情所感动，便用身体搭成一道跨越天河的桥，让牛郎织女在银河上相会，这座桥被称为"鹊桥"。最后，王母娘娘对牛郎和织女的事情也没有之前那么生气了，于是允许他们每年农历七月初七在鹊桥上相会一次。这个故事表达了人们对于美好爱情和幸福生活的歌颂和向往。

  2.《白蛇传》是中国古代广为流传的民间故事之一。故事伊始，白蛇精和乌龟精几百年来一直在湖中练习神力，以变成人形，成为不朽。乌龟想吃到少年许仙刚刚抛出的长生不老汤圆，但未能如愿，白蛇却先吃到了，于是白蛇获得了五百年的神力。白蛇十分感激许仙。然而，乌龟从此对白蛇又气又妒。由于不能长生不老，乌龟在仇恨中死去，转世为法海，法海仍然记得要向白蛇报仇。当白蛇变成人形时，以白素贞自称。十八年后，白素贞遇到了成年的许仙并嫁给了他，以表达自己的感激之情。这对夫妇经营着他们的生意，生活得很幸福。然而，复仇心切的法海打算破坏这对夫妻的关系，于是他找到许仙，让他在端午节期间让自己的妻子喝雄黄酒（中国人认为雄黄酒可以驱蛇或其他有毒动物）。白素贞以为她已经练就长生不老之身，雄黄酒伤不了她。然而，她在喝完酒后，却感到很不舒服，这迫使她暴露了自己的真身，幻化成了一条巨大的白蛇。许仙在发现自己的妻子是一条蛇后震惊不已，一命呜呼。白素贞对许仙的死很是沮丧，于是她从法海那里偷来了仙药，让许仙起死回生。许仙仍然爱着白素贞，即使她不是真正的人。法海并没有放弃拆散许仙和白素贞，他绑架了许仙并把他囚禁在金山寺。为了救出自己深爱的丈夫，白素贞带着妹妹小青一起对抗法海。然而，白素贞并没有救下许仙，她的法力因为怀孕而变弱了。许仙设法逃脱并见到了正在生产的妻子，白素贞生下了他们的儿子许仕林。法海趁此将白素贞囚禁在雷峰塔下。直到二十年后，小青法力变强，打败了法海，许仙白素贞一家人终得以团聚。

  3. 据说很久以前，边境一带住着一位老人。一天，他的一匹好马突然跑掉了。所有的邻居、亲戚和朋友都过来安慰他。然而，这位老人并没有感到不安。他向邻居们解释说，丢了那匹马并不一定是件坏事。谁也无法预测那匹马会逃跑，事情就这样发生了，而现在对此已经无能为力。"没有什么好担心的，"老人说，"如果马丢了，怎么知道不是件好事呢？"几个月过去了。有一天，老人丢失的马竟然回来了，并且还带回了一匹好马，一匹稀有而珍贵的母马。这件事震惊了整个村子，人们都向老人表示祝贺。但是老人并不高兴。他对大家说："有什么可祝贺的，这怎么就不能是一场灾难呢？"几天后，老人的独子骑上了那匹好马。这匹马不熟悉它的新主人，疯狂地奔跑，结果把年轻人摔倒在地，摔断了他的腿。摔断腿后，老人的儿子走路总是一瘸一拐的。人们听到后又来安慰老人。但是老人还是不着急。他甚至说这可能是件好事。在那一刻，他的许多邻居和朋友都认为他疯了，决定离开他。不久，老人家附近爆发了一场战争。年轻人被征召入伍，送到了前线。然而，老人的儿子却被允许待在家里，因为他身体残疾。这个故事告诉我们，当一件坏事发生时，并不一定意味着长期结果都是灾难性的。同样地，一个想当然的好事也会转变成不好的事。所以，当你遇到所谓不幸或幸运的事时，不要太沮丧或太高兴。顺势而为，一步一个脚印是最好的应对方法。

  4. 相传在两千多年前，燕国寿陵有一位少年。这位少年不愁吃不愁穿，可他就是缺乏自信心，经常无缘无故地感到事事不如人、低人一等。家里的人劝他改一改这个毛病，他则认为是家里人管得太多。不知不觉中，他竟开始怀疑自己的走路姿势，越看越觉得自己走路的姿势太笨太丑。有一天，他在路上听到几个人说，邯郸人走路姿势优美。他一听，对上了心病，急忙走上前去，想打听个明白。不料想，那几个人看见他，一阵大笑之后扬长而去。邯郸人走路的姿势究竟怎样美呢？他怎么也想象不出来，这又成了他的心病。终于有一天，他瞒着家人跑到遥远的邯郸学走路去了。一到邯郸，他感到处处新鲜，简直令人眼花缭乱。看到小孩走路，他觉得活泼、美，学；看见老人走路，他觉得稳重，学；看到妇女走路，摇摆多姿，学。就这样，不过半月光景，他连走路也不会了，路费也花光了，只好爬着回家了。后来，"邯郸学步"这个成语用来形容那些一味模仿他人，结果别人的优点没学来，自己的长处却丢光了的人。

5. 班超是东汉时期著名的外交家和军事家。公元73年，班超率领部下36人出使塔里木盆地各王国，首先到达鄯善国。起初国王热情地接待他们，但过了一段时间，鄯善王却拒不接见班超，态度也十分冷淡。班超得知匈奴也派使者来和鄯善王联络感情，因此鄯善王的态度才急转直下。班超召集部下，告诉他们情况危急。班超认为，不入虎穴，焉得虎子，只有冒着一切危险，当晚除掉匈奴使者才能化险为夷。晚上，班超带着他的36名部下潜入匈奴军营。他们兵分两路，一路拿着战鼓躲在营地后面，一路手执弓箭刀枪埋伏在营地两旁。他们一面放火烧帐篷，一面击鼓呐喊。匈奴人在混乱和恐慌中惊醒，以为有一支庞大的汉朝军队在攻击他们。他们中有30多人在伏击中丧生，其中包括匈奴使团团长，另有100多人在大火中丧生。第二天，班超手提匈奴首领的首级觐见鄯善王，鄯善王为之震惊，决定投靠汉朝，便和班超言归于好，成功结盟。

6. 曹植是三国人，天资聪颖，10岁就可以写一手好文章。有一次，他的父亲曹操看了他的文章后，非常惊讶地问："这是你写的吗？"曹植忙跪下说："我下笔就可以成章。如果父亲不相信，我愿意接受测试。"这时正好铜雀台落成了，于是曹操命自己的几个儿子各写一篇记文。曹植提笔便写下了名篇《铜雀台赋》，曹操这才相信曹植的文采的确高人一筹。后来曹植的哥哥曹丕做了皇帝。曹丕心眼小，容不下这个弟弟，找了个罪名要处死他，说："如果你能在七步之内作成一首诗，我就饶了你。如果不成，可不要怪我了。"曹植请他出个题目。曹丕说："就以兄弟为题目，但不许出现兄弟二字。"曹植走出六步吟了一首诗："煮豆燃豆萁，豆在釜中泣。本是同根生，相煎何太急？"曹丕听了，羞愧地放了他。曹植一生写下了许多杰出的文章，赢得了许多人的钦佩。晋朝诗人谢灵运有诗曰："天下才气共十斗，曹植一人占八斗。"今天，"才高八斗"便用来形容一个人很有文采。

7. 春秋时代，有个叫俞伯牙的人，精通音律，琴艺高超，是当时著名的琴师。俞伯牙年轻的时候聪颖好学，曾拜高人为师，琴技登峰造极，但他总觉得自己还不能出神入化地表现对各种事物的感受。伯牙的老师知道他的想法后，就带他乘船到东海的蓬莱岛上，让他欣赏大自然的景色，倾听大海的波涛声。他情不自禁地取琴弹奏，音随意转，把大自然的美妙融进了琴声，伯牙感受自己进入了一个前所未有的境界。老师告诉他："你已经学到了。"一日伯牙乘船游览，面对清风明月，他思绪万千，于是又弹起琴来，琴声悠扬，渐入佳境。忽听岸上有人叫绝。伯牙闻声走出来，只见一个樵夫站在岸边。伯牙当即请樵夫上船，兴致勃勃地为他演奏。伯牙弹起赞美高山的曲调，樵夫说道："真好！雄伟而庄重，好像高耸入云的泰山一样。"当他弹奏表现奔腾澎湃的波涛的曲调时，樵夫又说："真好！宽广浩荡，好像看见滚滚的流水，如无边的大海一般。"伯牙兴奋极了，激动地说："知音。你真是我的知音。"这个樵夫就是钟子期。从此二人成了非常要好的朋友。成语"高山流水"由此而来，用以比喻知己难遇或乐曲高妙。

Unit 13

民间工艺

Unit Goals

In this unit, you are going to
- grasp words and expressions concerning Chinese folk arts;
- acquire knowledge about Chinese folk arts which are the important part of Chinese rich cultural and art heritage;
- know how to translate the 把-Sentences into English;
- grasp translation skills of paragraphs on Chinese folk arts.

Related Words and Expressions

工艺品 craftwork; artwork
传统工艺品 traditional handicraft
剪纸 paper-cutting
中国结 Chinese knots
皮影戏 shadow play
鼻烟壶 snuff bottle
陶瓷 porcelain
青花瓷 blue and white porcelain
彩绘 color decoration; color painting
刻绘 engraved painting
泥塑 clay figurines
唐三彩 tricolor glazed pottery of the Tang Dynasty
刺绣 embroidery
蜡染 batik; wax printing
木雕 wood engravings
景泰蓝 Jing Tai Lan; Cloisonné
装饰 adornments; decoration
福寿 felicity and longevity
吉祥 lucky; auspicious, propitious; fortunate
祝你一帆风顺！Wish you a fair wind!
辟邪 drive away evil spirits; ward off evil spirits
增添喜庆气氛 add joyous atmosphere
庙会 temple fair

旅游纪念品 travel souvenir

享有……声誉 enjoy the reputation of...

达到鼎盛 reach its peak

独占鳌头 rank first; came out first (in)

获得社会意义 acquire considerable social significance

给……带来艺术价值 bring artistic values to...

造型优美 elegantly shaped

色彩绚丽 rich in color

装饰精美 delicately decorated

尊贵与财富的象征 a symbol of being noble and wealthy

华丽的龙袍 magnificent dragon robes

高水准工艺 high standard of craftsmanship

吉祥艺术 art of mascot

集多种工艺之大成 integrates the culmination of a variety of techniques

独树一帜 develop a school of one's own; develop one's own unique style; be highly original

丝绸之路 The Silk Road

养蚕 silkworm raising

退茧 cocoon unwinding

丝绸文化或蚕业 silk culture or sericulture

大胆的变化和夸张手法 bold variation and exaggeration

印章制作 seal carvings

签名图章 signature stamp

朱砂糊 cinnabar paste

不落俗套 depart from convention; be off the beaten track; not follow popular patterns; be unconventional

出土的陶器和青铜器 unearthed pottery and bronze ware

祭祀的器皿 sacrificial vessels

特权的象征 an emblem of privilege

各种各样的图案 diversified patterns

Lead-in Activities

1 **Answer the following questions.**

1) How many Chinese folk arts have you ever learned? What are your favorite ones?

2) Have you ever read any introductions about the technical skills of Chinese folk arts? Can you say something about them?

3) The Chinese knot is China's unique folk art of handwork, which fully embodies the wisdom of the Chinese people and profound cultural deposits. Do you know how to make a Chinese knot?

2 **Listen to a brief introduction to Chinese wood carving and fill in the blanks with the words you hear.**

Chinese wood carving has a time-honored history and is one of the traditional Chinese arts.

The earliest wood carvings _____ are believed to have been carved during the Warring States Period, about 3,000 years ago. In China, wood carving is mainly divided into three categories: _____, furniture carving and art carving. The wood carving decoration of ancient Chinese buildings (including gardens, temples, and palaces) _____ in world history. Carved furniture can be said to be _____ wood carving art, and it is both large-scale and very practical. Furniture decorated with woodcarving art _____ primitive simplicity and elegance. China's exported art carving furniture and carved mahogany furniture _____ fine, elegant carving, in a unique antique oriental style. Woodcarving handicrafts are an art form, created by highly skilled artisans _____, for both _____. These handicrafts are a _____. Chinese wood carving _____ for its impressively detailed structures and the beauty of its themes. Today, traditional wood carvings can be seen in private galleries and also on the decorations over residential areas on both sides of the Yangtze River.

3 Read the following passage and then do the exercises.

Chinese Porcelain

The West's trade with China has been at the forefront of globalization since the days of Marco Polo. Pieces of eight, minted out of South American silver, crossed the Pacific and were used up and down the coast of Asia. Indeed, interruptions in this silver trade ultimately helped bring on the collapse of the Ming Dynasty in China in the early 17th century. Later exchanges of tea and spices served to enrich Western merchants, particularly from Britain.

By the 18th century, British, Dutch, Portuguese, Swedish and American trade with China was so well established that the new wealthy merchant class emerged from the trade had taken to emulating the trappings of the landed gentry (乡绅), designing coats of arms and commissioning entire porcelain services on which to flaunt them. No marriage or promotion was complete without a specially made plate to commemorate it. This upward social mobility gave rise to a new phenomenon, the manufacture of Chinese porcelain and paintings for the export market.

Two centuries on, Chinese export porcelain attracts a quite different collector from those seeking Chinese porcelain proper. Whereas all Chinese treasures—whether jade, porcelain, lacquer, bamboo or rhinoceros horn—have an aesthetic appeal that prizes rarity, delicacy and symbolism above all, export porcelain speaks to the academic collector or, less politely, the "anorak" or "train-spotter." The form is based on Meissen or other soft-paste porcelain, but it is not really European. Nor is it particularly Chinese, although it was made there.

Instead, it is a bit of a mish-mash. It appeals to buyers who seek to complete a particular series defined by decorative patterns, special coats of arms or links between different families.

Elinor Gordon, who died at the age of 91, was the consummate American dealer/collector of Chinese export porcelain. She bought widely in Britain, Holland and Portugal, and for more than half a century sold her wares from her Pennsylvanian home and at antiques fairs up and down the East Coast. Her private collection, shows just how much American-related export porcelain she managed to gather together.

Many of the pieces feature complicated combinations of different coats of arms. Several pieces stand out, such as a grandly decorated orange oval platter of modest size. Estimated at $12,000-18,000, it belongs to a pattern known as "Fitzhugh," of which so few pieces were made it is suspected that they all were once part of the same service.

Several other pieces are connected to a single ship, the *Empress of China*, which in 1784 became the first American vessel to trade directly with China. The Society of the Cincinnati was founded in May 1783 for commissioned officers who had served in the continental army or navy during the American revolution. The founder, Major Samuel Shaw, was responsible for ordering all the services decorated with the society's badge. He first travelled to China on the *Empress of China* and spent more than ten years working the same route, dying at sea on a return trip in 1794. A plate from one of the earliest Cincinnati services, which is believed to have belonged to George Washington, is estimated to fetch $30,000-50,000, and another smaller, later Cincinnati plate $12,000-18,000.

John Morgan was a carpenter on the same first outward journey on the *Empress of China*, and died on the return. The ship's log notes that his effects included two punch bowls. Ms. Gordon owned several Morgan pieces, including a small tureen estimated here at $3,000-5,000 and a larger version, both with lids, estimated at $7,000-9,000.

1) Answer the following questions.
   (1) What's the major reason which ultimately helped bring on the collapse of the Ming Dynasty in China in the early 17th century?
   (2) What is the necessity to commemorate the complete marriage or promotion?
   (3) What is the name of the single ship, connected to several other pieces of porcelain, which in 1784 became the first American vessel to trade directly with China?
2) Translate the following words or expressions into English.
   全球化前沿
   西班牙古银币
   具有审美情趣
   古董交易会
   多风格混合物
3) Translate the following paragraph into English.
   中国瓷器是从陶器发展演变而成的。至宋代时，名瓷名窑已遍及大半个中国，是瓷业最为繁荣的时期。当时的钧窑、哥窑、官窑、汝窑和定窑并称为五大名窑。到了元代，被称为瓷都的江西景德镇出产的青花瓷已成为瓷器的代表。青花瓷釉质透明如水，胎体质薄轻巧，洁白的瓷体上敷以蓝色纹饰，素雅清新，充满生机。青花瓷一经出现便风靡一时，成为景德镇的传统名瓷之冠。

翻译技巧："把"字句(把-Sentences)

汉语的"把"字句是汉语中一种特有的句型，在结构上用特殊介词"把"字将宾语引出，放在谓语动词之前。"把"字句只用于主动句，目的是将宾语提前，以突出宾语，宾语之后的主要动词必须是及物动词，并且不能有其他宾语(能带双宾语的动词除外)。根据不同意义和作用，"把"字句可以分为以下几种类型。

1) 含有"处置"意思的"把"字句。在翻译含有"处置"意思的"把"字句时，常使用英语句型"动词＋宾语＋补语"(have sth/sb done)或"动词＋宾语＋状语(介词短语)"来处理。

例 1 原文 他生气时，就把自己关在房里看书。

译文 When he is angry, he has himself confined in the room, reading books.

2) 含有"致使"意思的"把"字句。这种类型的"把"字句，"把"字后面常接"累""忙""气""急""吓""热""感动"等动词，表示结果。翻译时通常使用英语中含有"致使"意义的动词。

例 2 原文 光线太暗，看书会把眼睛累坏的。

译文 It will strain your eyes to read in such dim light.

例 3 原文 他的病不见好转，真把我急死了。

译文 He is getting no better, so I am worried to death about him.

3) 带有双宾语的"把"字句。这一句式可翻译为"动词＋间接宾语＋直接宾语"或"动词＋直接宾语＋to＋间接宾语"结构。

例 4 原文 政府把贷款给了这家新公司。

译文 The government granted a loan to the new company.

4) 表示"把……当作……"的"把"字句。这一句式可以用"动词＋宾语＋as/for"或"动词＋间接宾语＋直接宾语"的句型来翻译。

例 5 原文 我把这首诗看作是本人的杰作之一。

译文 I regard the poem as one of my masterpieces.

5) 表示动作场所和范围的"把"字句。这种类型的"把"字句，在译成英语时，可根据句意灵活处理。

例 6 原文 他把抽屉翻了遍，也没有找到笔记本。

译文 He rummaged through all the drawers, but still could not find the notebook.

6) 含有祈使意味的"把"字句。这种类型的"把"字句，可直接译为英语中的祈使句。

例 7 原文 把收音机的音量调低些，我在看书呢。

译文 Turn down the radio because I am reading the book.

段落翻译

1. 中国结

中国结是中国典型的本土艺术，象征着团结、友谊、和平、热情和爱情。中国结源于古代，当时人们用系结的方式来记事。中国结在唐宋时期逐渐发展成一种饰品，自明清时期起盛行至今。制作中国结的材料多种多样，如棉线、丝绸、尼龙、皮革，甚至包括一些贵重金属。在古代，由于没有纽扣或拉链等现成的配件，人们不得不打结来固定衣服。随着社会的发展，中国结逐渐失去了原来的实际用途，演变成一种优雅、丰富多彩的工艺品。今天，中国结以其独特的形式、丰富的色彩和深刻的含义而受到人们的喜爱。

难点讲解：

1) "中国结源于古代，当时人们用系结的方式来记事"可处理成 when 引导的状语从句，译为"The Chinese knot originated in ancient times when people used knots to record events."。

2) "中国结在唐宋时期逐渐发展成一种饰品，自明清时期起盛行至今"说明了中国结发展的不同阶段。从结构上看，此句具有汉语中典型的"叙事多用并列结构"的特点，故可将 developed 和 prevailed 处理成并列谓语。本句可译为"Chinese knot developed gradually as a type of decoration during the Tang and Song dynasties, and prevailed from the Ming and Qing dynasties up to now."。

3)"在古代，由于没有纽扣或拉链等现成的配件，人们不得不打结来固定衣服"中"没有现成的配件"可用 there be 句型来翻译。全句可译为"In ancient times, people had to tie knots to secure their clothes because there were no ready-made accessories like buttons or zippers."。

2. 灯笼

灯笼是中国传统的手工艺品，也是中国的象征。它源于汉代，在唐宋时期最为繁盛。起初，人们在门口悬挂灯笼是用来辟邪，后来灯笼逐渐成为节日时增添喜庆气氛的装饰。灯笼的样式有很多，除了圆形和方形外，还有花、鸟、鱼等形状。灯笼通常以纸和丝绸为主要制作原料。灯笼的装饰是中国文化的重要组成部分。灯笼不但在中国历史上扮演着重要角色，对国际上的发明、创新也作出了巨大贡献。如今，每到元宵节，人们会制作漂亮的灯笼来欢庆节日。

难点讲解：

1)"灯笼是中国传统的手工艺品，也是中国的象征"中"是中国的象征"可处理为"灯笼"的同位语，以插入语的形式译出，全句可译为"Lantern, a symbol of China, is a traditional Chinese handicraft."。

2)"灯笼的样式有很多，除了圆形和方形外，还有花、鸟、鱼等形状"一句可拆分翻译。第一个分句"灯笼的样式有很多"总起，第二和第三个分句讲述灯笼的具体形状。本句可译为"There are many styles of lanterns, including round and square shapes, as well as shapes of flowers, birds, fish, etc. They are mainly made of paper and silk."。

3)"灯笼不但在中国历史上扮演着重要角色，对国际上的发明、创新也作出了巨大贡献"中的"不但……也"用"not only ... but also"连接。"作出巨大贡献"可译为 make tremendous contributions to。

3. 皮影

皮影是中国民间古老的传统艺术。据史书记载，皮影戏始于西汉，兴于唐朝，盛于清代。皮影戏所需要的皮影人是用驴皮或牛皮做成的，由一个或几个人控制，人们用光将它们反射到幕布上。表演时，艺人们在白色幕布后面，一边操纵皮影，一边用当地流行的曲调讲述故事，同时配以打击乐器和弦乐，整个表演具有浓厚的乡土气息。皮影戏的流行范围很广，并因各地表演的声腔不同而形成多种多样的风格。皮影戏在陕西和甘肃地区最为流行，经常在庙会、婚礼和葬礼等场合演出。陕西皮影造型质朴单纯，富于装饰性，同时又具有精致工巧的艺术特色。人物形体的整体轮廓简洁，线条优美生动且有力度，在轮廓内部以镂空为主，又适当留实，繁简得宜，虚实相生。皮影人物、道具、配景的各个部位，常常饰有不同的图案花纹，整体效果繁丽而不拖沓，简练而不空洞。每一个形象不仅局部精致，而且整体配合充实生动，从而构成完美的艺术整体。精致生动的皮影人形极具收藏价值，深受人们的喜爱。

难点讲解：

1)"皮影戏始于西汉，兴于唐朝，盛于清代"中"始于……兴于……盛于……"可分别译为 originated、thrived 和 reached its peak。本句可译为"Shadow play originated in the Western Han Dynasty, thrived during the Tang Dynasty, and reached its peak in the Qing Dynasty."。

2)在"表演时，艺人们在白色幕布后面，一边操纵皮影，一边用当地流行的曲调讲述故事，同时配以打击乐器和弦乐，整个表演具有浓厚的乡土气息"一句中，可把"艺人们在白色幕布后面，一边操纵皮影"处理成主句,其他部分处理为从属部分。本句可译为"During the performance, the artists manipulate the shadow puppets behind a white screen, narrating stories with popular local tunes, accompanied by percussion instruments and stringed instruments, creating a strong local flavor."。

3)"陕西皮影造型质朴单纯,富于装饰性,同时又具有精致工巧的艺术特色"一句可采用非限制性定语从句进行翻译,译为"Shaanxi shadow puppet is characterized by its simple and rustic style, which is rich in decoration and shows exquisite craftsmanship."。

4)"人物形体的整体轮廓简洁,线条优美生动且有力度,在轮廓内部以镂空为主,又适当留实,繁简得宜,虚实相生"可拆分成两句来翻译。第一句为"人物形体的整体轮廓简洁,线条优美生动且有力度",可译为"The overall outline of the character's shape is concise, with elegant, vivid and powerful lines.";第二句为"在轮廓内部以镂空为主,又适当留实,繁简得宜,虚实相生",可译为"The interior of the outline is mostly hollowed out, with appropriate solid parts, achieving a balance between complexity and simplicity, and a harmonious combination of emptiness and solidity."。

4. 泥塑

泥塑俗称"彩塑",是中国古老的民间艺术形式之一,它的历史可以追溯到新石器时代。泥塑可根据功用可分为宗教和民俗两类,前者主要供奉在佛寺道观,后者多为陈设品与儿童玩具。泥塑制作方法是在黏土里掺入少许棉花纤维,捣匀后,捏制成各种人物的泥坯,经阴干,涂上底粉,再施彩绘。泥塑发源于宝鸡市凤翔县,流行于陕西、天津、江苏、河南等地,其中天津"泥人张"的泥塑非常出名。创始人张明山不但继承了传统艺术遗产,还从绘画、戏曲、民间木版年画等艺术中吸收营养。"泥人张"制作的泥塑精美而生动,富有浓郁的地域风情。随着中国旅游业的发展,泥塑已经成为广受欢迎的旅游纪念品,受到世界各地游客的青睐。

难点讲解:

1)"泥塑俗称'彩塑',是中国古老的民间艺术形式之一,它的历史可以追溯到新石器时代"一句可译为"Clay sculpture, commonly known as 'colorful sculpture' in Chinese, is one of the ancient folk art forms in China, with a history that could be traced back to the Neolithic Age."。

2)"泥塑制作方法是在黏土里掺入少许棉花纤维,捣匀后,捏制成各种人物的泥坯,经阴干,涂上底粉,再施彩绘"可译为含有多个动词的并列句,如"The process of making clay sculptures involves mixing a small amount of cotton fiber into the clay, kneading it into various clay molds, drying them in the shade, applying a base powder, and then painting them with colors."。

3)"创始人张明山不但继承了传统艺术遗产,还从绘画、戏曲、民间木版年画等艺术中吸收营养"可译为"Zhang Mingshan, the founder, not only inherited the legacy of traditional art but also incorporated skills from painting, opera, and New Year woodblock painting."。

4)"泥人张制作的泥塑精美而生动,富有浓郁的地域风情"可译为"The clay sculptures made by 'Niren Zhang' are exquisite, vivid, and rich in regional characteristics."。

5)"随着中国旅游业的发展,泥塑已经成为广受欢迎的旅游纪念品,受到世界各地游客的青睐"中"受到世界各地游客的青睐"在翻译时需用被动语态。本句可译为"With the development of China's tourism industry, clay sculpture has become a popular souvenir and is favored by tourists from all over the world."。

5. 中国瓷器

中国瓷器是中国艺术的重要组成部分。唐朝时期,人们就在昌南建造窑坊,烧制出一种青白瓷。青白瓷色彩晶莹，有"人造玉器"的美称，因而远近闻名，并大量出口欧洲。当时，欧洲人还不会制造瓷器，因此中国特别是昌南镇的瓷器很受欢迎。中国瓷器经久耐用，质地轻薄，图案奇特，色彩明亮，质量上乘，在西方很受欢迎。瓷器促进了中国与外部世界之间的经济文化交流，并深刻地影响着其他国家的传统文化和生活方式。

难点讲解：

1)"青白瓷色彩晶莹，有'人造玉器'的美称，因而远近闻名，并大量出口欧洲"一句含有因果逻辑关系。全句可译为"The bluish white porcelain was translucent and had the reputation of artificial jade, so it became famous far and wide and was exported to Europe in large quantities."。

2)"中国瓷器经久耐用，质地轻薄，图案奇特，色彩明亮，质量上乘，在西方很受欢迎"可用被动句来翻译，译为"Chinese porcelain is known for its durability, thin texture, unique patterns, bright colors, and excellent quality, which made it highly popular in the West."。

3)"瓷器促进了中国和外部世界之间的经济文化交流，并深刻地影响着其他国家的传统文化和生活方式"可译为并列句，即"Porcelain has facilitated economic and cultural exchanges between China and the outside world and profoundly influenced the traditional culture and way of life of other countries."。

6. 剪纸

剪纸有着悠久的历史，是传统的民间艺术形式，它可以追溯到北朝时期。剪纸就是用剪刀将纸剪成各种各样的图案，其艺术造型浓郁质朴、生动有趣，有着独特的艺术魅力。这种民俗艺术的产生和流传与中国农村的节日风俗有着密切的关系，逢年过节抑或是在新婚等喜庆的日子，人们都会把美丽明艳的剪纸贴在雪白的墙上、明亮的玻璃窗上或门和灯笼上等，以此来烘托欢乐的气氛。在中国的传统文化中，剪纸可以反映生活的诸多方面。另外，中国人认为门上的红色剪纸可以给全家人带来好运和幸福。虽然其他艺术形式（如绘画）也可以传达类似的意义，但剪纸仍然以它的魅力脱颖而出。今天，剪纸主要用作装饰，或被用作赠送友人的礼物。剪纸艺术不仅是中国民间艺术中的瑰宝，也已成为世界艺术宝库珍贵的组成部分。

难点讲解：

1)"剪纸就是用剪刀将纸剪成各种各样的图案，其艺术造型浓郁质朴、生动有趣，有着独特的艺术魅力"一句较长，可采用分译法进行翻译。"有着独特的艺术魅力"可处理成现在分词短语。本句可译为"Paper-cutting involves using scissors to cut paper into various patterns. Its artistic style is rich, simple, vivid and interesting, possessing unique artistic charm."。

2)"这种民俗艺术的产生和流传与中国农村的节日风俗有着密切关系，逢年过节抑或是在新婚等喜庆的日子，人们都会把美丽明艳的剪纸贴在雪白的墙上、明亮的玻璃窗上或门和灯笼上等，以此来烘托欢乐的气氛"可拆分成两句来译。第一句为"这种民俗艺术的产生和流传与中国农村的节日风俗有着密切关系"，可译为"The origin and dissemination of this folk art form are closely related to the festival customs in China's rural areas."。第二句为"逢年过节抑或是在新婚等喜庆的日子，人们都会把美丽明艳的剪纸贴在雪白的墙上、明亮的玻璃窗上或门和灯笼上等，以此来烘托欢乐的气氛"，可译为"During festivals or joyful occasions such as weddings, people would decorate their homes with beautiful and vibrant paper-cuttings on white walls, bright glass windows, doors, lanterns, and more, creating a festive atmosphere."。

3)"虽然其他艺术形式（如绘画）也可以传达类似的意义，但剪纸仍然以它的魅力脱颖而出"一句可用让步状语从句进行翻译，译为"Although other art forms such as painting can also convey the similar meanings, paper-cutting still stands out with its unique charm."。

4)"剪纸艺术不仅是中国民间艺术中的瑰宝，也已成为世界艺术宝库珍贵的组成部分"可译为"Paper-cutting art is not only a treasure in Chinese folk art but also has become a cherished part of the world's art collection."。

7. 景泰蓝

景泰蓝是中国的一种传统艺术品，距今已有六百多年的历史。这种艺术品在明朝景泰年间盛行，制作技艺比较成熟，使用的珐琅釉多以蓝色为主，故而得名"景泰蓝"。景泰蓝又名"铜胎掐丝珐琅"，是一种在铜质的胎型上，用柔软的扁铜丝，掐成各种花纹焊上，然后把珐琅质的色釉填充在花纹内烧制而成的器物。它采用金银铜及多种天然矿物质为原材料，集美术、工艺、雕刻、镶嵌、冶金等专业技术为一体。景泰蓝典雅精美，具有独特的民族风格和浓厚的文化韵味。在明清两朝，景泰蓝都是皇家专用的器物饰品，象征着尊贵与财富。直到清朝后期才作为商品出现在市场上，景泰蓝也由此开始随着商船走向海外。

难点讲解：

1)翻译"这种艺术品在明朝景泰年间盛行，制作技艺比较成熟，使用的珐琅釉多以蓝色为主，故而得名'景泰蓝'"一句时，需注意汉语和英语的句法差异，适当添加连接词。此句可译为"Because this type of craftwork was popular in the Jingtai period of the Ming Dynasty when its craftsmanship was relatively mature, and the enamel used was mostly blue, the name 'Jing Tai Lan' came into being."。

2)"景泰蓝又名'铜胎掐丝珐琅'，是一种在铜质的胎型上，用柔软的扁铜丝，掐成各种花纹焊上，然后把珐琅质的色釉填充在花纹内烧制而成的器物"一句较长，可采用分译法进行翻译，译为"Cloisonné, also known as 'copper padding thread weaving enamel,' is a kind of utensil made of soft flat copper wire on the copper tire which is molded into various patterns and welded. The patterns are then filled with enamel colored glaze and fired to create enamelware."。

3)"它采用金银铜及多种天然矿物质为原材料，集美术、工艺、雕刻、镶嵌、冶金等专业技术为一体"可译为并列句"Cloisonné utilizes gold, silver, copper, and various natural minerals as raw materials, combining the techniques of fine arts, craftsmanship, carving, inlaying, and metallurgy."。

4)翻译"景泰蓝典雅精美，具有独特的民族风格和浓厚的文化韵味"一句时可将后半句处理成伴随状语，补充说明景泰蓝，此句可译为"Cloisonné is elegant and exquisite, showcasing a unique national style and rich cultural charm."。

5)"象征着尊贵与财富"可处理为同位语，译为 a symbol of being noble and wealthy，也可处理为伴随状语，译作 symbolizing nobility and wealth。

8. 刺绣

作为中国艺术中一颗璀璨的明珠，刺绣是用针和线在织物或其他材料上进行装饰的民间手工艺，在中国至少有两三千年的历史。中国刺绣主要有苏绣、湘绣、蜀绣和粤绣四大门类。刺绣主要用于生活用品和艺术装饰，如服装、床上用品、舞台、艺术品装饰等。据记载，中国最古老的刺绣可以追溯到商朝，在当时刺绣象征着社会地位。唐朝以前的绣品，多为实用及装饰之用，刺绣内容与生活和风俗有关。到了宋代，绣画逐渐流行。文人志士嗜爱书法及绘画，书画乃当时最高的艺术表现形式，以至于书画风格直接影响到刺绣的风格。随着经济的发展，刺绣逐渐走进普通人的生活。从华丽的龙袍到今日的时装,刺绣为中国人的文化和生活增添了许多乐趣。令人感到吃惊的是,在刺绣发展的整个过程中,人们感觉不到也说不出来有什么材质或技术上的变化。

难点讲解:

1)"作为中国艺术中一颗璀璨的明珠,刺绣是用针和线在织物或其他材料上进行装饰的民间手工艺,在中国至少有两三千年的历史"一句较长,可采用分译法进行翻译。译为"As a shining pearl in Chinese art, embroidery is a traditional handicraft that involves decorating fabric or other materials with needles and threads. It has a history of at least two or three thousand years in China."。

2)"唐朝以前的绣品,多为实用及装饰之用,刺绣内容与生活和风俗有关"中后半句可处理为介词短语作为补充说明,译为"Embroidery, before the Tang Dynasty, was mainly used for practical and decorative purposes, with motifs related to daily life and customs."。

3)"文人志士"可译为 scholar and literati。

4)"令人感到吃惊的是"可以理解为"这是一个令人吃惊的事实",可用"It is a striking fact that…"句型,也可直接用副词 surprisingly 来翻译。

9. 扇子

中国有着悠久的扇子文化,最早的扇子出现在三千多年前,由羽毛制成。我们的祖先在炎炎夏日,随手摘取树叶或猎取禽羽,用以障日挡风,这便是扇子的来源。在漫长的岁月中,小小的扇子除了实用之外,还蕴涵着中华文化艺术的智慧,凝聚了古今工艺美术之精华,是民族传统文物中的瑰宝。扇子之所以受人喜爱,除了可以扇风纳凉,还和扇子的雅致精巧及扇面的书画艺术分不开。扇面上的书法、绘画和诗歌为扇子增添了艺术价值,使扇子为历代收藏家所珍爱。汉唐时期,农业得到发展,丝绸和缎面扇子开始出现,并在文人雅士中成为一种时尚。他们通过在扇面上书写和绘画来展示自己的才能,扇子很快获得了非常大的社会意义。现在,随着人们生活水平的提高,扇子作为实用品的功能正在逐渐消退,更多人看重的是它的艺术性,并用之于收藏把玩。这一传统的工艺品正以其独特的艺术魅力焕发出新的活力。

难点讲解:

1)"我们的祖先在炎炎夏日,随手摘取树叶或猎取禽羽,用以障日挡风,这便是扇子的来源"可译为"Our ancestors would collect leaves or bird feathers at hand to shield themselves from the sun and wind during the scorching summer days, which was the origin of the fan."。

2)"在漫长的岁月中,小小的扇子除了实用之外,还蕴涵着中华文化艺术的智慧,凝聚了古今工艺美术之精华,是民族传统文物中的瑰宝"可译为并列句"Throughout the long period of time, the small fan not only served practical purposes but also possessed the wisdom of Chinese cultural art and contained the essence of traditional crafts and fine arts, making it an artistic treasure among national cultural relics."。

3)"为扇子增添了艺术价值,使扇子为……所珍爱"可译为"add artistic value to the fans and make them cherished by…"。

4)"汉唐时期,农业得到发展,丝绸和缎面扇子开始出现"中"农业得到发展"其实是"丝绸和缎面扇子开始出现"的原因,所以这里有一层因果逻辑关系,可用因果连词来表达,译为 due to the development of agriculture, silk and satin fans began to appear。

5)"这一传统的工艺品正以其独特的艺术魅力焕发出新的活力"可译为"This traditional handicraft is radiating new vitality with its unique artistic charm."。

拓展阅读

Chinese Silk

Silk and silk making is a vital feature of Chinese history and its ancient civilization. According to archeological evidence, silk and silk fabric emerged in China at least 5,500 years ago. Thousands of years ago, silk was also spread from Chang'an to Europe along the Silk Road, bringing not only pieces of colorful clothing and ornaments, but also the ancient and splendid oriental civilization. Since then, silk has almost become the transmitter and symbol of oriental civilization. Chinese silk is famous for its excellent quality, exquisite color and rich cultural connotation.

China is the hometown of silk, and silk is one of the important characteristics of Chinese civilization, which is closely linked with Chinese etiquette system, culture and art, local customs, science and technology, etc. Emperors used silk to show their authority, officials used silk to mark their ranks, literati scholars wrote poems praising silk, and painters splashed ink on silk fabric.

The cultivation of the silkworm could be traced back to the third century BCE. Silkworm raising and cocoon unwinding are now known as silk culture or sericulture. It takes about 25 – 28 days for a silkworm to grow old enough to spin a cocoon. Then farmers will pick them up and place them one by one onto piles of straws. Then each silkworm, with its legs stretched out, will attach itself to the straw and begin to spin.

The next step is unwinding the cocoons. The cocoons are heated enough to kill the pupae, which must be done at the right time. Otherwise, the pupas are bound to turn into moths. Moths will make a hole in the cocoon, which makes reeling useless. To unwind the cocoons, they are put into a basin filled with hot water at first. Then the reeling women find the loose end of the cocoons and twist them. Afterwards, the women carry the cocoons to a small wheel for unwinding.

At last, two workers measure them into a certain length and twist them into so called "raw" silk, which then are dyed and woven into cloth. It is a fact that about 1,000 meters can be unwound from one cocoon, while 111 cocoons are needed for a man's tie, and 630 cocoons are needed for a woman's blouse. Chinese people developed a new way by using silk to make clothes since the discovery of silk. This kind of clothes became popular soon. At that time, China's technology was developing fast.

Emperor Wudi of Western Han Dynasty decided to develop trade with other countries. Building a road became priority to trade silk. The Silk Road was built for that purpose. The Chinese Silk Road has lasted for many dynasties in history from Han, Tang till Qing. It begins from Chang'an, Shaanxi Province, via the west along Hexi Corridor in Gansu Province, to Xinjiang Uygur Autonomous Region. The Silk Road went across Middle Asia, South Asia and West Asia. Many countries of Asia and Europe were connected. Therefore, Chinese silk and many other inventions were brought to Europe via the Chinese Silk Road. Chinese silk became a symbol of wealth among them.

As one of the great inventions of ancient China, silk contributed a lot to the world civilization through the ancient Silk Road. Meanwhile, foreign cultures also entered China through the Silk Road, making the local culture more colorful. All in all, silk is a symbol of ancient Chinese culture and has made an indelible contribution to the development of human civilization in the world.

Exercises

1 **Match the English expressions in Column A with the Chinese translations in Column B.**

Column A	Column B
1 archeological evidence	a 文化内涵
2 colorful clothing and ornaments	b 退茧
3 transmitter	c 蚕业
4 cultural connotation	d 传播者
5 etiquette system	e 蛹
6 splashed ink	f 华美的服饰
7 cocoon unwinding	g 泼墨挥洒
8 sericulture	h 考古证据
9 pupae	i 不可磨灭的贡献
10 indelible contribution	j 礼仪制度

2 **Answer the following questions.**

1) What is Chinese silk famous for?

2) What are the significant meanings of the Chinese Silk Road?

翻译佳作赏析

《迢迢牵牛星》

佚　名

迢迢牵牛星，皎皎河汉女。
纤纤擢素手，札札弄机杼。
终日不成章，泣涕零如雨。
河汉清且浅，相去复几许。
盈盈一水间，脉脉不得语。

译文：

Far, far away the Cowherd Star

Anonymous

Far, far away the Cowherd Star;
Bright, bright riverside Weaving Maid.
Slender, slender her fingers are;
Clack, clack her shuttle's tune is played;
She weaves all day, no web is done;
Like rain her tears drop one by one.
Heaven's River's shallow and clear;
The two stars are not far apart.
Where brimful, brimful waves appear;
They gaze but can't lay bare their heart.

（许渊冲　译）

赏析：

《迢迢牵牛星》是创作于汉代的一首文人五言诗，被编入《古诗十九首》。此诗借神话传说中牛郎织女被银河阻隔而不得会面的悲剧，抒发了女子对离别的丈夫的相思之情，写出了人间夫妻不得团聚的悲哀。全诗共五句，其中六处用了叠音词，即"迢迢""皎皎""纤纤""札札""盈盈"和"脉脉"。除了"脉脉"这一叠音词，许渊冲巧妙地将其余五个叠音词直接翻译为"far, far""bright, bright""slender, slender""clack, clack""brimful, brimful"。这些叠音词的翻译使整首诗音节和谐，质朴清丽，情趣盎然，自然贴切，生动地传递了物性与情思，再现了原诗的意境之美、音韵之美和结构形式之美。此外，许渊冲的译文在一二句押了行尾韵"d"（Maid 和 played），在四五句押了行尾韵"t"（apart 和 heart），读来朗朗上口，韵律感十足，形式上给人简洁、清新之感。

翻译练习

1. 唐三彩是一种著名陶器，以黄、褐、绿为基本釉色。它的诞生可以追溯到唐朝以前。"三彩"是多彩的意思，并不是指三种颜色。唐三彩吸取了中国国画和雕塑的技巧，成为一种风格艺术品。它以造型生动、色彩丰腴而著称。千姿百态的骆驼俑，能让人们置身于一望无际的丝路大漠；而那些造型各异的胡人俑，展现了胡人留学、经商或者卖艺的经历，他们为大唐盛世增添了浓郁的异国色彩。唐朝文化融合了丰富多彩的异域民族文化，这些文化在唐三彩里都得到了很好的体现。在当时，唐三彩不仅在国内风行一时，还闻名海外，受到世界各地收藏者的推崇。

2. 谈起我国的吉祥艺术，不得不提到鼻烟壶。尽管它的历史不长，却浓缩了悠久的中国传统文化。鼻烟虽是舶来品，但鼻烟壶经过中国能工巧匠的精心打造，很快便成为一个独立、崭新的工艺美术品种。鼻烟壶的设计集书法、绘画、雕刻、镶嵌和中外绘画之大成，让人爱不释手，成为中国古代工艺繁荣发展的一个缩影。鼻烟壶所蕴含的吉祥文化，不仅在装饰中体现得淋漓尽致，还体现在材质、造型等方面。鼻烟壶尽管体量袖珍，却彰显了多种工艺技艺，被广大收藏爱好者视为珍贵文玩。

3. 筷子是中国古代发明中一种具有鲜明民族特色的进食工具，反映了中国饮食的文化特色。中国人使用筷子的历史可以追溯到商代，距今已有三千多年。筷子可谓是中国的国粹，既轻巧又灵活，在世界各国餐具中独树一帜，被西方人誉为"东方的文明"。筷子形状和种类多种多样，从雕刻着彩画或书法的金筷子到可再生的竹筷和木筷，不一而足。筷子已成为中国文化的重要标志，是人类历史的重要组成部分。

4. 中国有句古话："黄金有价玉无价。"在中国人的心目中，玉这种美丽的宝石无比重要和珍贵。浙江河姆渡遗址出土的一件玉器已有七千多年的历史。在新石器时代中后期，玉器更受欢迎，它已经从用于祭祀的器皿变成了特权的象征，在一些高级官员的坟墓里都能发现玉器。对于官员使用玉器有严格的规定，以不同的图案显示不同的等级。秦朝皇帝使用玉玺，这种做法一直在之后的朝代中沿用。春秋以来，玉雕技术迅速发展，玉器雕刻精美绝伦。这一时期的龙凤纹玉器，至今仍十分珍贵。在明代，除了用于装饰，玉器还有更多的实际用途。中国的工匠们受佛教或儒家思想的影响，在玉器上雕刻各种各样的图案，以表达不同的含义，流行的图案有"佛驱邪""鱼发财""鹿平安""桃长寿""蝙蝠祝福"等。一些中国人还认为，由于玉石含有一些好的成分，佩带玉石可以使身体健康，有平衡阴阳和驱除疾病的好处。玉象征着美丽、高贵和纯洁，在许多中国成语和短语中被用来形容美丽的人和美德。当父母给孩子（大多是女孩）起名时，"玉"字也很受欢迎。儒家思想还认为"君子比德如玉"。

5. 蜡染据说早在秦末或者汉初就已经出现，但它最初作为成品出现是在唐朝。西南部少数民族发现蜡可以用于染布，并掌握了蜡染的技艺。自此，蜡染在贵州少数民族地区代代传承，并在不同的地区广泛流传。苗族在蜡染方面有着独特的绘画和手工染色技艺。作为中国最具有少数民族特色的艺术之一，蜡染产品的种类有很多，如墙上挂饰、邮包、书包、桌套等。蜡染图案色彩丰富，大多数以写实为基础。蜡染手工艺者在绘制图案时使用了大胆的变化和夸张手法，这种夸张和变化出自天然的想象，因而富有无穷的魅力。

6. 印章制作是一种结合书法和雕刻的古老艺术。中国的古代印章主要分为官印和私印两大类。印章是一种带有汉字的图章，通常用于在文件、办公文书、合同、艺术品或类似物品上证明身份。中国印章通常由石头、木头、竹子、塑料、象牙、红墨水和朱砂糊等制成。私人印章在非正式场合被用作个人图章，这些非官方图章被称为"印"。艺术家们创作了独特的印章，作为代表他们身份的签名图章。这些印章雕琢自然，不落俗套。

7. 中国杂技是中国传统表演艺术的瑰宝，有两千多年的悠久历史。它也是最受人们欢迎的传统艺术形式之一。在古代，杂技与音乐、舞蹈有关，在当时的文化中扮演着重要的角色。汉唐时期，杂技在内容、种类和技巧上得到进一步发展。自宋朝以来，杂技从宫廷传到民间。然而，杂技表演者的社会地位不断下降。明末清初，杂技被国外引进，在西方社会广受欢迎。中华人民共和国成立后，杂技也获得了新的生命和更好的发展。

Unit 14

生态环境

Unit Goals

In this unit, you are going to
- grasp words and expressions concerning ecological environment;
- acquire knowledge about Chinese ecological environment;
- know how to translate negation sentences from Chinese into English;
- grasp translation skills of paragraphs on ecological environment.

Related Words and Expressions

可持续发展战略 sustainable development strategy
环保产品 environmentally-friendly products
低碳经济 low-carbon economy
减排，减少温室气体排放 reduce greenhouse gas emission
可再生资源 renewable resources
保护森林资源 protect forest resources
环境歧视 environmental discrimination
能源制造 energy production
生态平衡 ecological balance
太阳能 solar energy
自然资源 natural resource
森林资源 forest resource
绿色能源 green energy
碳排放 carbon emission
再生水 recycled water
污水处理 sewage treatment
森林砍伐率 deforestation rate
水土流失 soil erosion; water loss and soil erosion
湿度 humidity
倾盆大雨 downpour
臭氧层变薄 depletion of the ozone layer
石油 petroleum
居住环境破坏与物种灭绝 habitat destruction and species extinction
原料 raw materials

商业捕鱼 commercial fishing
灾难 catastrophe
自然灾害 natural disasters
水污染防治 water pollution control
核污染防治 nuclear pollution control
世界环境日 World Environment Day
酸雨 acid rain
适应性强的物种 adaptable species
植树造林 afforestation
农业生物技术 agricultural biotechnologies
空气污染物 air pollutants
人工环境 artificial environment
生物多样性 biological diversity; biodiversity
生物资源 biological resources
气候变化 climatic change
淡水保护 conservation of freshwater

Lead-in Activities

1 Answer the following questions.

1) What do you think are the most challenging ecological problems our world and our country are faced with now?

2) Do you think protecting ecological environment is important for us human beings? Why?

3) How can the world cooperate as a whole to protect our ecological environment?

2 Listen to a brief introduction to China's ways of meeting ecological challenges and fill in the blanks with the words you hear.

Building a shared future for all life on Earth is _____. Faced with various ecological challenges, all people are members of a community where they _____. China adheres to the philosophy of _____ and has made remarkable progress in this area.

China desires to _____ the international community to _____ the importance of respecting, following and protecting nature, to actively share its experience in advancing ecological civilization, to _____ green development and a _____ _____ mode of production and life, and so to jointly build a shared future for all life on Earth, _____ a global ecological civilization.

3 Read the following passage and then do the exercises.

Circular Targets Plastic Waste

Nine central government bodies have jointly issued a circular on phasing out disposable plastic products, vowing to ensure timely fulfillment of the 2020 target by rolling out law enforcement campaigns at both local and national levels.

Clarifying the responsibilities of each of the bodies and local governments, the document will help address the overlap of duties in the governance of disposable plastic items and pave the way for promoting more environmentally friendly substitutes, the production of which is currently enough to meet the emerging demand, experts said.

Unveiled on July 24, the circular demanded each provincial-level government draft plans by the middle of next month to phase out disposable plastics in their regions. Meanwhile, cities at prefecture level and above should specify measures to be taken for their 2020 targets.

Gao Xing, coordinator of the plastic initiative with the Worldwide Fund for Nature Beijing Office, applauded the initiative for stressing the responsibility of local governments **in the phaseout** efforts. The WWF launched its global plastics initiative, **No Plastics in Nature**, in 2018.

"It included clear requirements for local governments to roll out specific and effective measures to cope with plastic pollution," he said.

However, Gao also called on the Chinese government to introduce guidelines in a timely manner on the definition, production standards, identification and recycling of substitutes for disposable plastic products.

The duties of the nine government bodies are all specified in the circular.

Different levels of commerce authorities and administrations for market regulation, for example, will be responsible for supervising the phasing-out work in the retail sector, marketplaces, catering businesses and exhibitions. Evidence of violations will be transferred to law enforcement teams at ecology and environment departments, it said.

All local governments should launch enforcement campaigns in key sectors such as shopping malls and supermarkets by the end of August. A joint inspection by the nine central government bodies will be organized by the end of the year, it said.

Wen Zongguo, a professor from the School of Environment at Tsinghua University, said the specification of the duties of different government bodies is important for the country to combat plastic pollution.

"Plastic pollution control involves various government bodies," he said. "The overlapping responsibilities and gaps in supervision management can only be addressed through cooperation of these bodies after their duties are specified."

The circular was released to ensure the implementation of a guideline published in January, which pledged to effectively curb plastic pollution in the country's major cities in five years.

The guideline demanded non-degradable plastic products be phased out gradually. Non-degradable plastic bags, straws and tableware will be the first to be affected.

Disposable plastic straws will be prohibited nationwide in restaurants by the end of the year. In addition, the use of disposable plastic tableware will be banned in dine-in restaurants and scenic spots across the country by the end of the year, and then be expanded to all other disposable plastic products by the end of 2022.

Meanwhile, non-degradable plastic bags are expected to disappear from some major consumption sectors, including shopping malls, supermarkets and restaurant takeout services, in large cities by the end of this year and then in all major Chinese cities and urban areas in coastal regions by the end of 2022.

Zhang Lijun, deputy head of the China General Chamber of Commerce, said the ban will stop the annual consumption of about 300,000 metric tons of disposable plastic straws, tableware and bags by the end of 2022.

The country is currently capable of supplying over 400,000 tons of degradable plastic annually, and also has abundant raw materials such as paper and bamboo to produce substitutes, she said.

1) Answer the following questions.

(1) Who will be responsible for supervising the phasing out work in commercial places?

(2) What is important for China to combat the plastic pollution, according to scholars?

(3) What specific measures are expected to be taken for the nationwide plastic control activity?

2) Translate the following words or phrases into English.

一次性塑料制品

环保替代品

展开执法行动

执行准则

丰富的原料

3) Translate the following paragraph into English.

长久以来，中华文化强调人与自然和谐相处，认为这样人类才能幸福生活。但在20世纪后期，随着工业化进程的加快，环境在某种程度上也遭到破坏。针对这一问题，中国政府已经采取积极的应对措施，并取得了明显的成效。

翻译技巧：否定句（Negation Sentences）

汉英两种语言都有肯定和否定形式。汉译英时汉语的否定形式通常也可以译成英语的否定形式。但由于两种语言在否定概念的表达方面有所差异，翻译时也应根据具体语境选择恰当的翻译策略。

汉语和英语中的否定形式均可分为完全否定、部分否定和双重否定三种。针对不同的否定形式应采用不同的译法，使原文和译文意义相符、功能相似。英语中表示否定有两种方法，一是借助词汇，如使用否定词，或含有否定意义的动词、名词、形容词、副词、连词、介词等；二是借助结构和表达方式，如使用表示否定意义的比较结构等。英语表示否定意义的方式比汉语丰富。在汉译英时，应该充分考虑英语的表达习惯，使译文尽可能准确、地道。

例1 原文 他永远也忘不了亲眼见到她的那一天。

译文 He will never forget the day when he saw her with his own eyes.

评析 原文中的否定词用 never 来翻译，将汉语的全部否定译成英语的全部否定。

例2 原文 这家书店里几乎找不到几本好书。

译文 Few of good novels can be found in this book store.

评析 原文中的部分否定用英语中的否定词 few 译出，将汉语的部分否定译成英语的部分否定。

例 3 原文 没有你的帮助我是无法按时完成这项任务的。
译文 I could not have finished the task without your help.
评析 原文中的双重否定译成英语的双重否定。

例 4 原文 我还没来得及插句话，他就给我量好了尺寸。
译文 Before I could get in a word, he had measured for me.
评析 原文中的否定结构在译文中变为肯定结构，意思仍为否定。

例 5 原文 赶快把这封信寄出去。
译文 Don't lose time in posting this letter.
评析 原文中的肯定形式译成英语的否定形式，句意不变。

例 6 原文 所有的学生都不去参加音乐会。
译文 None of the students will go to the concert.
评析 原文否定的是谓语动词，译文否定的是主语，否定部分在翻译过程中发生了转变，但原文句意未改变。

段落翻译

1. 西部建设

西部大开发（China's Western Development Policy）是我国中央政府制定的一项政策，目的是"把东部沿海地区的剩余经济发展能力（surplus capacity of economic development）用以提高西部地区的经济和社会发展水平、巩固国防"。加速西部地区发展，是缩小地区差距、实现共同富裕的中国特色社会主义的本质要求；是进一步扩大国内需求、保持国民经济持续、快速、健康发展的客观要求；是改善全国生态环境、实现可持续发展的急切要求；也是维护社会稳定、民族团结和边疆安全的迫切要求。目前西部大开发取得的成就显著，东西部地区的差距正逐渐缩小。

难点讲解：

1）在"西部大开发是我国中央政府制定的一项政策"中，"是我国中央政府制定的一项政策"可处理为定语，译为 a policy made by the Central People's Government of China。其中过去分词短语"made by…"作 policy 的后置定语。

2）"剩余经济发展能力"中的"剩余能力"可译为 surplus capacity。

3）"提高……经济和社会发展水平"可译为 enhancing the economic and social development。

4）"缩小地区差距"可译为 narrow the gap between different regions。narrow 作形容词意为"狭窄的"，作动词意为"使变窄"，引申为"缩小"。

5）"共同富裕"可译为名词短语 collective prosperity。

6）"扩大国内需求"可译为 expanding domestic demands。

2. 环境保护

过去 10 年，海平面升高和森林破坏的速度都是前所未有的：生态恶化、物种灭绝、臭氧层被破坏、温室效应、酸雨等一系列环境问题已经严重影响到人类的生存环境。环境恶化导致的问题之一就是水资源短缺。2022 年全球人口已增长到 80 亿，环境保护面临更大的压力。中国作为一个发展中国家，面临着发展经济和保护环境的双重任务。中国将环境保护视为一项基本国策，对生态环境和生物多样性的保护是环保工作的重点。

难点讲解：

1）第一句为附加成分众多的长句，可采用分译法译为两句："Sea level rose and forest were destroyed at an unprecedented rate during the last decade. A series of environmental problems such as the deterioration of ecosystem, the extinction of bio-species, damage to the ozone layer, the green-house effect, acid rain, have posed a serious threat to human living conditions."。

2)"2022 年全球人口已增长到 80 亿，环境保护面临更大的压力。"一句中"2022 年全球人口已增长到 80 亿"，可采用介词短语译为 With the global population having increased to eight billion in 2022，以使译文表达简练。

3. 环境污染

在当今人口越来越多、社会越来越工业化的世界，人类居住的环境日益受到污染。人口的增长导致对地球有限的水资源和土地资源的需求不断增长。中国是发展中国家中的大国，工业化正在快速发展，环境问题也越来越受到人们的重视。环境保护是中国的一项基本国策。近年来，政府采取了很多措施来加强环境治理，如建立了世界闻名的生态工程"三北防护林工程"(the Three-North Shelter Forest Program)。此外，中国也在大力发展自然保护区，颁布了《环境保护法》(The Law on Environmental Protection)，加强环保意识和环保教育。目前，环境治理已取得明显成效，城市环境和农业生态环境得到了很大改善，工业污染防治能力也大大提高。

难点讲解：

1）第一句"人类居住的环境日益受到污染"中的"污染"可译为 upsetting，作为对本段 polluting 的同义词替换使用，以增强译文语言的表达丰富性。

2)"发展中国家中的大国"可译为 a major developing country。

3)"越来越受到人们的重视"可译为 getting more and more attention。

4)"自然保护区"可译为 natural reserves。

5）翻译"环境治理已取得明显成效"时可使用被动语态，译为 distinct achievements have been gained in environmental governance。

4. 气候问题

全球气候变暖是近年来各国一直热议的话题。很多人认为全球变暖会使全球降水量重新分配，冰川(glacier)和冻土(permafrost)消融，海平面上升，破坏自然生态系统的平衡，威胁人类的居住环境。也有人认为全球变暖对有些地区是坏事，对有些地区却是好事。比如，南北极的寒冷地区由于温度升高，冰川会融化，动物栖息地减少；而在寒冷地区，天气变暖意味着可以将农作物种植范围扩大。20 世纪 90 年代以来，气候问题日渐被世人关注并演化为一个全球政治议题。过去 20 年的气候谈判展现出气候政治博弈的复杂局面，利益主体的分化和博弈主题的扩展使气候政治这一全球性难题出现。

难点讲解：

1)"破坏自然生态系统的平衡"可译为 do harm to the balance of natural ecosystem。

2)"威胁"可直接译为 threat，也可译为 cause negative effect on。

3)"对……是坏事/好事"可译为"be bad/good for…"。

4)"被世人关注"可译为 become a global concern。

5）最后一句为长句，句式较复杂，其主干为"气候谈判展现出复杂局面"，可译为 Climate negotiation have ended in a complicated situation。

5. 垃圾分类

近年来,中国政府正在努力推行垃圾分类政策。垃圾分类要求人们将垃圾投放至不同的垃圾桶,通过不同的清理、运输和回收方式,使之变成新的资源。垃圾分类可以减少垃圾处理量,降低处理成本,减少土地资源的消耗,对社会、经济、生态三方面都有益。垃圾分类不仅关乎人类的生存质量,也会对地球上其他的生物产生积极影响。因此我们要自觉保护环境,做好垃圾分类。

难点讲解:

1)第一句中的"努力推行垃圾分类政策"可译为 implement the policy of garbage classification with great effort。

2)第二句为长句,由三个短句组成。"要求人们……"可以用 require sb to do 来翻译。"通过不同的清理、运输和回收方式,使之变成新的资源"可看作是"人们将垃圾投放至不同的垃圾桶"的结果,可用 so that 连接,加强句子逻辑。

3)"垃圾分类可以减少垃圾处理量,降低处理成本,减少土地资源的消耗,对社会、经济、生态三方面都有益"一句的主干可理解为"它可以减少……降低……减少……",三个谓语动词可以分别用 reduce、decrease 和 cut down 来翻译,后接不同的宾语。"对社会、经济、生态三方面都有益"则可处理成现在分词短语"benefiting…",表示结果。

4)"自觉保护环境"可译为 consciously protect the environment。

6. 可持续发展

可持续发展是 20 世纪 80 年代提出的一种新的发展观。这种模式要求在保护环境的条件下发展经济,既要满足当代的需求,又不能损害后代人的利益。它的核心思想是确保经济、资源和环境的协调发展,目的是让子孙后代也能享受充分的资源和良好的环境。可持续发展是中国的一项基本国策。目前中国正集中精力节能减排,加快资源节约型和环境友好型工业体系的建设,加大环境保护力度,提高生态文明(ecological civilization)的水平。

难点讲解:

1)第一句中的"发展观"可译为 concept of development;"20 世纪 80 年代提出的"可处理为定语从句或过去分词作后置定语。

2)"这种模式要求在保护环境的条件下发展经济"中的谓语"要求"后的从句要用虚拟语气;"发展经济"可采用被动语态,即 economy be developed。

3)第三句"它的核心思想是……目的是……"前后分句关系不大,可分译成两句,即"The core idea is to…"和"The goal is to…"。

4)第五句较长,主语是"中国",谓语是"正集中精力",其他部分为宾语。因此需将"加快……的建设,加大……力度,提高……水平"转化为名词或动名词形式,如"accelerating…, making more efforts to…, raising…"。

拓展阅读

Reading A

Achievements Seen in Wildlife Protection

Cameras placed for wildlife surveillance in both Southwest and Northeast China have recently captured rare activities of Asian elephants and Siberian tigers, both of which are endangered species under State protection.

On Friday, forest rangers in Yunnan province reported that a herd of Asian elephants with 17 members had traveled tens of kilometers from its habitat in Mojiang County to Yuanjiang County.

As the country's only habitat for Asian elephants, Yunnan has built a comprehensive protection and alert system for the species. The Asian elephant population in the area has surged from less than 200 in the 1980s to about 300 now.

During the group's two-day journey, drones and cameras helped record its route and activities, and alerts were sent to local residents based on this information. As a result, no conflicts were reported between the elephants and local residents.

Last Wednesday, surveillance cameras at the Hunchun branch of the Northeast China Tiger and Leopard National Park in Jilin province revealed that a Siberian tiger and her three offsprings were roaming in the park. One of the tiger cubs even came close to the camera and sniffed at it.

The park, which is in Jilin and Heilongjiang provinces, has been listed since 2015 as one of the country's 10 pilot national parks. In the past five years, the Siberian tiger and Amur leopard—two species noted as critically endangered on the International Union for Conservation of Nature's Red List of Threatened Species—have seen their numbers steadily increase. The total population of the Siberian tigers in the wild now stands at 27, and there are 42 Amur leopards.

"Currently, tigers and leopards can be seen at almost all of the mountains in the park," said Feng Limin, a biologist from Beijing Normal University in charge of the park's wildlife surveillance work.

"We've kept tracking this tiger mother for a long time. She gave birth to three cubs last May and these young tigers are all in a very healthy condition."

The annual Earth Day falls on Thursday, and its theme this year is "Restore Our Earth." Countries are being urged to focus on restoring the world's ecosystems through natural processes, emerging green technologies and innovative thinking.

Zhang Zhizhong, director of the wildlife protection department at the National Forestry and Grassland Administration, said multiple departments and social organizations in China have made steadfast conservation efforts to protect the country's biodiversity by focusing on habitat protection, afforestation and wildlife conservation.

As one of 17 countries in the world with mega-biodiversity, China is home to nearly 10 percent of all plant species and 14 percent of animals on the planet. Between 2016 and 2020, the country established many nature reserves that now cover 18 percent of its land area and protect 90 percent of the country's plants and 85 percent of its wild animals.

In October, the 15th meeting of the Conference of the Parties to the Convention on Biological Diversity, also known as COP 15, which will be the biggest biodiversity summit in a decade, is scheduled to take place in Kunming, Yunnan province.

On Tuesday, President of the 75th Session of the UN General Assembly Volkan Bozkir pledged that efforts must be made to make progress on the "Road to Kunming," reaffirming his strong support for boosting biodiversity.

"We must continue to make progress on the 'Road to Kunming' and the goal of a 2020 Framework on Biodiversity," he said on Tuesday in remarks addressed to the high-level Raising Ambition for Nature event, organized by the Group of Like-Minded Megadiverse Countries, a group of countries with the majority of Earth's species.

Zhang Jun, China's permanent representative to the UN, told the same event that a high level of political importance must be attached to the COP15.

"Biodiversity is the foundation for human survival and development. We should explore a path of harmonious coexistence between man and nature through COP15," he added.

"There is only one Earth. We must protect the ecological environment as much as we take care of our eyes. We must take environmental issues seriously at all times, not only during meetings and conferences," he said.

Exercises

 Match the English expressions in Column A with the Chinese translations in Column B.

Column A   Column B

1   wildlife surveillance   a   恢复生态系统
2   endangered species   b   和谐共存
3   forest ranger   c   增加生物多样性
4   restore ecosystem   d   自然过程
5   natural process   e   野生动物监测
6   conservation efforts   f   多数物种
7   boost biodiversity   g   濒危物种
8   majority of species   h   生态环境
9   harmonious coexistence   i   保护工作
10 ecological environment   j   森林管理员

Answer the following questions.

1) How have multiple departments and organizations in China made efforts to conserve biodiversity?

2) What are the results of placing cameras for wildlife surveillance?

Reading B

Environmental Protection in China

China consistently holds that economic development should be coordinated with environmental protection; protection of the environment is a common task for mankind, but the economically developed countries should take more responsibility in this respect. It always maintains that the strengthening of international cooperation should be based on respecting national sovereignty, the protection of the environment and the spurring of development cannot be done without peace and stability in the world, and both practical interests of various countries and long-term interests of the world should be considered in handling environmental problems.

While a series of measures for solving its own environmental problems are being taken, China has participated, actively and in a practical manner, in international cooperation in the environmental protection field and made sustained efforts to promote global environmental protection as a common task of mankind.

China supports and actively participates in the environmental activities launched by the UN organizations. China has been a member state of the successive UN Environment Program Governing Council and fruitful cooperation has been carried out between China and the UNEP. In 1979 China joined the UNEP's "Global Environment Monitoring System," "International Registry of Potentially Toxic Chemicals" and "International Environmental Information System." In 1987 a head-office for research and training in international desertification control was established by the UNEP in Lanzhou, capital of northwest China's Gansu Province. China has passed its experiences and techniques on controlling desertification and building ecological agriculture onto many countries through the UNEP. By 1996 a total of 18 units or persons in China had won the "Global 500" title awarded by the UNEP. Good cooperative relationships have been forged between China and the UN Development Program, the World Bank, the Asian Development Bank and other international organizations. At present, an effective mode of cooperation for the use and management of multilateral funds of the Montreal Protocol on Substances that Deplete the Ozone Layer and the Global Environmental Facility as well as loans from the World Bank and the Asian Development Bank has been established. This has played an active role in promoting prevention and control of China's pollution and in improving environmental management ability. China is a member of the UN Committee on Sustainable Development, set up in 1993, and has played a constructive role in this high-level political forum on the global environment and development. China has kept a close cooperative relationship with many countries like the UN Economic and Social Commission for Asia and the Pacific and other relevant organizations and has made contributions to environmental causes and the development of the Asian and Pacific regions through participating in the Northeast Asia environmental cooperation, the Northwest Pacific Action Plan, and the Regional Coordinating Unit for the East Asian Seas Action Plan.

China has actively developed bilateral cooperation in the field of environmental protection. Over the past ten-odd years China has successively signed bilateral environmental protection cooperation agreements and memorandums of understanding with many countries like the United States, the Democratic People's Republic of Korea, Canada, India, the Republic of Korea, Japan, Mongolia, Russia, Germany, Australia, Ukraine, Finland, Norway, Denmark, and the Netherlands. Exchanges and cooperation have been carried out in environmental planning and management, global environment problems, pollution control and prevention, protection of forests and wild animals and plants, marine environment, climate change, air pollution, acid rain and sewage disposal and important achievements have been made in these respects. China has also taken part in the Global Learning and Observation to Benefit the Environment, as proposed by the United States.

In order to promote further international cooperation in the environment and development field, China set up the China Council for International Cooperation on Environment and Development in April 1992, composed of more than 40 leading specialists and well-known public figures from China and other countries, to be responsible for submitting proposals and advisory opinions to the Chinese government. The Council has put forward valuable concrete proposals on energy and the environment, biodiversity protection, ecological agriculture, resources accounting and the pricing system, public participation and the implementation of the environment laws and regulations, which have aroused the attention and response of the Chinese government.

China took an active part in the preparations for and in attending the UN Conference on Environment and Development. It made great efforts for the smooth convening of the Conference. China has taken part in all the preparatory meetings of the Conference and played a constructive role in discussions and negotiations concerning international environment conventions. In June 1991 the Ministerial Conference of Developing Countries on Environment and Development, proposed by China and held in Beijing, was participated in by 41 developing countries, and the Beijing Declaration published by it set forth the principled stand of the developing countries on environment and development, making substantial contributions to the preparation of the UN Conference. In line with the requirements of the first meeting of the Preparatory Committee for the UN Conference on Environment and Development, China worked out the Report on the Environment and Development of the People's Republic of China, which gave an overall exposition on the current situation of China's environment and development, put forward strategic measures for coordinated development of China's environment and economy and set forth China's principled stand on the problems of the global environment, which have received favorable comments from the international community. In June 1992 Song Jian, state councilor and director of the Environmental Protection Commission of the State Council, led a delegation from the Chinese government to the UN Conference on Environment and Development. China's Premier Li Peng was present at the summit meeting of the Conference and made an important speech proposing the strengthening of international cooperation in the field of environment and development, winning positive comments from the international community. On behalf of the Chinese government, Li Peng took the lead in signing the United Nations Framework Convention on Climate Change and the Convention. Since 1979 China has signed a series of international environmental conventions and agreements, including the Convention on International Trade in Endangered Species of Wild Fauna and Flora, International Convention for the Regulation of Whaling, Vienna Convention for the Protection of the Ozone Layer, Basel Convention on Control of Transboundary Movements of Hazardous Wastes and Their Disposal, Montreal Protocol on Substances that Deplete the Ozone Layer (revised version), Framework Convention on Climate Change, Convention on Biological Diversity, Convention on Combating Desertification, Convention on Wetlands of International Importance Especially as Waterfowl Habitat, and 1972 London Convention.

China always conscientiously carries out its responsibilities for international environmental conventions and agreements which it has signed, approved or joined. Under the guidance of

China's Agenda 21, in order to conscientiously undertake its promised duties China has worked out some important documents and state programs or action plans, including the 21st Century Agenda on Environmental Protection, Action Plan for the Conservation of Biodiversity, Action Plan for Forestry in the 21st Century Agenda, and the 21st Century Marine Agenda. The Chinese government approved the State Plan for Gradually Eliminating Substances that Deplete the Ozone Layer which put forward a plan and policy framework for eliminating controlled materials as well as measures for controlling or banning the production and extensive use of substances which deplete the ozone layer. In July 1994, with the support of the UN Development Program, the Chinese government successfully held in Beijing the High-level International Round-Table Conference on Agenda 21, which contributed to the promotion of the nation's sustainable development. To provide legal basis for preventing environmental pollution by the importation of wastes, in November 1995 China published the Emergency Announcement on Strictly Controlling Trans-Boundary Movement of Wastes to China, and in March 1996 it published the Provisional Regulations on Environmental Protection and Management of Wastes' Importation.

Exercises

 Match the English expressions in Column A with the Chinese translations in Column B.

Column A		Column B	
1	global environmental protection	a	沙漠治理
2	desertification control	b	多边基金
3	forge cooperative relationship	c	生物多样性保护
4	multilateral funds	d	加强污染预防
5	promote pollution prevention	e	环境规划
6	improve environmental management	f	全球环境保护
7	environmental planning	g	环境监测系统
8	environmental monitoring system	h	铸造合作关系
9	coordinated development of environment and economy	i	环境与经济和谐发展
10	conservation of biodiversity	j	增强环境管理

 Answer the following questions.

1) What should be considered in handling environmental problems?

2) How has China participated actively in international environmental protection?

翻译佳作赏析

《枫桥夜泊》

张　继

月落乌啼霜满天，江枫渔火对愁眠。

姑苏城外寒山寺，夜半钟声到客船。

译文：

Mooring by Maple Bridge at Night

by Zhang Ji

At moonset cry the crows, streaking the frosty sky;
Dimly lit fishing boat beneath maples sadly lie.
Beyond the city wall, from Temple of Cold Hill,
Bells break the ship-borne roamers dream and midnight still.

（许渊冲　译）

赏析：

以原诗的题目《枫桥夜泊》为例，诗人仅用四字便简单明了地交代了地点、时间及事情。许渊冲选用了直译的方式，直接使用了 Maple Bridge 作为"枫桥"的译文，简洁明了。对于"泊"一字，许渊冲使用了 moor 来翻译，在《牛津英语词典》中 moor 意为"to attach a boat, a ship to a fixed object or to the land with a rope moor"。mooring 还有另外一层意思，就是"荒野、旷野"。在荒野之中，只有一艘靠岸的小船被绳子固定，形单影只，给人一种荒凉之感。而在最后的介词使用上，许渊冲选择了 at，具有很强的目的性。

在译文押韵方面，许渊冲采用了 aabb 的形式，如 sky 对 lie，Hill 对 still。他将这首诗歌翻译得十分有节奏感，传达了"音美"。

在"月落乌啼霜满天"的翻译中，"乌啼""霜满天"按照正常语序翻译是 the crows cry、the frosty sky streaking，而译者在这里使用了倒装语序，把状语 at moonset 提前，使整个句子倒装。在"江枫渔火对愁眠"的翻译中，译者使用了 dimly 和 sadly lie。dimly 指暗淡和昏暗，一语双关，既指渔火光线的昏暗，又表现出诗人内心的压抑与孤寂，非常符合"意美"。在"寒山"的翻译上，许渊冲也另辟蹊径，没有直接将寒山译为 HanShan，而是将其中的文化内涵翻译了出来。"寒山"寓有文化内涵，象征与世无争的生活哲学。而在 20 世纪 50 年代，欧美诗歌中也有类似的意象，就是 Cold Hill，这同"寒山"的意义十分吻合。break 一词用得恰到好处。寂静无声的夜晚被凄凉所淹没，诗人倍感愁思和寂寞，寒山寺的钟声恰如其分地出现，打破了夜晚的寂静，同时也唤醒了沉浸在哀伤中的诗人。

翻译练习

1. 我们应该追求人与自然和谐。山峦层林尽染，平原蓝绿交融，城乡鸟语花香。这样的自然美景，既带给人们美的享受，也是人类走向未来的依托。无序开发、粗暴掠夺，人类定会遭到大自然的无情报复；合理利用、友好保护，人类必将获得大自然的慷慨回报。我们要维持地球生态整体平衡，让子孙后代既能享有丰富的物质财富，又能遥望星空、看见青山、闻到花香。

2. 为应对工业化过程所带来的环境污染、生态系统退化等严峻挑战，中国政府倡导并建设生态文明。生态文明思想继承了中国古代"天人合一""道法自然"的优秀传统思想，是以人与自然、人与人、人与社会和谐共生、良性循环、全面发展、持续繁荣为基本宗旨的文化伦理形态。

3. 面对日益严重的环境问题，低碳经济的关注度越来越高。虽然对于低碳经济的界定有很多种，但人们普遍承认，低碳经济是以低能耗、低污染、低排放为基础的经济模式，是人类社会继农业文明、工业文明之后的又一次重大进步。低碳经济的实质包括能源高效利用、清洁能源开发和追求绿色 GDP，核心是能源技术和减排技术创新、产业结构和制度创新以及人类生存发展观念的根本性转变。在我国经济发展的关键时期，进一步协调低碳经济与发展的关系，保护地球的生态环境，事关中国人民乃至世界人民的福祉。

4. 空气质量不仅关乎人类的生存质量，也影响着地球上其他的生物。随着工业及交通运输业的不断发展，大量的有害物质被排放到空气中，严重危害人类和其他生物的生存环境。因此，防治大气污染、控制污染排放尤为重要。植物能过滤掉（filter out）各种大气污染物，森林的作用尤为显著，所以绿化造林（afforestation）是防治大气污染的有效措施。

5. 交通拥堵是世界各大城市共同面临的问题。交通拥堵不仅影响了城市生活的效率和质量，而且带来了环境污染、能源紧张等一系列社会问题，严重制约了城市的发展。要想解决这一问题，良好的公共交通是必不可少的。实行低票价政策，是实现公交优先的基本保证。从长远来看，则要大力发展轨道交通（rail transportation），缓解路面拥堵问题。

Bibliography

参考书目

蔡基刚. 英汉汉英段落翻译与实践[M]. 上海：复旦大学出版社，2002.

常俊跃，霍跃红，王焱，赵永青. 中国文化(英文版)[M]. 北京：北京大学出版社，2018.

陈宏薇，李亚丹. 新编汉英翻译教程[M]. 上海：上海外语教育出版社，2013.

陈文伯. 译艺：英汉双向笔译[M]. 北京：群言出版社，2008.

程爱民. 中国概况(英文版)[M]. 上海：上海外语教育出版社，2019.

程裕祯. 中国文化要略(第4版)[M]. 北京：外语教学与研究出版社，2017.

创想外语. 用英语介绍中国双语阅读[M]. 北京：中国水利水电出版社，2019.

邓炎昌，刘润清. 语言与文化－英汉语言文化对比(新版)[M]. 北京：外语教学与研究出版社，2018.

董晓波. 英汉比较与翻译[M]. 北京：对外经济贸易大学出版社，2013.

董晓波. 缤纷中国：中国文化英语读本[M]. 北京：北京交通大学出版社，2011.

杜瑞清. 新世纪汉英大词典(第二版)[M]. 北京：外语教学与研究出版社，2016.

冯庆华. 汉英翻译基础教程[M]. 北京：高等教育出版社，2020.

符存，王倩，张玲. 中国文化概况[M]. 北京：中国人民大学出版社，2020.

付满. 巅峰训练[M]. 吉林：吉林出版集团有限责任公司，2015.

高黎，崔喜哲. 用英语介绍中国[M]. 北京：中国水利水电出版社，2022.

国务院侨务办公室，国家汉语国际推广领导小组办公室. 中国文化常识[M]. 北京：高等教育出版社，2007

黄建滨. 中国文化英语阅读教程[M]. 上海：上海外语教育出版社，2018.

乃逯. 中国文化释疑[M]. 北京：北京语言文化大学出版社，1999.

李荫华. 全新版大学进阶英语综合训练(第3版)[M]. 北京：外语教学与研究出版社，2015

廖华英. 中国文化概况(修订版)[M]. 北京：外语教学与研究出版社，2022.

龙毛忠，贾爱兵，颜静兰. 中国文化概览[M]. 上海：华东理工大学出版社，2009.

秦洪武，王克非. 英汉比较与翻译[M]. 北京：外语教学与研究出版社，2010.

商舞，邢星. 中级口译培训教程[M]. 武汉：武汉大学出版社，2016.

束定芳. 中国文化英语教程[M]. 上海：上海外语教育出版社，2016.

司显柱，曾剑平. 汉译英教程(第3版)[M]. 上海：东华大学出版社，2021.

孙致礼. 新编英汉翻译教程(第3版)[M]. 上海：上海外语教育出版社，2022.

王宏，胡静道. 梦溪笔谈(大中华文库汉英对照)[M]. 成都：四川人民出版社，2008.

王宏. 《梦溪笔谈》译本翻译策略研究[J]. 上海翻译，2010，(1)：18-22.

王蕙. 中国社会与文化翻译教程[M]. 北京：清华大学出版社，2023.

王振国，李艳琳. 新汉英翻译教程[M]. 北京：高等教育出版社，2017.

王志茹，陆小丽. 英语畅谈中国文化[M]. 北京：外语教学与研究出版社，2019.

习近平. 习近平谈治国理政(英文版)：第二卷[M]. 北京：外文出版社，2018.

许建平. 英汉互译实践与技巧[M]. 北京：清华大学出版社，2018.

许渊冲. 诗经：汉英对照[M]. 北京：五洲传播出版社，中华书局，2020.

许渊冲. 中诗英韵探胜[M]. 北京：北京大学出版社，2010.

许渊冲. 许渊冲译唐诗三百首(汉英双语)[M]. 北京：中译出版社，2021.

姚宝荣. 中国文化汉英读本[M]. 西安：西安交通大学出版社，2013.

叶朗，朱良志. 中国文化读本[M]. 北京：外语教学与研究出版社，2019.

印晓红. 汉英语篇翻译教程[M]. 北京：清华大学出版社，2017.

余同元. 中国文化概要(修订版)[M]. 北京：人民出版社，2018.

张白桦. 翻译基础指津[M]. 北京：中译出版社，2017.

张培基. 英译中国现代散文选[M]. 上海：上海外语教育出版社，2007.

张培基. 英译翻译教程(修订本)[M]. 上海：上海外语教育出版社，2018.

赵云利，刘景琳，王云，等. 用英语介绍中国传统文化[M]. 北京：知识产权出版社，2023.

郑和平. 英译汉实用教程[M]. 广州：中山大学出版社，2006.

郑树棠. 新视野大学英语Ⅰ[M]. 北京：外语教学与研究出版社，2015.

中国思想文化术语编委会. 中国传统文化关键词[M]. 北京：外语教学与研究出版社，2019.

周仪，廖建思. 中国文化概论[M]. 重庆：重庆大学出版社，2019.

Benjamin A. Elman. *A Cultural History of Civil Examinations in Late Imperial China*. Berkeley：University of California Press，2000.

Shiuon Chu. Failure Stories：Interpretations of Rejected Papers in the Late Imperial Civil Service Examinations. *T'oung Pao*，101(1/3)，2015.

Feifei Ma & DanDan Zhao. Analysis of the Abolition of the Imperial Examination System and the Development Trend of the Stratum of Scholars in Qing Dynasty. *Proceedings of 2018 International Workshop on Advances in Social Sciences（IWASS 2018）*. Francis Academic Press，2018.

Michael Dillon. *History of China：From Earliest Times to the Last Emperor*. Beijing：China Translation & Publishing House，2017.

Wolfram Wilss. *The Science of Translation：Problems & Methods*. Shanghai：Shanghai Foreign Language Education Press，2001.

参考网站

https://baijiahao.baidu.com

https://baike.baidu.com

https://cet4.koolearn.com

https://cet46.wendu.com

https://cet6.koolearn.com

https://cet4-6.xdf.cn

http://cpc.people.com.cn

https://easylearn.baidu.com/edu

http://edu.sina.com.cn

http://en.ce.cn

http://en.chinaculture.org

https://en.jinzhao.wiki

Bibliography

https://fashion.sohu.com

https://ishare.ifeng.com

http://jhsjk.people.cn

https://journey-to-the-west-xiyouji.fandom.com

http://language.chinadaily.com.cn

https://mtoutiao.xdf.cn

https://news.cgtn.com

http://news.cntgol.com

http://news.sdchina.com

http://news.zhuoyixuan.com

https://nobelliterature.com

https://ru.hujiang.com

https://view.inews.qq.com

https://wap.peopleapp.com

https://wenku.baidu.com

https://whc.unesco.org

https://zhuanlan.zhihu.com

https://www.bilibili.com

https://www.bmy.com.cn

ttps://www.britannica.com

https://www.cchatty.com

http://www.cctv.com

http://www.china.org.cn

http://www.chinadaily.com.cn

https://www.chinadiscovery.com

http://www.chinakongmiao.org

https://www.chinanews.com

https://www.chinatravel.com

https://www.cma.gov.cn

https://www.dyhzdl.cn

http://www.enread.com

https://www.fx361.com

http://www.gov.cn

https://www.hjenglish.com

https://www.iesalc.unesco.org

https://www.imsilkroad.com

https://www.jiuzhai.com

https://www.jstor.org

http://www.kekenet.com

http://www.mwr.gov.cn

https://www.renrendoc.com

http://www.rmzxb.com.cn
https://www.sohu.com
https://www.topchinatravel.com
https://www.travelchinaguide.com
https://www.visitourchina.com
https://www.wenmi.com
http://www.xinhuanet.com
http://www.yrcc.gov.cn
http://www.zhongguodiqing.cn
https://www.zgbk.com
http://ylj.suzhou.gov.cn